LOOKING DOWN THE CORRIDORS

ALLIED AERIAL ESPIONAGE OVER EAST GERMANY AND BERLIN 1945–1990

KEVIN WRIGHT AND PETER JEFFERIES

FOREWORD BY AIR VICE-MARSHAL MIKE JACKSON CB FRAES, RAF (RETD)

The History Press

D1343062

The views and opinions expressed are those of the authors alone and should not be taken to represent those of Her Majesty's Government, MoD, HM Armed Forces or any government agency.

Cover illustration
Front: Chipmunk over Brandenburg Gate. (Crown Copyright)

First published 2015

This paperback edition published 2017 by
The History Press
The Mill, Brimscombe Port
Stroud, Gloucestershire, GL5 2QG
www.thehistorypress.co.uk

British Library Cataloguing in Publication Data.
A catalogue record for this book is available from the British Library.

ISBN 978 0 7509 7947 4

Typesetting by Thomas Bohm, User design
Printed and bound by CPI Group (UK) Ltd

Contents

FOREWORD BY AIR VICE-MARSHAL MIKE JACKSON CB FRAeS, RAF (RETD)

Formerly Director General Intelligence and Geographic Resources, Defence Intelligence Staff (DIS); OC Joint Air Reconnaissance Intelligence Centre; Defence and Air Attaché Warsaw; OC 60 Squadron

Sun Tzu wrote in his famous treatise *On the Art of War* that 'tactics without strategy is the noise before defeat', while 'strategy without tactics is the slowest way to victory'. In the prologue to this book you see the central theme rightly described as reconnaissance operations being part of an intelligence campaign. Air reconnaissance is a collection tactic which helps to feed an intelligence strategy, and each connects with the other in a continuous relationship of supply and demand, which Sun Tzu would have recognised.

Looking Down the Corridors describes collection operations which were amongst many in the strategic intelligence campaign to penetrate the secrets of the Warsaw Pact during the Cold War. They were complementary with other aerial reconnaissance activity, as well as with intelligence collection work on the ground – in particular by the Allied Military Liaison Missions accredited to the Soviet Forces in Berlin, and by the Defence Attachés in neighbouring Warsaw Pact countries.

However, these were exceptionally significant operations because they took place in such a 'target rich' environment, and because they could provide evidence that could not be surpassed. The 'Prague Spring' case is a perfect example of how they could impact at the very highest levels, and respond in real time. More often the Corridor missions satisfied specific intelligence requirements, to update and maintain the long-term Indicators and Warning watch, and to provide the fine detail that helped the technical intelligence community to analyse and assess the weapons and systems capabilities of the other side. While this was less dramatic it was also vital work, often producing unique results.

Inevitably the aircrew and the flights themselves attract attention, but I am glad to see that the other actors in this story also receive the credit that is due to them. The ground crew who serviced the aircraft and sensors were even more in the shadows than the aircrew, but nothing would have happened without their professional and strictly discreet efforts, which in some cases involved keeping venerable systems punching well above their weight and beyond their natural life. On the other hand they also had to master the intricacies of some of the most advanced sensors of the time.

Then there were the interpreters. It may be true that the camera never lies, but the images can often deceive and conceal, as more than one impatient operational commander has learnt to his cost. The artful science of the imagery analyst was absolutely fundamental to these operations. It is a skill that has evolved over many years, keeping pace with the technology of both the collector and the target, to make the most of every pixel while seeing through the veil of ambiguity that nature or the opposition might assemble.

As for security, it could be that these operations were better concealed from our own side than from the opposition. It is true that from the national level in capital cities down to individuals within the operating squadrons, the 'need to know' principle was rigorously applied and to this day has kept the story restricted to a few insiders. On the other hand, there are plenty of incidents that suggest that the other side was aware that reconnaissance flights were taking place. Suspicious Soviet air traffic controllers, rudely finger-waving East German soldiers, messages written in the snow, not to mention aggressive approaches by opposition fighter aircraft, all point that way. What they could not have known was the sheer quantity and quality of information that was being collected.

Looking Down the Corridors is the story of the persistent and imaginative application of aerial reconnaissance to one of the most successful intelligence campaigns of the Cold War.

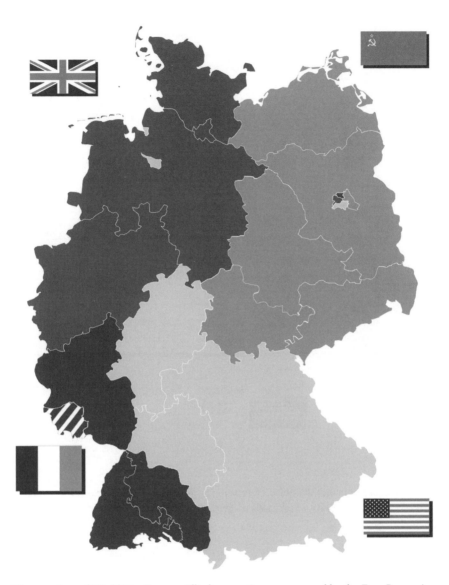

The post-Second World War German Allied occupation zones agreed by the Four Powers in 1945. (Wikimedia Commons)

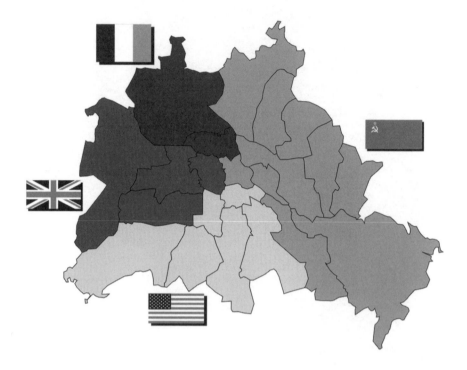

The division of Berlin into the Allied Occupation Sectors created meandering boundaries through and around the city which made policing and protecting them extremely difficult. (Wikimedia Commons)

Prologue

In July 1968 the 'Prague Spring' crisis in Czechoslovakia was coming to a head. In East Germany at the Soviet garrison of Dallgow-Döberitz, just west of Berlin, the Divisional Commander of 19 Motor Rifle Division had been given orders to prepare his unit to move to an unspecified destination. In the barracks, vehicles had been formed into unit columns ready to move out.

At RAF Gatow in West Berlin, an apparently innocuous Percival Pembroke light transport aircraft took off, bound for RAF Wildenrath in West Germany. However, this was no ordinary Pembroke. Concealed in its fuselage were five powerful reconnaissance cameras. As it passed over Dallgow-Döberitz the camera doors in the belly opened and the scene below was recorded.

On arrival at RAF Wildenrath the film magazines were rapidly removed and transferred to the headquarters complex at Rheindahlen where they were processed and passed to the Army and Royal Air Force photographic interpretation units for analysis. The very high level of activity in the garrison was swiftly reported to local intelligence staffs, the Ministry of Defence in London and select members of the Allied intelligence community.

Later that morning a single-engined Chipmunk training aircraft from the RAF Gatow Station Flight took off for an apparently normal local flight. This aircraft was another 'wolf in sheep's clothing'. The crew were drawn from the British Military Liaison Mission (BRIXMIS) and the flight's purpose was to covertly photograph Soviet and East German installations in the Berlin Control Zone. It too passed over Dallgow-Döberitz and the activity recorded this time by a 35mm hand-held cameras operated by the observer from an open cockpit.

On its return the film was processed at the BRIXMIS Headquarters in West Berlin and the initial results were reported to the intelligence staff at the Joint Headquarters at Rheindahlen, the Ministry of Defence in London and the French and US Liaison Missions in Berlin.

The photographs provided visible and verifiable proof that the Soviets were preparing for some form of military action. After studying all the available intelligence, it was agreed that these forces were probably being prepared to intervene in Czechoslovakia. They did so a few days later on 20 August 1968.

This was just one incident in the life of two covert British aerial photographic reconnaissance operations that were part of one of the most understated and successful intelligence campaigns of the Cold War. They were authorised at the highest political and military levels, conducted in great secrecy and the aircrew flying the missions would have faced serious consequences if their aircraft had come down in East Germany. The operations' existence was known only to a select few. Similar programmes were conducted by the United States and the French, and much of the collected information was exchanged between all three.

This book traces those operations from the early days of the Cold War to their conclusion in 1990 with German reunification. It covers British operations in detail but also those of the French military and the US Army and Air Force. It is dedicated to the people who took part, from the men and women who prepared and handled the aircraft, the aircrew who spent many anxious hours plying the Corridors and the Berlin Control Zone (BCZ) at no small risk to themselves, the photographers who processed the film and the photographic interpreters who spent many long, painstaking hours analysing the images and writing reports.

Even twenty-five years after the operations' end, their activities have remained largely in the shadows of the Cold War, many details still cloaked in secrecy. In recording some of the vast range of the activities they undertook, we cannot hope to recapture the seriousness of the daily tasks and the tensions. However, what stands out most of all is the professionalism of all those involved, whatever their responsibilities. They all played their part. Shining through most clearly is their gentle discretion, modesty and the sometimes wry, wickedly self-deprecating, dark humour that often shields the sense of dedication and determination that is the hallmark of servicemen and women worldwide. For those who participated in these operations we hope you will now be able to answer the question 'What did you do in the Cold War?' more openly.

Acknowledgements

Our first thanks go to Air Vice-Marshal Mike Jackson, a former OC 60 Squadron and later OC Joint Air Reconnaissance Intelligence Centre and Director General Intelligence and Geographic Resources of the Defence Intelligence Staff, for writing the Foreword. We could not have found anyone with more knowledge and authority on all aspects of British Corridor and Allied operations.

There are a great number of people to thank who have all played different parts, but without their collective goodwill we would not have got very far. It is normally invidious to nominate people individually but the efforts of John Bessette who is the 7499th Group Historian in the US calls for special mention because he is a repository of knowledge about all things Corridor related. We thank him for his personal assistance and for introducing us to many contacts in the United States who provided us with so much information. Hugo Mambour in Belgium, who runs the authoritative 'Red Stars over Germany' website about the Soviet 16th and 24th Tactical Air Armies, has helped us enormously with information on French operations and effected introductions to some participants and shared his material on the US Army's BCZ operations.

Thanks to various organisations and associations whose members and archives have provided us with a great deal of assistance, material support and introductions: 60 Squadron Association, RAF Air Historical Branch (AHB), BRIXMIS Association, Friends of the Intelligence Corps Museum (FICM), Intelligence Corps Association, Medmenham Association and Archive, the Military Intelligence Museum and Archive, and finally The National Archives at Kew.

Many individuals have given of their time freely, regaled us with their memories, raised topics and answered a great number of questions, including Francis Bacon, Chris Benn, Bob Boothman, David Brain, Steve Bridgewater, Phil Chaney, David Clark, David Cockburn, Ray Dadswell, Len Davies, John Denman, Frank Doucette, Ben Dunnell, John Elliot, Paul Fallon, Neil Fearn, Charles Garrad, Chris Halsall, David Hamilton, Marcus Herbote (Gutersloh Spotters Group), Paul Hickley,† David Hollinshead, Will Jarman, Alan (Fred) Judge, Brian King, Peter Kirkpatrick,

Lionel Lacey-Johnson, David Laidlaw,† Bert Lewer, Jim Lewis,† Steve Lloyd, Charles (Dizzy) Lynas,† Roy Marsden, Vance Mitchell, Mike Neil, Hans Neubroch,† Mike Palmer, Dallas Payne, Des Pemberton, Roland Pietrini, Vincent Robertson, Stewart Ross, Rod Saar, Andrew Scott, Brian Terry, Nick Watkis, John Webber, Peter Williams, George Young and Robert Zoucha, as well as others who wish to remain anonymous.

For the images we would very much like to thank Peter Seemann and Ralf Manteufel in particular for the large number of pictures they provided of Corridor and BCZ aircraft at Tempelhof, but also Manfred Faber, Dallas Payne, Ian Powell, David Hamilton, Aldo Bidini and Lionel Lacy-Johnson for their contributions, which are all greatly appreciated. A special mention must be made of Group Captain, now Air Commodore, Steve Thornber for his help in ensuring the declassification of official imagery and the Medmenham Collection for supplying the majority of it.

And last, but not least, thank you to our long-suffering partners Sue and Valerie, who have tolerated us vanishing into our work rooms/studies to put it all together and supported us throughout.

If we have missed anyone out, please accept our sincerest apologies – it was not deliberate.

We know that there are many parts of this story to be told and more to be added to those which we have discussed. We would welcome contact with anyone involved in these fascinating operations over the years. If you have anything you would like to add or tell us about then please email us at: lookingdownthecorridors@gmx.com.

Kevin Wright and Peter Jefferies, 2015

TIMELINE OF EVENTS

Year	Germany	International
1945	*May* VE Day – End of war in Europe HQ 21 AG and 21 AGPIU locate in Bad Oeynhausen HQ 2TAF and PID 2TAF locate in Bad Eilsen	President Harry S. Truman becomes US president following death of Franklin D. Roosevelt Clement Attlee elected British PM
	July Potsdam Conference attended by President Truman (USA), Prime Minister Attlee (Britain) and General Secretary Stalin (USSR) *15 July* HQ 2TAF renamed HQ BAFO PID 2TAF becomes PID HQ BAFO BAFO Comms Sqn formed from 2TAF Comms Sqn	
	August HQ 21 AG renamed HQ BAOR 21 AGPIU renamed APIU (BAOR)	*August* VJ Day – End of the war against Japan and end of the Second World War
	10 October BAFO Comms Sqn renamed BAFO Comms Wg	
	November Four Powers agreement establishes the Berlin Air Corridors and Control Zone	
	December Berlin Air Safety Centre established	

Year	Germany	International
1946	*February* Berlin Air Safety Centre starts operations	*March* Churchill's 'Iron Curtain' speech at Fulton, Missouri
	Spring USA starts photographic reconnaissance flights over Russian Occupied Zone using 10 RG: 45 RS and 10 PCS	*August* US McMahon Act prohibits sharing atomic information with other nations, including Britain
	45 RS re-equips with A-26 Invader to fly reconnaissance missions in Corridors and BCZ	
	Britain starts photographic reconnaissance flights in Corridors and BCZ using Dakota, Mosquito and Spitfire PR XIX aircraft	
1947	APIU (BAOR) and PID HQ BAFO combine to form JAPIC (G) at Bad Eilsen	
	27 September BAFO Comms Wg renamed BAFO Comms Sqn	*September* USAF formed from USAAF and becomes an independent service
1948	Britain starts photographic reconnaissance flights in the Corridors and BCZ using Avro Anson aircraft	*April* President Truman announces Marshall Plan for economic recovery in Europe
	June Deutschemark introduced to Western Sectors of Berlin Soviets leave Berlin Kommandatura never to return Berlin blockaded. Start of Berlin Airlift	*October* Lt Gen. Curtis LeMay is appointed C-in-C SAC
	1 November 7499 SS forms at Fürstenfeldbruck AB from 'X' Flight 45 RS and Det 'A' 10 RG. Equipped with RB-17, RB-26 Invader, C-47 and C-54 aircraft	

Year	Germany	International
1949	Spitfire PR XIX of II(AC) Sqn RAF start flying unofficial missions in the Corridors and BCZ	
	May Berlin blockade lifted but Airlift continues	*May* North Atlantic Treaty signed and NATO formed
	September End of Berlin Airlift Federal Republic of Germany (FRG) founded	
	October German Democratic Republic (GDR) founded	
1950	Soviet claims that Corridor and BCZ altitude limits are between 2,500 and 10,000ft and only unarmed transport and training aircraft can use them	*June* Korean War starts. North Korea invades South Mutual Defence Assistance Programme signed with USA
	7499 SS moves to Wiesbaden AB	
1951	II (AC) Sqn Spitfire PR XIX flights in Corridors and BCZ stop because of move to Köln-Wahn	Winston Churchill elected British PM
	3 May 497 RTS forms at Wiesbaden from photographic and PI elements of 45 RS and 10 RG	
	July 497 RTS transfers to Shaw AFB in the USA	
	August First C-54 flights by 7499 SS	
	1 September HQ BAFO renamed HQ 2TAF BAFO Comms Sqn renamed 2TAF Comms Sqn	

Year	Germany	International
1952	*24 January* 497 RTS returns to Schierstein Compound	
	21 March US-owned RB-45C crewed by RAF personnel flies down Centre Corridor at high altitude to assess Soviet response. This was the precursor to Operation Jiu-Jitsu flights	
1953	Western Allies unofficially accept Soviet unilaterally imposed restrictions on heights and aircraft types allowed to use the Corridors and BCZ	Dwight D. Eisenhower elected US president
	C-97A 49–2952 Pie Face starts Corridor flights from Rhein-Main	
	PID element of JAPIC (G) becomes PID HQ 2TAF	
	12 March RAF Lincoln shot down by the Soviets near the North Corridor with loss of seven lives	*March* Georgi Malenkov becomes leader of USSR
	17 June Workers' uprising in East Berlin put down by Soviet and East German authorities	*3 June* Queen Elizabeth II crowned
	November RB-17G leaves 7499 SS service	*July* Korean War armistice signed at Panmunjon
1954	2TAF Comms Sqn moves to RAF Wildenrath near the Dutch–German border	
	One DHC-1 Chipmunk T10 forms RAF Gatow Station Flight and is used by BRIXMIS for visual reconnaissance flights	
1954 to 1955	Army and RAF HQs and PI units move to JHQ complex at Rheindahlen JAPIC (G) ceases to exist and the two PI units are co-located but autonomous	

Year	Germany	International
1955	7499 SG forms at Wiesbaden from 7499 SS. Group consists of three squadrons: 7405 SS, 7406 SS and 7407 SS	Anthony Eden elected British PM
	May First C-118 joins 7405 SS	Nikolai Bulganin and Nikita Khrushchev are joint leaders of the USSR
		July First Four Power summit at Geneva to open dialogue and reduce Cold War tensions
1956	Cabinet approves use of the RAF Gatow Station Flight Chipmunk for photographic collection operations by BRIXMIS	
	Percival Pembroke starts to replace the Avro Anson on British Corridor photographic flights	*23 October to 10 November* Hungarian uprising. Soviet troops from GSFG despatched to help quell it
	FRG becomes independent nation state BMG and BOZ disbanded Whitehall becomes directly involved in the staffing and authorisation processes of British Corridor and BCZ flights	*November* Suez crisis. Britain, France and Israel co-operate to retake the Suez Canal. Serious rift in Anglo-American relations
1957	French start Corridor and BCZ flights from Lahr using C-47 Gabriel I-IV	Harold Macmillan replaces Anthony Eden as British PM
	First signs of construction sighted at Glau. Became the first SA-2 Guideline site in the forward area	*November* USSR launches Sputnik 1, the first artificial satellite
1958	Intelligence Corps assumes responsibility for provision of all British Army PIs	Nikita Khrushchev becomes leader of the USSR
	May First T/CT-29 arrives at 7405 SS to replace C-47s	Charles de Gaulle forms new French government to deal with war in Algeria
	July Last RB-26 Invader leaves 7405 SS Det 1, 7406 SS (Slick Chick) ceases operations	
	December Last C-54 flight by 7405 SS	

Year	Germany	International
1959	USA sends C-130 aircraft down the Corridors at 25,000ft to exercise its rights to fly at any altitude along them Robust Soviet reaction ensures that this is never repeated	Charles de Gaulle elected French president
	1 January HQ 2TAF renamed HQ RAFG (2TAF) PID HQ 2TAF becomes PID HQ RAFG (2TAF) 2TAF Comms Sqn becomes HQ RAFG Comms Sqn	*Summer* President de Gaulle orders USA to remove its nuclear weapons from France
	July BRIXMIS Chipmunk flight acquires close-up photographs of SA-2 Guideline equipment at Glau	
1960	APIU (BAOR) renamed PI Coy (TINTU)	*1 May* US U-2 shot down over Sverdlovsk in USSR
	Following shooting down of U-2 and the deteriorating Berlin situation, the British embargo all photographic flights in the Corridors and BCZ. Other training and transport flights continue US and French continue reconnaissance flights	
	Last C-47 mission flown by 7405 SS	
	January Last C-118 flight by 7405 SS	
1961	RAF Corridor and BRIXMIS Chipmunk photographic flights controlled directly from London. Flights are in single figures to be executed within a set time	*January* John F. Kennedy elected president of USA
	16 August Berlin Wall built dividing the city	

Year	Germany	International
1962	British restrictions on RAF Corridor and BRIXMIS Chipmunk flights relaxed with authorisation devolved to senior military officers in Germany and Berlin	
	Pembroke Mod 614 programme started to fit F.96 cameras	*October* Cuban Missile Crisis
	PI Coy (TINTU) renamed PI Coy (BAOR)	
1963	C-97 Stratofreighters start 7405 SS Corridor and BCZ flights	Alec Douglas-Home replaces Harold Macmillan as British PM
	French C-47 Gabriel I-IV replaced by Nord 2501 Noratlas Gabriel V	*November* President John F. Kennedy assassinated and succeeded by VP Lyndon B. Johnson
1964	Satellite imagery renders Corridor and BCZ flights I&W requirement less important	Harold Wilson elected British PM
		Aleksandr Kosygin and Leonid Brezhnev become leaders of USSR
		USA introduces operational reconnaissance satellites
1965	PI Coy (BAOR) renamed 6 (PI) Coy on formation of Int Gp (BAOR)	
1966	French move Corridor and BCZ flights to Metz-Frescaty following French withdrawal from NATO	
		March President de Gaulle announces French withdrawal from NATO by 1967. US forces given notice to leave France
1967	*October* 497 RTS redesignated 497 RTG	*June* Six-day War between Israel and Arab states

Year	Germany	International
1968	Second DHC-1 Chipmunk allocated to RAF Gatow Station Flight	Leonid Brezhnev becomes leader of the USSR
	July 19 MRD seen formed into unit columns prior to deploying to Czechoslovakia	
	August T/CT-29 leave 7045 SS	*20 August* Soviet military intervention in Czechoslovakia in response to Dubçek government's reforms (Prague Spring)
	1 October 7407 SS disbands	
1969	*3 February* HQ RAFG Comms Sqn redesignated 60 Sqn RAF	Richard Nixon elected president of the USA
		Georges Pompidou elected French president
1970	6 (PI) Coy renamed 6 Int Coy (PI)	Edward Heath appointed British PM
		March Nuclear Non-Proliferation Treaty between Britain, USA and USSR ratified
1972	*17 January* Pembroke XL954 intercepted by three MiG-17s in the South Corridor	*May* Strategic Arms Limitation Treaty (SALT 1) signed
	1 March 7499 SG disbands	
1973		*October* Yom Kippur War in Middle East and oil crisis
1974	7406 SS disbands and becomes 7580 SS	Harold Wilson elected British PM
		Gerald Ford elected president of the USA
		Valéry Giscard d'Estaing elected French president
1975	7405 SS moves to Rhein-Main AB 7405 SS receives first C-130E-II to replace C-97 Stratofreighters	

Year	Germany	International
1976		James Callaghan replaces Harold Wilson as British PM
1977	7405 SS becomes 7405 OS	Jimmy Carter elected president of the USA
		Soviets deploy SS-20 Sabre in Europe
1979	6 Int Coy (PI) renamed 6 Int Coy	Margaret Thatcher elected British PM
	December NATO deploys Pershing and Ground Launched Cruise Missiles (GLCM) in Britain and Germany	*December* USSR invades Afghanistan
1980	*December* 35 MRD appears to be preparing for intervention in Poland	Start of Polish Solidarity Crisis
1981		Ronald Reagan elected president of the USA
		François Mitterrand elected French president
1982		Yuri Andropov becomes leader of the USSR
		April to June Falklands War between Britain and Argentina
1983	7580 OS forms at Rhein-Main AB	*November* GLCM arrive at Greenham Common
1984		Konstantin Chernenko becomes leader of the USSR
1985		*March* Mikhail Gorbachev becomes leader of the USSR
1986	Berlin nightclub bombed, causing US service casualties	*15–16 April* Operation Eldorado Canyon – USA attacks suspected terrorist targets in Libya from British bases
1987		USA and USSR sign Intermediate Nuclear Forces Treaty – Pershings, GLCMs and SS-20 Sabre are to be withdrawn from Europe

Year	Germany	International
1989	60 Sqn RAF – Hawker Siddley Andover partially replaces Percival Pembroke	Year of collapse of Soviet power in Eastern Europe
	June First C-160G Transall Gabriel VI delivered to Metz-Frescaty	
	3 July First operational Corridor and BCZ flight by C-160G Transall Gabriel VI	
	26 October Last French Nord N2501 Noratlas Gabriel V flight	*November* Berlin Wall comes down
1990	*29 September* Last Corridor flight by 7405 OS	John Major replaces Margaret Thatcher as British PM
	30 September RAF Corridor and BRIXMIS Chipmunk flights cease	*August* Iraq invades Kuwait
	3 October FRG and GDR reunified as Germany	
	31 December Berlin Air Safety Centre closes	
1990 to 1994	French continue BCZ and other photographic flights over Soviet and East German targets	
1991	497 RTG moves to RAF Molesworth in UK	
	23 January 7405 OS and 7580 OS disband	*January to February* First Gulf War
	Spring British PM authorises formation of JAC at Molesworth	*May* Greenham Common GLCM deactivated
		July Warsaw Pact dissolved
		December USSR dissolved
1992	*April* 60 Sqdn disbands at RAF Wildenrath, later reforms at RAF Benson	
1994	Last Soviet Western Group of Forces troops leave Germany	

Introduction

Our account of Allied operations along the Berlin Air Corridors, in the Berlin Control Zone (BCZ) and along the Inner German Border (IGB) does not start in Germany. The early chapters outline the intelligence collection methods available to the Western Allies, examining the development of their efforts to gather airborne intelligence on the Soviet Union and Eastern Europe. A key thread throughout is the extent of Anglo-American co-operation as the United States, supported by Britain, began its worldwide airborne intelligence collection effort. After a brief interregnum following the end of the Second World War, the two co-operated extensively in collecting photographic imagery as the British provided bases and undertook some overflights at the behest of the USA. Under President Eisenhower the Americans began a huge effort to capture as much photographic and signals intelligence as they could of the Soviet Union – particularly through the U-2 and related programmes. Domestic politics in both countries and international incidents impacted on the conduct of programmes in Germany and elsewhere. It established the overall framework of intelligence gathering in Europe within which Corridor and BCZ flights operated.

Chapter 2 concentrates on post-war Germany, how its division required the four wartime allies to find a way of coexisting. This was especially important in relation to West Berlin and access to the city from the Western occupation zones through the establishment of the Air Corridors, BCZ and Berlin Air Safety Centre (BASC). The Cold War saw a huge concentration of military forces facing each other across the Inner German Border and around Berlin which became a running political sore, potential military flashpoint and 'hot spot' for the collection of intelligence via every possible means.

The substantive part of the book concentrates on the conduct of Corridor missions, BCZ and some IGB collection flights. These are covered in three chapters that examine US, British and French activities respectively using a combination of available official records and the recollections of participants from all levels. Chapter 6 looks, with an emphasis on British operations, at Allied flights by all three countries within (and occasionally beyond) the BCZ; their origins, equipment and experiences.

The final three chapters look at how collected photographic imagery was processed, exploited, recorded, reported and shared from the perspectives of those doing the work. Via examples, they detail some successes and outline a few 'wild goose chases'. The final chapter considers what the Soviet and East German military probably knew about Allied Corridor and BCZ flights and explores why, for the most part, they largely tolerated this constant observation for over forty years.

We may have been the ones to bring the material together for this project, but without the very generous assistance of many people we would never have been able to tell such a detailed and fascinating story.

COLD WAR AIRBORNE INTELLIGENCE GATHERING: TECHNOLOGY AND POLITICS

It is clear that the main element of any United States policy toward the Soviet Union must be that of long-term, patient but firm and vigilant containment of Russian expansive tendencies.

The Sources of Soviet Conduct (George Kennan, 1947)

The Sources of Intelligence

Throughout the Cold War the size, composition and technological quality of Soviet and Warsaw Pact forces was constantly improving. To keep abreast of these developments, the Western intelligence community voraciously gathered information from all available sources. The generation of reliable, wide-ranging, verifiable intelligence was vital in providing political and military decision-makers with the most accurate assessed intelligence available.

All intelligence disciplines were employed against the Soviets. Operationally each was narrowly defined and had its individual strengths and weaknesses, but effective collation and fusion helped to reduce the individual disciplines' deficiencies. An outline of the main disciplines used by Western intelligence agencies in Cold War Germany is useful in understanding intelligence collection methods.

Signals and Communications Intelligence (SIGINT–COMINT/ELINT)
SIGINT is the overarching term applied to the collection of communications intelligence (COMINT) and electronic intelligence (ELINT). SIGINT's capabilities cover both tactical and strategic communications and electronic emissions. These included radio transmissions between military forces, armies, aircraft, ships and headquarters, as well as radar and data links. SIGINT can provide invaluable intelligence on current and strategic activities, organisations, military formations and

manufacturing. However, it only 'hears' what is going on and requires confirmation by other means.

Photographic and Imagery Intelligence (PHOTINT/IMINT)

Photographic and Imagery Intelligence provides a permanent, tangible record by exploiting ground, airborne and space-based imagery. PHOTINT refers to optical photography, whereas IMINT encompasses multi-spectral sensors such as infrared and radar. Extracting intelligence from imagery, just like SIGINT, requires skilled, well-trained and experienced personnel. Imagery is far from infallible as it can be deceived by careful camouflage, sophisticated deception plans, and hiding equipment or physical activity from view whilst the collection platform is overhead and these measures are still used against satellites with their predictable orbits. Imagery's value is its ability to produce details of new items of equipment, monitoring fixed operating locations and watching the movement of equipment and personnel. It can also help to confirm, or refute, information gathered from other sources.

Human Intelligence (HUMINT)

As its name suggests, Human Intelligence covers the acquisition of information and intelligence from human sources and is perhaps the most familiar form of intelligence collection. It can come from virtually any human interaction. More commonly this can mean casual and social meetings with local populations, formal and informal contact between diplomatic and military personnel, defectors and 'agents in place' (spies). HUMINT often manages to capture the information and perspectives that are not easily seen by external observers or technical means, including the state of military and civilian morale, levels and effectiveness of training, the overall competence of troops, equipment reliability, readiness and routine military practices. A key advantage, and complication, of HUMINT is its flexibility because humans not only collect information, but they also interpret and explain it. Explaining the reasons behind why something is done can sometimes be more valuable than just noting that it is being done. HUMINT has significant limitations: the age of the information is one, as much is likely to be very time sensitive. Another key consideration is the source's own agenda and motivation.

One particularly valuable form of HUMINT sources were military and defence attachés who were trained to make informed and expert observations, and interpret them. They often took photographs to support their observations. Most were generally permitted to tour in their host country overtly. But in less friendly regimes their movements were often constrained by embassy policies, local regulations and local security force activities. Attachés have to work within the constraints of acceptable diplomatic practice. In extremis, they can be declared persona non grata and expelled from the country, resulting in political embarrassment and the loss of their unique capability until they can be replaced, which may take some time.

The sharing of intelligence gathered by separate agencies and states can multiply the amount of information available and contribute to the assembly of a more comprehensive intelligence picture.

The UK–US Intelligence Relationship and Co-operation

Richard Aldrich has observed that extensive US–UK security co-operation is rooted in the areas of atomic and intelligence exchange.[1] This co-operation is often characterised as the 'Special Relationship' which developed between Britain and the US during the Second World War. Intelligence sharing has certainly always been a major element of that relationship. It included the US presence at Bletchley Park where wartime enemy communications were broken and at the Allied Central Interpretation Unit (ACIU) at RAF Medmenham where air photography was exploited. Both sides sought the continuance of this mutually beneficial relationship after the end of the war. In March 1946, before the well-known 'UK–USA Agreement' formalised the SIGINT relationship, an agreement on the 'exchange of photographic cover of every description on a world-wide basis' had been concluded between Air Vice-Marshal (AVM) Elmhirst of the RAF and General George McDonald, USAAF (Head of USAAF intelligence).[2] In its haste to demobilise, the USA neglected airborne reconnaissance capabilities significantly so it was not surprising that the embryonic USAF intelligence branch looked instinctively to the RAF for support.[3] Although US Army officialdom had officially banned such contact, there were very practical reasons why early US air intelligence efforts retained a significant focus on the UK.

The Nazis' Photographic Legacy

In May 1945 British and US units overran a number of Luftwaffe intelligence centres in the heart of the German Reich. They recovered a remarkable imagery collection covering the western part of the Soviet Union that had been assembled by the Luftwaffe. For the next two decades this photography was a vital part of British and American targeting intelligence. They gathered together this huge photographic collection, under Operations Dick Tracy and GX, from a number of dispersed locations. These ranged from a barn near Reichenhall, through partially burned photography found in barges, with some of the best said to be from Hitler's retreat at Berchtesgaden and yet more from Vienna and Oslo. Totalling over 1 million prints it required nearly 200 officers to manage the collection. In October 1945 the duplication effort moved from Pinetree in Essex to RAF Medmenham in Oxfordshire. Work on piecing the material together continued beyond 1949.[4] More photography was purchased from two unidentified 'gentlemen of Europe' in 1958 and Dino Brugioni mentions the discovery, of hitherto unknown material, moved from Berlin to a Dresden basement at the end of the war, which was found in 1993.[5] The combined collection provided a detailed photographic record of Soviet Russia as far as the Ural Mountains and had begun to be amassed well before the Nazi invasion in 1941. Significant updating and replacement of this imagery was not possible until the advent of satellite imagery after 1960.[6] This collection was the basis of the continuous Anglo-American photographic intelligence exchanges throughout the Cold War but was not restricted to just Soviet-focused material.

Cold War: Spy Planes and Politics

Cold War Intelligence Collection Flights (ICF) saw ever more sophisticated platforms being employed, ranging from balloons to aircraft and ultimately space-based satellites. The consolidation of Soviet control over Eastern Europe, the Berlin Airlift, the exploding of the USSR's first atomic bomb, the Korean War and other events rapidly accelerated the USA's desire for detailed targeting information. Besides the technological issues involved, extensive political bargains were struck between Britain and the USA to co-ordinate their deepening intelligence co-operation.

This combined British and US collection effort soon became extremely provocative as both countries engaged in deep-penetration overflights of the USSR, flouting its borders and breaching its sovereignty. The precise start of these long-range overflights in Europe is difficult to identify but in 1950, after the start of the Korean War, was a watershed in the process. A series of six meetings between prime minister and president took place in Washington during December 1950. The talks suddenly kick started military nuclear co-operation between the two, based largely on a series of 'informal understandings'. The deliberate ambiguity that seems to surround these meetings may well have included agreement on the collection of necessary intelligence for targeting purposes. US historian Cargill Hall refers to one meeting between Attlee and Truman, asserting (although admitting no archival material has emerged to support this) that the British agreed to join the USA in a co-ordinated overflight programme of the USSR. The details of this element of the 'understandings' were probably presaged by a conference at RAF Benson in October 1950 to discuss Cold War intelligence collection priorities. Hosted by RAF Bomber Command, attended by representatives from the War Office, Air Ministry, Admiralty, US and Canadian armed forces, it established early primary tasks for photographic collection.[7] These included discovering evidence of the Soviet ability to mount long-range air attacks on Britain and to use submarines against Western surface ships. Reporting the movement of Soviet ground forces, undertaking air survey and updating targeting maps to support a future strike force were all seen as important priorities. Some of these tasks would have necessitated direct overflight of Soviet and satellite territory and both states were prepared to accept the inherent risks of such a policy as an intensified overflight programme got under way.[8] By the spring of 1951 preparations were well advanced for the arrival of USAF B-45/RB-45 bomber and reconnaissance aircraft at RAF Sculthorpe in Norfolk.[9]

Operation Jiu-Jitsu

In 1951, well before the advent of the U-2, the British received a US request for the RAF to undertake a small number of radar reconnaissance missions over targets in the western USSR. The loss of a US Navy Neptune aircraft on a Far East peripheral flight in November 1951, together with an approaching election year and the high risk of losing a US overflight, have all been suggested as reasons for the USA seeking British support. The RAF duly obliged by forming the suitably anodyne 'Special Duties Flight' commanded by Squadron Leader John Crampton now deceased.

In late February 1952, after the selected crews had been trained on the RB-45 in the USA, Crampton was told that the flight's mission was to simultaneously fly three different routes to acquire 'radarscope photography' of airbases, missile sites and other important targets using the US-owned RB-45s that now sported RAF markings. The final case justifying the mission was made in a summary paper of February 1952 and approved by Prime Minister Churchill.[10] A gentle probe of the defences flying over the Soviet Zone of Germany for thirty minutes or so provoked no Russian reaction in March and the flight was ready for operations.[11] On 17 April, the three aircraft, flying at 36,000ft over the Baltic, after an air refuelling, split up to fly their separate routes. One followed a northerly track covering targets in the Baltic republics, another a Central route that went well beyond Minsk and approached Moscow, while the Southern mission went beyond Kiev and close to Rostov-on-Don in the Ukraine. The flights' results were viewed as a considerable success and the 'Special Duties Flight' then dispersed, only to be briefly reactivated in the autumn of 1952.[12]

This reactivation was short-lived because not all the Cabinet sub-committee ministers involved were comfortable with the flights. Anthony Eden, the Foreign Secretary, strongly objected to this second flight because he regarded it as of being of greater importance to the USA than to the UK: 'The information to be obtained by "Jiu-Jitsu II" is required primarily for the general atomic offensive on the USSR and not for the special attacks on Soviet bomber bases, which are so important for the defence of the United Kingdom.'

He questioned why the UK should undertake these highly risky flights when the USA was not prepared to do so itself. Ministerial colleagues accepted Eden's objections and the US authorities were informed of their decision and the proposals quietly dropped.[13]

The 'Special Duties Flight' came together for a final mission on 28–29 April 1954. The Northern and Central routes were much the same as before but the Southern route over the Ukraine went even further eastwards. Crampton's aircraft, on the latter route, encountered significant and prolonged anti-aircraft fire as it approached Kiev and night fighters were also launched to engage it.

Operation Jiu-Jitsu established an important precedent, clearly demonstrating how closely the two nations could integrate their efforts when there were perceived mutual interests.

Stepping Up the Surveillance

In the mid 1950s the USA faced great difficulties in collecting strategic intelligence on the Soviet Union. The huge landmass and the closed nature of the Soviet state and society meant very little useful information was overtly available to verify Soviet claims of military technical advances and a rapidly growing nuclear arsenal. The main means to gather this information was through photographic and signals intelligence. Peripheral SIGINT and shallow penetration photographic ICFs in Europe and Soviet Asia yielded valuable information but at a significant loss of life.[14] Even so, the flights were not providing the material really sought by US military planners and politicians.

Eisenhower's presidency oversaw a huge growth in technical intelligence gathering. Large budgets, rapid technological advances, careful management and some hugely talented individuals all played their part. The president demonstrated considerable political skill and practical statesmanship in managing the many divergent demands facing him. Many, including Eisenhower, were seriously concerned about the possibility of a surprise attack by the USSR. Congress was pressing for details of Soviet technology and military dispositions to justify the continual demands for huge increases in US defence spending to counter the growing 'Communist threat'. This pressure was compounded by the C-in-C, Strategic Air Command (SAC) – General Curtis LeMay – Congress, and the military generally, who pursued aggressive intelligence collection programmes for targeting purposes. Eisenhower had to manage these demands and balance them with efforts to improve relationships with the USSR's post-Stalinist leadership.

At a practical level, a lot of signals intelligence could be collected by distant monitoring posts and peripheral ICFs that did not violate sovereign airspace or borders. Photographic intelligence, of the quality required for targeting, needed either close proximity peripheral missions or direct overflights to discover Soviet bomber bases, missile sites, industrial complexes, command and nuclear secrets.

Eisenhower, who had been the Allied Supreme Commander in Europe in the Second World War, was acutely aware of what high-quality photographic intelligence could offer. Whilst not shy of developing the collection means, he was well aware that overflights of Soviet territory were highly provocative and tantamount to a declaration of war. There were also worries about domestic reactions, particularly from US public opinion, if its own government was seen to be so flagrantly violating international law.

The USA developed mechanisms for the political control of sensitive peripheral and overflight programmes intended to mitigate their inherent risks. It also established the political and military controls necessary for their management which lasted beyond the Cold War's end. To avoid duplication and 'overspill' most peripheral missions and the Corridor programmes were co-ordinated through agreed monthly schedules. However, deep-penetration flights remained firmly subject to presidential scrutiny and authorisation. Most US deep-penetration overflights took place during the Eisenhower presidency. The original 'broad approval' process quickly became subject to more rigorous controls. In the early days, Staff Secretary General Andrew Goodpastor recalls authorisation discussions being just between the Chairman of the Joint Chiefs – General Nathan Twining or Admiral Arthur Radford. Later Secretary Dulles, or the CIA's Richard Bissell, would provide Eisenhower with a memo detailing the justification for the flight and a proposed routing. The president would examine the individual mission proposals in detail.[15] The possible intelligence gain was weighed against the likely political embarrassment if something went seriously wrong. Eisenhower also came to insist on the tighter specification of flight dates and the length of time for which the flight authorisation remained valid.[16] Knowledge of operations was initially kept to a very small group, with Staff Secretary Goodpastor acting as political 'cut out' to enable presidential deniability in the event of a disaster.

In the USA the continuing fears about the 'bomber and missile gaps' fed by senior military officers and many in Congress were further exacerbated by Khrushchev's regular pronouncements on the rapid advances of Soviet military technology. Without hard evidence the USA was unable to sort fact from exaggeration and outright fiction.

Preparing for the U-2

There were a number of projects reaching fruition that pushed photographic and SIGINT capabilities forward by large orders of magnitude. The secret development of the U-2 reconnaissance aircraft was followed by an even more ambitious programme that produced the SR-71 Blackbird. Many advances were facilitated through Eisenhower's 1954 establishment of the 'Technological Capabilities Panel'. The Panel pushed forward huge leaps in camera, lens and film technologies that were harnessed for the overflight programmes. Even more sensitive were the resources being invested to create viable space-based reconnaissance satellites to ultimately replace the need for manned overflights. However, until their arrival, politicians had little option other than to authorise ever more risky manned overflights to get the information they so desperately sought. By 1955, the U-2 had reached an advanced stage of development and was almost ready for operations.

The Four Power conference at Geneva in July 1955 addressed a wide range of political issues, including the future of Germany, the prospects for a surprise attack and arms control matters. It was there that Eisenhower launched his 'Open Skies' initiative on 21 July. This sought agreement for each side to conduct mutual overflights, to collect imagery of military installations and activities. Had the proposal been accepted it would have significantly reduced the US photographic intelligence deficit of the USSR. Whilst the locations of most major US military installations were already well known to the Soviets, the reverse was definitely not true. The proposal was quickly rejected by the Soviets, well aware that it would have represented a major asymmetric 'information loss' for them. Nikita Khrushchev's son, Sergei, years later wrote that his father very much feared that US overflights would quickly reveal Soviet weaknesses and perhaps have encouraged the USA to mount a pre-emptive attack whilst the 'balance of forces' was still in their favour.[17] The Soviet rejection of Open Skies removed the last internal hurdle to Eisenhower's authorisation of operational U-2 flights.

The U-2's radical design meant it could operate at such high altitudes that it initially flew well above Soviet air defences. Eisenhower was briefed that the poor performance of Soviet air defence radars might even mean that the U-2s would not be detected at all. After a flurry of flights in July 1956, one of which flew over Moscow itself, the programme was put on hold after the receipt of a Soviet protest note. The note misidentified the type of aircraft used, but it described the flights' routes with sufficient accuracy to demonstrate that the U-2s were not only being detected, but also successfully tracked by Soviet air defences. This revelation saw a significant decline in Eisenhower's early enthusiasm for the project and it seems he was prepared to halt further U-2 overflights even at that early stage.[18]

However, these few U-2 flights successfully ended the 'bomber gap' myth within SAC and the Administration. Bomber base photographs showed clearly that there were not masses of Bison bombers poised to strike at the Continental United States. The Administration's concern about the sensitivity of U-2 derived information was such that it was not prepared to share the revelations even with congressional leaders, so the public political debate raged on. The flights yielded far greater quantities of photography than the combined efforts of the British and US overflights had cumulatively produced until that time. However, the better-quality imagery from operations such as the Berlin Corridor flights was used to compare and positively identify some of Soviet hardware seen on U-2 photography.[19]

Although still wary of deep-penetration flights, Eisenhower authorised a few further U-2 overflights of the USSR. They were conducted mainly from Peshawar in Pakistan, between June and October 1957, to cover a wide range of targets in the Soviet Far East. But major U-2 operations over the USSR had already peaked. Whilst peripheral flights continued, attempts at positive political engagement with the USSR made continued U-2 overflights a counterproductive activity, given how closely the Soviets were tracking them. Richard Bissell explained the president's reluctance to authorise further overflights was for 'fear of being shot down and simply fear of provocation'.[20] Staff Secretary Goodpastor has stated that 'it always distressed Eisenhower that he was doing this, and it was only out of necessity – an ugly necessity'.[21]

After a Soviet Far East overflight out of Japan, on 1 March 1958, the strength of Soviet protests persuaded Eisenhower to put a brake on further missions. Increasing tensions over Berlin provided another justification for keeping the U-2s away from the Soviet bloc. Eisenhower warned that further overflights might provide a superficial justification for Khrushchev to move on Berlin, though other Administration members doubted it.[22] But numerous other flights continued over Eastern Europe, China, Indonesia, Indo-China and Middle East. There were no further U-2 missions over the Soviet Union for more than a year until the president reluctantly authorised two more individual flights in July and November 1959 because Soviet ICBM testing had recommenced and fears of the 'missile gap' continued to gather weight in US military and congressional circles. The CIA's Richard Bissell credited the U-2 missions with providing 'ninety percent of our hard intelligence information about the Soviet Union' in 1959, illustrating the paucity of available sources at the time.[23]

Britain and the Black Aircraft

In January 1956, just prior to the start of U-2 operations, the USA had sought British agreement to base U-2 aircraft at RAF Lakenheath in Suffolk, which was occupied by the USAF. The US intention was to mount an initial series of overflights from the base. But just prior to the commencement of their operations, there was a major, though unrelated, intelligence incident that politically embarrassed the government and significantly changed the political controls applied to all future British intelligence operations.

MI6 had mounted a botched operation to collect intelligence on the new propeller design of the Soviet Sverdlov-class cruiser *Ordjoninkidze*. It was moored in Portsmouth harbour, having brought the Soviet leaders, Nikita Khrushchev and Nikolai Bulganin, to Britain for a ten-day official visit. On 19 April 1956, Commander Lionel 'Buster' Crabb, RNVR, dived on the vessel and disappeared although it was fourteen months before his body was finally recovered. Much of the subsequent political scandal was played out in the British national press. The Head of SIS, John Sinclair, was sacked and replaced by the Head of MI5, Dick White, and the PM (Anthony Eden) ordered a review of UK intelligence operations.[24] Eden contacted President Eisenhower and requested a postponement of the proposed U-2 operations from Lakenheath, saying 'this is not the time to be making overflights from here'.[25] The USA consequently rapidly transferred operations to Wiesbaden and Giebelstadt in West Germany, from where the early U-2 flights over Eastern Europe and the Soviet Union were conducted.

The Suez debacle of 1956 saw Harold Macmillan become PM in January 1957. He, too, had been shaken by the successive espionage revelations that rocked the British establishment. He much preferred intelligence issues to be kept out of the public gaze and so took a significant interest in them. Like Eden and Eisenhower, Macmillan was keen to ensure that the intelligence operations did not undermine ongoing diplomatic discussions with the post-Stalin Soviet leadership. The conduct of intelligence operations needed to be much more sensitive to the daily political priorities. Political risk calculation was now a major driver in the conduct of intelligence operations by Britain and the USA.[26] However, for both Eisenhower and Macmillan events almost seemed to conspire to wreck their desire to keep intelligence issues in the shadows. Revelations about Soviet agents within the British establishment and the shooting down of US reconnaissance aircraft soon shone far too much light on intelligence topics for the comfort of those involved.

After Suez, Anglo-American relations quickly returned to normal and Britain regularly began to receive U-2 imagery. Information and copy images were briefed to

an RAF Air Commodore (and his assistant) based in Washington DC, then brought
to Britain to be shown to the PM, key military staff, government ministers and
officials.[27] Following the precedent set by Operation Jiu-Jitsu, the USA became interested in British participation in the U-2 programme. This would be a risk reduction
measure for the USA and provide another political decision-making centre for grant-
ing flight authority. British interest gathered pace during 1957. After seeing examples
of the imagery, Macmillan agreed that four RAF pilots would be trained to fly the
U-2, after which they deployed to Adana (now Incirlik Air Base) in Turkey during
November 1958.[28] In December 1958 a final exchange of letters confirmed the operational arrangements in which Macmillan reserved the right to be the final approving
authority for all flights using RAF pilots. He then quickly exercised it by preventing
British pilots undertaking overflights of the USSR, concerned as he was about the
growing tensions over Berlin and his own planned visit to the Soviet Union in early
1959. The political fallout from any overflight incident involving an RAF-piloted U-2
would have been extremely embarrassing to the British government and undoubtedly lead to renewed accusations of 'political ineptitude' in the media. Instead, the
RAF crews were employed on overflights of Middle Eastern targets.[29]

   In late 1959, Macmillan relented and authorised an RAF-piloted U-2 mission
over the USSR. On 6 December 1959, Squadron Leader Robert (Robby) Robinson
undertook Operation High Wire (Mission 8005) from Peshawar in Pakistan to Adana
in Turkey routing via Kuybyshev, Engels airfield and Kapustin Yar missile test range.[30]
The mission's photography was excellent but did not provide further ICBM intelligence as these were tested at the Tyuratam missile range (Baikonur). On 5 February
1960, Squadron Leader John McArthur left Peshawar to conduct Operation Knife
Edge (Mission 8009) that routed via Tyuratam again, followed by the Kazan Aircraft
Plant and then turned south to photograph a stretch of the Soviet rail network before
landing at Adana. No missile sites were detected but a new bomber, NATO code
name 'Backfin', was imaged at Kazan.[31]

Time Running Out: The Final U-2 Flights over the USSR

According to the National Security Agency (NSA) history of the U-2, two of the
final three successful overflights of Soviet territory were undertaken from Peshawar
by RAF pilots, with the final successful flight launched on 9 April 1960 flown by a US
pilot. The objectives of these final flights were largely to gather imagery to inform the
raging 'missile gap' debate. They covered targets including Dzhezhkazgan, Kapustin
Yar, Kazan, Kybyshev, Kyzylespe, Lake Balkash, Semipalatinsk and Tyuratam.[32]

   Eisenhower authorised a further deep-penetration flight for April 1960. The flight
(Mission 4154), also known as Grand Slam, was to route from Peshawar to Bodø
in Norway, overflying mainly nuclear-related sites. The flight suffered a series of
postponements because of a combination of poor political co-ordination, adverse
weather and equipment problems. The president insisted that the final date for the

flight would be 1 May 1960 – partly because of the forthcoming Paris summit scheduled for 14 May. On 1 May, after a late take-off from Peshawar, it climbed to its 68,000ft penetration height. Soviet air defence radars picked it up before it crossed the Soviet–Afghan border. After photographing the Tyuratam Missile Test range, the U-2 set course for Chelyabinsk near Sverdlovsk. At just over 70,000ft it appears to have been struck by an SA-2 Guideline surface-to-air missile (SAM), although this has been disputed. The pilot, Francis Gary Powers, managed to bail out, but was soon captured and later put on show trial in Moscow. The aircraft, despite having fallen from such a high altitude, remained largely intact and was later publicly displayed in Moscow. The cockpit and other wreckage of this U-2 are still in the Central Armed Forces Museum in Moscow. To put the U-2 missions over the Soviet Union into perspective, there were only twenty-four flights from 4 July 1956 until 1 May 1960.[33]

Immediately all peripheral missions, overflights and some Berlin Corridor missions were suspended. Sometime after this very public loss, Britain and the USA cautiously recommenced peripheral reconnaissance activities. On 1 July 1960 a USAF RB-47H, launched from RAF Brize Norton, was brought down by a Soviet MiG-19 fighter in international airspace off the Kola Peninsula with the loss of four crew, the rest being interned by the Soviets. This incident did nothing to defuse already tense relations between the superpowers and the political repercussions over the loss of these aircraft rumbled on into the 1960 Kennedy/Nixon presidential election campaign.

The shooting down of the two aircraft was seminal in the conduct, control and co-ordination of British and US ICFs. A heavily redacted, undated, summer 1960 Memorandum on all forms of aerial reconnaissance from the Eisenhower Archive details the levels of aerial activity. It also outlines the co-ordination of ICFs between the US military services and the British, largely achieved by agreeing flight timetables to eliminate possible confliction.[34] Prior to this there had been occasions when peripheral flights had taken place at the same time and in similar locations as penetrative overflights and these clearly needed to be de-conflicted.[35] In the early days many flight authorisations were handled in very short chains from the Pentagon and State Department to the White House, with 'go' messages being transmitted by key 'staff officers' (legmen) to senior commanders using personal codes. This may have been a satisfactory procedure when there were small numbers of flights, but as the numbers increased, they required stronger co-ordination.[36] The USAF's 'Special Activities Group' in the Pentagon was established to monitor all activities and to rapidly collect the details of any incident to ensure its timely reporting.[37] Even this system was too fragmented so Eisenhower decided to co-ordinate all of these activities in one place. This gave birth to the Joint Reconnaissance Center (JRC), under the JCS, that became responsible for the monitoring of all reconnaissance operations. It was in place just before Eisenhower left office in 1961.[38] At that time the JRC was co-ordinating around 500 flights per month graded as 'critical', 'sensitive', 'unique' or 'routine'. It maintained a monthly 'activities book' of planned flights from which to brief the JCS and the CIA.[39] These sensitive flights would recieve political approval from a small committee known by various names including: 'Special Group',

'303 Commitee' and '40 Commitee', consisting of top defence department, intelligence agency and administration representatives. The most sensitive missions, including overflights, usually required Presidential assent. Later in 1961 JRC progrannes were coordinated with other intelligence gathering efforts within the newly created National Reconnaissance Office (NRO).[40]

Big Safari

A key driving force that enabled the huge growth of intelligence collection operations were the rapid advances in technology. Whilst White House policy established the parameters of operations the technology had to be blended into suitable aircraft (and later satellites). For the US Air Force much of this was undertaken by Big Safari, which began in the shadows of the early Cold War and continues to this day. Beginning in 1952, this USAF Program Office grew rapidly and enabled the Air Force to develop and acquire specialist reconnaissance equipment. Individual programmes would generally pair a project with a selected contractor to develop, install and test the required equipment as efficiently as possible. Little fuss, little bureaucracy and as much secrecy as necessary were key features of Big Safari projects. Even today the Office continues to support significant numbers of projects at any one time.

The USAF has used a bewildering and confusing number of project and operation names connected with reconnaissance. In the early years most were comprised of two words with some using female names. Examples are: Wanda Belle, Nancy Rae, Pie Face, Sun Valley and Witch Doctor. Under Big Safari the naming system became more formalised, with the first word identifying the project's originating Command. So 'Rivet' belonged to Air Force Logistics Command, 'Senior' to HQ USAF, 'Creek' to HQ USAFE and 'Comfy' to the USAF Security Service (USAFSS). Renaming projects to suit the operational organisation of the day caused further confusion. For example, the ELINT C-130A/B programmes Sun Valley I and II, later became Rivet Victor, but there were many inconsistencies that all added to the camouflage.[41] Big Safari project aircraft were constant participants in European overflight, peripheral and Corridor operations throughout the Cold War.

The British connection with the US ICF programme did not end with the early U-2 flights. During the rest of the Cold War, the successors to the original U-2 (TR-1, U-2R and U-2S) were based in Britain variously at RAFs Alconbury, Mildenhall and Fairford, from where they launched missions covering an area from the Barents Sea to southern Europe and the Balkans. From the early 1970s, RAF Mildenhall hosted Detachment 4 of the 9th Strategic Reconnaissance Wing that flew the SR-71 Blackbird and U-2R Dragon Lady. There was also the RAF Akrotiri-based U-2 flying Olive Harvest missions that monitored the ceasefire positions surrounding Israel following the 1967 and 1973 Arab-Israeli wars and flew more secretive peripheral missions. Even today RAF Mildenhall continues to host RC-135 Rivet Joint aircraft from the 55th Strategic Wing to fly SIGINT ICFs in USAFE's area of interest and beyond.

Through their worldwide network of Cold War air bases, the USA and Britain could mount ICFs that covered the majority of the USSR's periphery and some of its Far Eastern interior. This was the stage on which the Cold War airborne intelligence battle was to be played out. Fear of conflict was at its highest in Europe, but it was across partitioned Germany, with its unique occupation status, that the likely protagonists faced each other across a common border in huge numbers. Considered a probable ignition point for any future general war, Germany provided the respective intelligence communities with a unique window on the others' military forces and activities. These opportunities were quickly seized upon by both East and West to generate valuable streams of intelligence.

Notes

1   R. Aldrich (1998), 'British Intelligence and the Anglo American "Special Relationship" during the Cold War', *Review of International Studies*, Vol. 24, No. 3, p. 331.
2   Aldrich (2001), *The Hidden Hand: Britain, America and Cold War Secret Intelligence* (London: John Murray Books), p. 213.
3   Ibid., p. 207.
4   Ibid., pp. 206–17.
5   D.A. Brugioni (2010), *Eyes in the Sky: Eisenhower, the CIA and Cold War Aerial Espionage* (Annapolis, MD: Naval Institute Press), pp. 50–2.
6   Aldrich (2001), p. 210.
7   Ibid., pp. 394–5.
8   P. Rodgers (2001), 'Photographic Reconnaissance Operations', *RAF Historical Society Journal*, No. 23, pp. 69–70.
9   R. Cargill Hall and C.D. Laurie (2003a), *Early Cold War Overflights 1950–1956: Symposium Proceedings*, Vol. 1: *Memoirs* (Washington DC: Office of the Historian, National Reconnaissance Office), pp. 2–3.
10 R. Cargill Hall and C.D. Laurie (2003b), *Early Cold War Overflights 1950–1956: Symposium Proceedings*, Vol. 2: *Appendixes* (Washington DC: Office of the Historian, National Reconnaissance Office), Doc 22–1, p. 444.
11 J. Crampton (1997), 'RB-45 Operations', *Air Intelligence Symposium*, RAF Historical Society, Bracknell Paper No. 7, p. 124.
12 H. Wynn (1997), *RAF Nuclear Deterrent Forces* (London: HMSO), p. 112.
13 The National Archive, AIR 19/1126: PM/52/149, Anthony Eden to PM, 28 November 1952.
14 The first major loss of life resulted from the shooting down of a US Navy PB4Y-2 reconnaissance aircraft over the Baltic Sea on 8 April 1950 in which ten men were killed.
15 A. Goodpastor, 'Cold War Overflights: A View from the Whitehouse', in Cargill Hall and Laurie (2003a), pp. 40–1.
16 Brugioni (2010), pp. 118–19, p. 153.
17 Ibid., p. 133.
18 M.R. Beschloss (1986), *Mayday: Eisenhower, Khrushchev and the U-2 Affair* (London: Faber & Faber), p. 133.
19 Brugioni (2010), p. 149.
20 Beschloss (1986), p. 150.
21 Ibid.
22 Ibid., p. 151.

23 Ibid., p. 5.
24 See Chapter 4.
25 Beschloss (1986), p. 116.
26 R. Aldrich (2011), *GCHQ* (London: Harper Press), p. 203.
27 Brugioni (2010), pp. 170–1.
28 A fifth, Squadron Leader Christopher Walker, had been killed during training in the USA in July 1958. G.W. Pedlow and D.E. Welzenbach (1992), *The Central Intelligence Agency and Overhead Reconnaissance, 1954–1974* (Washington DC: History Staff, CIA), p. 155.
29 Ibid., Appendix D, pp. 337–8.
30 Ibid., p. 164.
31 Ibid., p. 167.
32 Ibid., Appendix D, pp. 337–8.
33 Ibid., p. 175.
34 www.eisenhower.archives.gov/research/online_documents/aerial_intelligence/ Summer_1960.pdf.
35 R.K. Rhodarmer, 'Recollections of an Overflight "Legman"', in Cargill Hall and Laurie (2003a), p. 20.
36 Ibid., pp. 20–2.
37 www.eisenhower.archives.gov/research/online_documents/aerial_intelligence/ Summer_1960.pdf.
38 Brugioni (2010), p. 359, and F.L. Smith, 'Overflight Operations: Another View', in Cargill Hall and Laurie (2003a), pp. 35–6.
39 Pedlow and Welzenbach (1992), pp. 189–90.
40 Rhodarmer, in Cargill Hall and Laurie (2003a), p. 29.
41 W. Grimes (2014), *The History of Big Safari* (Bloomington, IN: Archway Publishing), pp. 1–3, 31.

Germany and Berlin Divided: Cockpit of Cold War Intelligence Gathering

Soviet power ... does not work by fixed plans. It does not take unnecessary risks. Impervious to logic of reason and ... highly sensitive to logic of force ... If the adversary has sufficient force and makes clear his readiness to use it, he rarely has to do so.

The Sources of Soviet Conduct (George Kennan, 1947)

The division of Germany and Berlin in 1945 cast a shadow well beyond the end of the twentieth century. Until its end in 1990 it was profound, shaping much of Europe's political, economic, military and social landscape for that era. It resulted from the early failure by the four wartime allies to adequately manage the huge complexities of a defeated Nazi Germany, coupled with the rapidly growing distrust and disputes between them.

By mid 1943 it was clear that Germany was beginning to lose the war. The Allied Powers (Britain, Soviet Union and United States) began making tentative plans to deal with the defeated Axis powers of Germany and Japan. Even at this early stage the tripartite division of Germany was proposed with a similar treatment for Berlin.

At Yalta in February 1945, Stalin, Churchill and Roosevelt made further major decisions on the structure of the post-war world to follow imminent Nazi defeat. The leaders knew that victory in Europe was practically assured, so discussions looked at arrangements for its future borders. France was to be given a role in Germany's post-war governance, with its own occupation zone, created from territory already allocated to Britain and the USA. However, the conference discussions over Germany's future were largely inconclusive.

Following the German unconditional surrender on 8 May 1945, Allied leaders met at Potsdam between 17 July and 2 August 1945 to negotiate the detailed terms for ending the war and determining Europe's post-war borders. However, by this time the political environment had already changed significantly. Following Roosevelt's untimely death, the USA had a new president in Harry S. Truman. In Britain, the

July General Election swept the Labour Party to power and Clement Attlee replaced wartime Prime Minister Winston Churchill. Continuity rested with Josef Stalin and the Soviet Union.

The decisions taken at the conferences laid the foundations for East–West relations for the next forty-five years. It soon became apparent that differences in the wartime Allies' ideology and views of the post-war world were growing and good relationships were unlikely to survive long after Nazi defeat.

Ultimately Yalta and Potsdam were largely inconclusive with respect to the central issue of what to do with post-war Germany. The question was certainly too complex to resolve quickly. It was also complicated by the actors' vastly different conceptions, or more accurately, an insufficiently common conception, of what post-war Germany should look like. Within the individual Western governments there were highly contrasting views. US Treasury Secretary Morganthau had proposed a permanent dismemberment of Germany. This 'year zero' option, called for the removal of all significant industrial capability from the country. Others favoured some limited reconstruction to enable Germany to make new reparations. At the opposite end of the scale, many felt that the punishments inflicted by the Versailles Treaty on Weimar Germany after the First World War had been too severe. In particular the huge reparations had sown the seeds for the growth of Nazism, so a repetition of this was to be avoided at all costs.

Stalin's short-term concerns were much more pragmatic. He was determined to ensure that the remaining industrial capacity, at least in the Soviet Occupation Zone (SOZ), was rapidly dismantled and moved eastwards. This was seen as the 'first instalment' of future reparations to compensate the USSR for its massive wartime losses.

There was a clash of political wills: the Soviets wanted a subservient German state that could never again become a major European threat, either economically or militarily. On the other side, the Western Allies wanted Germany to become an economically viable and politically independent entity in Europe, albeit without any international presence or armed forces. This would relieve them of the considerable economic and political burdens of governing their occupation zones. The Soviets' initial aspiration was to persuade the Western Allies to leave Berlin and ultimately Germany. Stalin did not expect British and US forces to remain in Germany for long and believed they could be persuaded to leave by the judicious application of pressure. In the face of often opposing views, attitudes on both sides hardened and relations between the former wartime Allies deteriorated further.

The Allied leaders agreed the status of a demilitarised and disarmed Germany under four Allied occupation zones. The zones had been determined largely by the Allied forces' dispositions at the time of the German surrender, with some later adjustments. The reconstitution of a national German government was postponed indefinitely, and the Allied Control Commission (ACC) – composed of the four occupying powers – would govern the country in the interim.

Each zone was governed by a Military Government, headed by a Military Governor, usually the senior military officer from the respective occupying state.

Most complex of all was Berlin, former capital of the Reich, which was divided into four sectors that were to be governed in a similar fashion to the main occupation zones. This seemingly straightforward decision created a Western enclave deep inside the SOZ that became a running sore for the next forty-five years.

Whilst political partition was created, in theory the German economy was to be managed as a single unit. If the political problems were proving intractable, economic issues were of an even more profound nature. Financially bankrupt, the British and French could not afford to support their occupation zones for very long. The Soviets' removal of industrial capacity from their occupation zone and East Berlin showed little sympathy for the German population under their control. The USA also quickly realised that maintaining its own occupation zone was prohibitively expensive – especially when it was continually being called upon to provide additional resources to support the other Allies' zones. It rapidly became apparent to the Western Allies that the regeneration of the German economy was urgent and essential, even if only to stave off immediate economic disaster. To counter political stagnation and kick start economic renewal the British and American Zones became a single economic entity in 1948, known as the 'Bizone', that the French Zone later joined. The creation of the Deutschemark (DM) as the Western Zones' currency was soon followed by the Marshall Plan for European economic recovery. Moscow viewed these actions as measures designed to marginalise its influence and control. They certainly hardened the growing divisions between the Western and Soviet occupation zones.

The Soviets continued to maintain large armed forces and were known to be aggressively pursuing a nuclear weapons programme hidden away from prying eyes in the USSR's huge continental interior. In the face of this, the British and Americans quickly discarded their early plans to rapidly demobilise their considerable wartime forces in Germany. Initially they had just wanted to leave sufficient there to maintain and administer their occupation zones. However, they soon found it necessary to return men and equipment into their occupation zones to meet the growing Soviet threat. Stalin was determined to ensure that the SOZ remained under direct control until there was a final settlement of the 'German question'.

Operating in Berlin

Whilst high politics was moving towards formal partition, British, French, Russian and US military and German civilian personnel tried to make those arrangements that had been agreed work as best as they could. Inevitably their daily activities were affected by the high-level negotiations and decisions. Daily interactions were not always smooth. They were frequently full of inconsistencies, fed by a growing combination of distrust, fear, competing ideology, realpolitik and simple uncertainty. On the ground, relationships between the Western Allies and the Soviets were not the closely orchestrated, well co-ordinated competition that is often alluded to. They were more a continuous mixture of 'make-and-mend' contacts between the Western and Soviet administrations as they tried to cope with constantly changing priorities. They were based on a combination of formal rule-driven behaviour, locally evolved informal processes, the application of common sense and equally often the complete absence of any apparent rationale whatsoever. This was at its most obvious in Berlin.

After the Potsdam Conference it was apparent that progress would be slow. The Soviets often took a very 'legalistic' approach to working with the Western Allies. They would generally stick very closely to the wording of any agreement, often interpreting it in ways that obstructed and frustrated wider Western objectives. A very early example of this was the Soviet foot dragging over allowing the Western Allies to occupy their agreed Berlin City Sectors, until forced to concede. It was a precursor of things to come. Equally they would sometimes try to stretch a point too far, or try to push the Allies well beyond the detailed wording of any agreement. In such situations, when challenged, they usually stepped back, but if unchallenged they quietly accepted the gain made.

Creation of the Air Corridors and Berlin Central Zone (BCZ)

The day-to-day practicalities of managing the Western Sectors of Berlin meant that organised access was vital. Between May and November 1945 air access to Berlin was a 'free for all' in the SOZ's airspace. This unco-ordinated approach to air traffic management was potentially dangerous and certainly not conducive to good air safety. Air traffic into Berlin needed to be properly co-ordinated, controlled and regulated if incidents and accidents were to be avoided.

In summer 1945, to ensure the safe passage of the British and US delegations to the Potsdam Conference, two ad hoc controlled air corridors were established over the SOZ. The Western Allies' understanding was that these corridors were a temporary measure for the conference's duration. However, afterwards the Soviets formally complained to the Western Allies that they were flying outside the 'agreed corridor' and this would not be tolerated, indicating that they had no intention of returning to the previous 'free for all' air access.[1]

Detailed discussions followed to formalise Air Corridors over the SOZ that would provide the Western Allies with regulated air access to Berlin. During the discussions the Commander of the Soviet Forces in Germany, Marshal Zhukov, explained at least part of the Soviets' rationale for formalising the Air Corridors. The British recorded his statement that corridors were necessary 'to prevent your aircraft from observing Russian armies'.[2] On 30 November 1945 the agreement establishing the three Air Corridors to the Western Zones was signed by the wartime Allies.[3] The Soviets probably felt that the Air Corridor concession would cost them little – there were only a small number of air movements into Berlin at the time, carrying mail and a few passengers. It provided greater safety for their flights, constrained the movements of Western aircraft and reduced the possibilities of flights over sensitive Soviet installations. And when the Western forces withdrew from Berlin, as intended, the concession would become redundant.

The three Corridors were each 20 statute miles wide and connected Berlin to Hamburg, Hannover and Frankfurt-am-Main respectively. The Corridors terminated in the 40-statute-mile diameter BCZ, also known as the 'Chucker' or 'Chukka'. The centre point of the BCZ was a pillar in the cellar of the Allied Control Authority building on Kleistpark in Berlin. The reason for using statute miles, rather than the nautical miles normally used in aeronautical matters, is attributed to General Montgomery who, when asked what sort of miles were to be used, is said to have responded, 'Proper miles of course.'

Berlin Air Safety Centre (BASC)

The Corridor agreement also established the BASC to co-ordinate air traffic in the Corridors going to and from West Berlin and within the BCZ. It was one of only two Four Power organisations that continued to operate in Berlin throughout the Cold War following the Soviet walk-out from the Berlin Kommandatura in 1948.

The BASC operated for twenty-four hours a day all year round until its closure on 31 December 1990. Each of the Four Powers was represented by a Chief Controller, with a Deputy and General Duty Controller, all of whom were Air Force officers. The Soviets generally had both a controller and an interpreter on duty.[4] The BASC did not speak directly to aircraft but worked closely with the Berlin Air Route Traffic Control Centre (BARTCC) based at the US Tempelhof Airbase. BARTCC was manned and operated by the Americans and provided the physical control of flights and air traffic facilities such as radar coverage and controllers. The simplest procedure required a flight plan to be filed with BASC two hours before departure. The flights origin in the Western Zone(s) and termination in Berlin, or vice versa, would be verified. After confirming the flight's eligibility to use the Corridors and BCZ through meeting conditions such as nationality and aircraft type, the BASC produced a flight safety card agreed by all the national representatives. The flight would then be cleared to transit the Corridors and BCZ. Any traffic not meeting these requirements had their flight safety card stamped 'Safety of flight not guaranteed', usually by the Soviet representative. This did not prevent such flights proceeding but they did so at the operator's risk and were still obliged to obey BARTCC instructions. Departure and arrival information was generally passed by telephone and teleprinter between the Berlin airfields, Berlin ATC, the ATCCs at Hannover and Frankfurt and the BASC. Besides air traffic co-ordination, the BASC's responsibilities included the logging of protests of Corridor and BCZ infringements.

The Corridor agreement did not cover every detail of operations, so there were inevitably differences of interpretation between the Western Allies and the Soviets from the outset. Frequently 'custom and practice' came to fill the less clearly defined areas of the Corridor agreement. A new 'restriction' or 'objection' would sometimes be raised by the Soviets to some 'excess' they felt that Western aircraft were perpetrating. The new restriction would usually be rejected by one or more of the Western powers. They would then deliberately flaunt the newly applied restriction to test any Soviet reaction – more often than not there was none. But the Western powers often made some accommodation, such as tacit recognition, slightly modified behaviour, or reaching an informal compromise. This would see a general acquiescence in practical terms by the Western Allies – without formal recognition – when they felt that it did not affect their vital interests.

An example was the Soviet assertion that the Corridors were only to be used for the resupply of Western garrisons in Berlin and therefore flights should be restricted to unarmed transport aircraft only. Their claim was rejected by the Allies. Following the Berlin Airlift, the Soviets again pressed their case and claimed that the Allies were not permitted to fly 'combat aircraft' in the Corridors, despite having done so previously. Again, this claim was rejected by the Allies. They then between themselves revisited the claim and, whilst still rejecting the Soviet position, it became 'custom and practice' that only unarmed transport and training aircraft used the Corridors and BCZ.

Similarly the Soviets denied the right of Allied aircraft to operate either above 10,000ft or below 2,500ft. This was another attempt to turn an agreed procedure into a rigid rule. Eventually the Western Allies reluctantly, but not formally, accepted the Soviet height restrictions in the Corridors being between 3,500ft and 10,000ft and in the BCZ from 2,500ft to 10,000ft.[5] In 1959 the US flew a C-130 into Berlin at 25,000ft to assert its access rights but the subsequent robust Soviet protest meant that it was never repeated.

The Corridors and BCZ were only open to aircraft of the four wartime powers. Other nations' aircraft wishing to use the Corridors and BCZ had to obtain prior permission from the BASC. East and West German registered aircraft were prohibited from using them at any time. Initially only military flights were permitted to use the Corridors and BCZ, but this was later extended to include civilian airliners and scheduled services by airlines from all four of the wartime Allies. These operated to and from the city to cater for the needs of residents, business and governments.

Berlin Under Stress

As relations between the wartime Allies deteriorated elsewhere in the world, much attention continued to be focused on Germany and Berlin. Both were simultaneously a cause of poor relations and indicators of the widening competition between the two blocs. The partition of Germany gathered pace and developments in Soviet and Western Zones began to parallel each other. In the SOZ, socialist economic reforms had taken place particularly in the agricultural and industrial sectors. The Social Democrats in the SOZ had been efficiently emasculated and forced to join with the Socialist Unity Party (SED), effectively eliminating any opposition to the Communists.

In early 1948, talks started in London between the Western Allies on the future of Germany, involving representatives from the Länder Assembly. It progressed to the creation of an Assembly, a Basic Law and ultimately the declaration of the Federal Republic (FRG) in September 1949, to be based in Bonn. Mirroring political developments in the West, the constitution of the Deutsches Demokratik Republik (DDR) with its civilian government in Berlin was declared in October 1949. Predictably, each side refused to recognise the other's arrangements for German governance.

The Soviet blockade of West Berlin from 24 June 1948 until June 1949 was the first major crisis over the city and an early Cold War confrontation. It indicated Stalin's growing impatience with the continued presence of Western forces in the city. As relationships between East and West had spiralled downwards, a long-term settlement of the German question was becoming increasingly unlikely.

Berlin lay some 100 miles inside the SOZ and although the Western Allies had surface access by road, rail and water, these were never formally agreed as the Air Corridors were. By unilaterally closing the surface routes, the Soviets' apparent objectives were to drive the Western Allies from Berlin and starve the civilian populace into accepting Soviet rule. The crisis could have easily escalated into a general European war. The decision to supply the city solely by air was a courageous one, in what is still frequently referred to as 'the greatest humanitarian airlift in history'. The Allies (predominantly the USA and Britain) flew close to 278,000 flights carrying in more than 2.3 million tons of supplies into the city, costing the lives of seventy-one military personnel.[6] Although the blockade was lifted in June 1949, the airlift continued until September to accumulate reserves in the city in case of a repeat. Among the huge number of supply aircraft heading to Berlin during the airlift there were occasional British and US reconnaissance flights, trying to discover Soviet military dispositions and intentions.

During the blockade the Soviets threatened to increase their own air exercises, which would impinge on the Corridors. Indeed they did so in September 1948 but punctiliously filed their activities with BASC.[7] Anti-aircraft firing practice and mock air engagements continued into October and caused some problems, particularly for traffic in the Northern Corridor. Western objections were met by Soviet counter accusations of infringements and threats to cancel the Corridor agreements. Similarly, in the final stages of the airlift in May 1949, more Soviet air exercises and ground firing threatened to interrupt the Corridors again.[8] Whilst Soviet harassment of airlift traffic was not uncommon, they never took systematic action to deliberately bring down aircraft involved in it. Perhaps somewhat ironically it was Soviet insistence on the formalisation of the Air Corridors into the city in 1945 that ultimately assured its survival in 1948–49.

By the end of the 1940s US–Soviet relations had become very fractious. Away from Germany, there had been tensions between the two over the Soviets refusal to withdraw troops from Iran and threats to Turkey over access through the Black Sea to the Mediterranean. Communist parties and movements were being electorally successful in Western Europe and the rest of the world. Throughout Eastern Europe the Americans, British and French could only watch the installation, in rapid order, of Communist governments in Czechoslovakia, Poland, Hungary, Albania, Romania and Bulgaria, all under Soviet domination. In Asia the defeat of the Chinese Nationalists and the ascent of the Communists, the partition of Korea and Communist insurgencies across much of the territory recently occupied by the Japanese were just some of the early disputes.

The Second Berlin Crisis

In the years following the airlift, reconstruction and managing practicalities were the priority in Berlin. Berlin became a particular focus for friction between East and West again between 1958 and 1962 in what was later known as the 'second Berlin crisis'. Tensions centred on a whole series of issues: Berlin's status as a Western 'outpost' in the East, the haemorrhaging of East German citizens to the West via the city, U-2 deep-penetration flights over the USSR, the creation of the FRG, NATO plans to allow German aircraft to carry nuclear weapons and restrictions on official travel that led to the 'face off' at 'Checkpoint Charlie' in October 1961. It was only the near disaster of the Cuba crisis in October 1962 that finally took the focus away from Berlin. The city was an obvious place for the Russians to apply pressure on the Western Allies because of its vulnerability. Afterwards, in an August 1963 speech, Khrushchev described the problem Berlin posed for the West in typical manner: 'Berlin is the testicle of the West. When I want the West to scream, I squeeze on Berlin.' It may be a rather earthy analysis but it captured its vulnerability succinctly.

In November 1958 an increasingly confident Nikita Khrushchev had quickly generated tension by demanding that the West stop using West Berlin as 'a springboard for intensive espionage, sabotage and other subversive activities'.[9] Although not imposing a blockade, he threatened that if the West did not withdraw its forces from the city, within six months, the USSR would conclude a separate peace treaty with the East German government. The Soviets also expressed preparedness to hand over control of the Air Corridors to the GDR. Whilst this was unacceptable to the West, simply not to have engaged with Khrushchev would have left the problem unresolved and possibly risked further escalation. Significant pressure on Khrushchev to reach a settlement over Berlin was being exerted by the East German leader Walter Ulbricht. Having no direct control over the city, Ulbricht was struggling to stem the haemorrhaging flow of East Germans going to the West through Berlin, and demanded the Soviets put a halt to it. In the United States President Eisenhower stated American intentions to stand firm on Berlin and in December, despite further Soviet demands, the three Western Allies firmly rejected Khrushchev's demands for them to leave Berlin.

British Prime Minister Harold Macmillan visited the USSR for two weeks in late February 1959 when Khrushchev indicated his willingness to let the deadline slip if the West agreed to a summit to discuss the matter. From the great comfort of fifty-plus years later, it is apparent that Khrushchev's ultimatum was a negotiating tactic to try to restart the stalled 'German question' discussions. Nevertheless this was an excellent example of Khrushchev's 'testicle squeezing' upon the West and it had the desired effect. Macmillan and Eisenhower agreed to a preliminary Foreign Ministers meeting at Geneva in May 1959 with a full summit scheduled for May 1960 in Paris. That conference was ultimately scuppered by the shooting down of Powers' U-2 high over the heart of the USSR on May Day 1960.

What Faced NATO?

On 9 July 1945, the Group of Soviet Occupation Forces Germany (GSOFG) was formed from elements of the 1st and 2nd Belorussian fronts, becoming an Army of Occupation. These occupation forces were subsequently maintained at close to war-time levels, soon considerably outnumbering the combined Western forces facing them. In 1949 they were renamed the 'Group of Soviet Forces in Germany' (GSFG), which remained in being until 1 June 1989 when they became the Western Group of Forces (WGF) as the Soviet hold on Eastern Europe began to unravel. This formation stayed in Germany until 1994 when the total withdrawal of Russian forces was completed. These forces were huge, supplemented until 1990 by the GDR's own military services.

At the height of the Cold War, GSFG could muster 21 Tank and Motor Rifle (armoured infantry) Divisions grouped into 5 armies and a single front that each possessed its own subordinate units. In total they consisted of nearly 500,000 personnel with some 6,100 Main Battle Tanks (MBTs), 8,000 armoured vehicles, 4,300 artillery pieces which included 600 multiple rocket launchers and 200 surface-to-surface missile systems, 1,200 air defence systems (including surface-to-air missile systems), 310 attack helicopters and 350 transport and utility helicopters. The 24 (later 16) Tactical Air Army provided fixed-wing air support to GSFG. Helicopter units were usually subordinated to the relevant Army-level formation, except for one regiment that was a front-level asset. The Tactical Air Army possessed around 610 fighter aircraft, 320 fighter-bombers, 50 attack and 120 transport helicopters.

The huge Soviet presence was supplemented by the GDR's forces, consisting of the East German Army – the National Volksarmee (NVA). The NVA had six Tank and Motor Rifle Divisions grouped into two Military Districts (MD) and the Ministry of National Defence (MND), each of which had directly subordinate units of its own. There were also five reserve Motor Rifle Divisions. These forces consisted of 180,000 personnel and operated around 2,700 MBTs, 5,400 armoured vehicles, 1,700 artillery pieces (including 200 multi-barrel-rocket-launchers (MBRL)) and 700 air defence systems, including SAM systems. There were also some 40 attack and 110 transport helicopters. The East German Air Force consisted of two Air Divisions and could muster around 450 fighter aircraft, 90 fighter-bombers, 50 attack and 120 transport helicopters. The East German Navy was composed of three flotillas based on the Baltic coast. It was predominantly a coastal force but did have a considerable amphibious warfare capability plus three squadrons of helicopters.

The four Border Guard (Grenz Truppen) commands were in essence another Military District but without heavy armour and self-propelled artillery. The Border Guard had around 47,000 personnel and besides small arms they also operated some obsolescent armoured vehicles and artillery pieces.

The Soviets and East Germans occupied nearly 900 installations at some 400 locations in the GDR. These included over 55 airfields and 150 major training areas and ranges. About 40 per cent of these locations lay either directly beneath or adjacent to (up to 20 miles outside) the Corridors and BCZ. There were also other locations that could be seen from the air along the Baltic Coast of the GDR and near the German–Czechoslovakian border. The installations in the GDR that could be viewed from the Corridors, BCZ and their immediate environs are listed in the appendix. Beyond any doubt this was an intelligence 'target rich environment' and for the next forty years both sides conducted an intelligence battle across the IGB using all means at their disposal.

Intelligence Resources

Both sides possessed a formidable array of assets in Germany to acquire the intelligence sought by national governments, military staffs and Germany-based commands. The Western Allies' assets included HUMINT: the division of Germany presented many opportunities for HUMINT exploitation. West Germans could travel to visit families in the GDR, although reciprocal trips were not possible. Such movements of people provided one source of information. Civilian employees of the Allied forces were required to report any visits to the GDR and on their return were usually debriefed by military or civil security authorities. There was also a constant flow of refugees from the East as well as defectors and controlled sources (spies).

A key and very successful resource was the unique presence of the Allied Military Liaison Missions (AMLMs) created after Allied occupation of Germany by the war-time Allies.

Allied Military Liaison Missions
Because the GDR was diplomatically unrecognised, there were no Western military attachés based there. Their nearest equivalents were the three Allied Military Liaison Missions (AMLMs), which were far more valuable. Established in 1946 and 1947 under individual agreements between the respective Western Commanders-in-Chief and the Soviet Commander-in-Chief, they were accredited with a quasi-diplomatic status. The British Mission's full title was the British Commanders'-in-Chief Mission to the Soviet forces in Germany, mercifully shortened to 'BRIXMIS' or 'The Mission'. The British, Americans and French had Mission Houses in Potsdam, also the home of the Soviet military headquarters until it moved to Zossen-Wünsdorf. The houses were where all Mission touring activity started and generally finished. Although the Mission houses were 'sovereign' territory, like an embassy, the locally employed East German staff reported the comings and goings at the houses. Mission members' activities, both official and personal, were closely monitored and reported, and communications were believed to have been monitored and intercepted and were accordingly regarded as insecure. The AMLMs' close proximity to Berlin meant that they also maintained HQs co-located with their own national headquarters in West Berlin, which gave them much more security, freedom and flexibility.

Reciprocal Soviet Military Liaison Missions were located in each of the three Western Zones. The Soviet presence in the British Zone was known as 'the Soviet Commander-in-Chief's Military Liaison Mission to the Commander-in-Chief

British Army of the Rhine', shortened to 'SOXMIS'. During its existence SOXMIS was located in Bad Salzuflen, Lübbecke and Bünde in special compounds but these were never sufficiently close to the GDR for them to have a separate HQ like the Allies in Berlin, so they were always rather more isolated in their operations.

BRIXMIS's primary official purpose was, according to the agreements, to maintain liason between the staff of the two Commanders-in-Chief and their military governments in the Zones to prevent incidents or events escalating to higher levels. Although emphasis quickly shifted onto intelligence collection the liaison function remained a core task throughout the Mission's existence. Because of this liaison function, and some of the personal relationships created, serious incidents, including the detention of Mission staff, could often be resolved without involving respective Commanders-in-Chief, diplomats or politicians.

BRIXMIS's intelligence collection included military and civil targets. To carry out these intelligence-gathering tasks BRIXMIS personnel were always unarmed, in working, not combat, uniform, and 'toured' throughout the GDR in specially marked military cars. They compiled visual, written and photographic reports on the activities they observed. Up to thirty-one British military personnel, referred to as being 'on pass', could be accredited to the GSFG Headquarters as being with BRIXMIS at any one time. They had relative freedom of movement within the GDR and their vehicles were regarded as being 'sovereign' territory and, in theory at least, inviolable. However, access was far from unfettered. The Missions were forbidden from penetrating designated 'Permanent Restricted Areas' (PRA), which theoretically placed the area out of bounds. Unsurprisingly, PRAs protected the high-value intelligence targets, including many of the Soviet and East German garrisons, airfields, major logistics facilities and training areas. PRAs were detailed on published maps. There were also designated Temporary Restricted Area (TRA) that were time limited, usually created to cover major military exercises or troop movements, often linking PRAs together. Unofficial 'Mission Restricted' signs, planted in the German countryside, were generally ignored by the Missions because they had no agreed official status and frequently became treasured souvenirs for Mission members. All these restrictions nevertheless inhibited Mission activities. However, the Soviets managed the imposition of PRAs and TRAs carefully because overuse ran the risk of provoking tit-for-tat restrictions on the Soviet Missions in the FRG.

The Missions deployed into the GDR every day, including Christmas Day, to observe activities, equipment and personnel. They recorded details, took photographs and sometimes returned with items of equipment and even, on a few occasions, pieces of ordnance. They had to be experts in military equipment recognition, learn Russian or German to a required standard and develop good photographic and later video skills. The aim was to get as close as possible to the opposition by stealth or using bluster and trickery to obtain the information they sought. For many Mission personnel this posting was often regarded retrospectively as a highlight in their military careers. Some experienced difficulty in returning to 'regular' soldiering afterwards. It was certainly a high-stress posting for many. In the early 1980s, following the Soviet invasion of Afghanistan, when East–West relations were particularly sour, Mission work became particularly dangerous. During this time there were two fatalities. Adjutant Chef Mariotti of the MMFL was killed in a deliberately engineered traffic accident in 1984, and in 1985 Major Nicholson of United States Military Liaison Mission (USMLM) was shot and killed by a Soviet guard close to a military installation at Ludwigslust. Throughout the Missions' existence there were many incidents of Soviet and East German forces causing physical injury to Mission members by administering beatings if they compromised an observation point, or during the detention of a 'Tour'.

The Mission's exploits were truly remarkable and are too numerous to describe in detail, though mention of a few of their intelligence 'scoops' gives an idea of what they achieved.

In 1966, BRIXMIS personnel liaised with Soviet military personnel who were trying to access the wreckage of a Yak-28 Firebar aircraft that had crashed into the British part of the Havelsee Lake in Berlin. Officially this meant keeping the Soviets away from the crash site until it and the crew's bodies could be recovered and returned by British forces.[10] Unofficially, they were co-ordinating the underwater removal of parts, including its then state-of-the-art radar, which were quickly spirited away to the UK for scientific examination. BRIXMIS successfully managed to stop the incident from becoming anything more than a very tense stand-off and illustrates BRIXMIS's liaison function in an exemplary fashion.

BRIXMIS members were expected to use their initiative and daring to gather intelligence. One Tour came upon a stationary train carrying BMP-2 armoured infantry combat vehicles (AICVs). A 'current priority intelligence requirement' was to discover the main armaments' calibre. A Tour member sneaked onto the train and pushed an apple into the weapon's muzzle before the train moved off, or he was shot at by a Soviet sentry. In 1987 the British Army tactic of 'acquisition' came into play when a Tour 'acquired' a sample of Explosive Reactive Armour (ERA) – 'it came off in me and Sir' – removed from a stationary Soviet T-80 MBT when no one was close by. At the time the composition and operation of ERA was a very high priority technical intelligence target.

The BCZ also gave BRIXMIS the opportunity to use the RAF Gatow-based Chipmunk aircraft for airborne observation and photography, covered in Chapter 6. There are several books about BRIXMIS and its operations that give comprehensive insights into their activities and modus operandi and they are highly recommended. They include works by Tony Geraghty, Steve Gibson and Major General Peter Williams.[11]

SIGINT: British, French and US forces engaged in significant SIGINT collection activities in Germany and Berlin. They utilised a network of ground-based listening posts, overlooking GDR territory. British airborne SIGINT assets operated peripheral flights mainly from the UK, where the necessary infrastructure existed to process the information collected. The French airborne effort originally flew from Germany before switching to Metz-Frescaty in 1966 when France withdrew from NATO. They too maintained ground-based listening stations. The US effort was largest of all with a major network of monitoring facilities and air assets. Most US airborne SIGINT assets were located in Germany, but they were frequently detached for periods of temporary duty across continental Europe from 1946 until 1974. From then most operations were undertaken by UK-based aircraft.

PHOTINT/IMINT: The existence of the Corridors and BCZ gave the Allies a unique situation that could be used to their advantage for the collection of PHOTINT/IMINT. The Corridors were internationally agreed and controlled airspace. Its rules allowed access to Berlin for some of the Western Allies' military and civilian aircraft. Aircraft using the Corridors and BCZ belonged to units on the published ORBAT and generally carried unit markings, flown by uniformed crews in airspace they were perfectly entitled to use. Whilst the risks to manned overflights of Soviet territory grew, Corridors and BCZ flights could be executed at comparatively low physical and political risk.

Being able to fly close along the IGB and through an important portion of East German airspace along the Corridors and around Berlin meant airborne intelligence gathering was an irresistible activity. All three Allies mounted their own airborne intelligence-gathering operations of varying scale and scope. The technical aspects of mounting equipment in a suitable aircraft and flying the missions could be difficult enough, but they were relatively straightforward when compared to the sensitive political risks attached to such activities elsewhere. To be at their most effective these flights required proper preparation, co-ordination and integration into the normal transport and training traffic going about its lawful occasions in the Corridors and BCZ.

Thus the stage was set for the execution of some of the most audacious ICFs of the Cold War that provided almost daily surveillance of installations in the GDR.

Notes

1   The National Archive, PRO AIR 55/257, Draft reply from Montgomery to Zhukov, 20 September 1945.
2   W.J. Boyne (2012), *The Berlin for Lunch Bunch*. Available at: http://www.airforcemag.com/ MagazineArchive/Pages/2012/July%202012/0712berlin.aspx.
3   The National Archive, PRO AIR 55/257, Allied Control Authority, Air Directorate, Committee of Aviation, Flight Rules for Aircraft Flights in Air Corridors in Germany and Berlin Control Zone, DAIR/P(45)71 Revised, 31 December 1945.
4   The National Archive: PRO DEFE 71/128, BASC Operations and Communications, pp. 1–2. This file provides a comprehensive description of BASC/BARTCC procedures.
5   In the 1946 agreement the BCZ is defined as 'the air space between ground level and 10,000 ft'. The National Archive, PRO AIR 55/257, Allied Control Authority, Air Directorate, Committee of Aviation, Flight Rules for Aircraft Flights in Air Corridors in Germany and Berlin Control Zone, DAIR/P(45)71 Revised, 31 December 1945.
6   R.G. Miller (1998), *To Save a City: The Berlin Airlift 1948–49* (Washington DC: Bolling AFB). Available at: http://www.afhso.af.mil/shared/media/document/AFD-101001–053.pdf, p. 109.
7   A. and J. Tusa (1988), *The Berlin Blockade: Berlin in 1948* (London: Hodder & Stoughton), pp. 291–2.
8   Ibid., p. 457.
9   J. Smith (1998), *The Cold War* (London: Blackwell) (2nd edn), p. 43.
10 The National Archive: FO 1042/226.
11 Details of these can be found in the bibliography.

3

AMERICAN CORRIDOR AND OTHER RECONNAISSANCE FLIGHTS

The US airborne intelligence collection effort in Europe was huge. Between 1945 and 1990, USAFE flew around 10,000 flights in the Berlin Corridors and BCZ – an average of a flight every one and a half days, which dwarfed British and French efforts. USAFE also conducted 'non-corridor' 'peripheral flights', from Federal Germany, as far afield as the Baltic Sea in the north, along the IGB and Czech-German border and south to the Adriatic, the Mediterranean and Black and Caspian seas. It also managed early penetration overflights over Eastern Europe before the arrival of the U-2. This extensive programme was conducted in conjunction with the discreet, passive and active support of other governments, including Denmark, West Germany, Greece, Norway, Sweden, Turkey and others.

European operations not only involved USAFE, but also other USAF commands, the US Navy, US Army and CIA. Most programmes were highly compartmentalised; a considerable number were very short-term and often overlapped with each other. They frequently used the same, or very similar aircraft, operating from the same bases, using crews and missions often mounted against the same 'targets'. These many operations were often interrelated and significantly impinged on Corridor and BCZ flights. The majority of the missions were launched from Wiesbaden and Rhein-Main (Frankfurt-am-Main International Airport) Air Bases. The Americans' efforts to disguise many of these operations made them even more impenetrable to outside observers – as they were meant to be.

US Units and Their Genealogy

On 1 November 1948, the 7499th Support Squadron (7499 SS) was formed at Fürstenfeldbruck Air Base (AB), near Munich, from the 45th Reconnaissance Squadron (45 RS) and elements of the 10th Photo Charting Squadron (10 PCS) and

10th Reconnaissance Group (10 RG). The squadron's inventory included A-26 Invaders, RB-17s, C-47 Skytrains and C-54 Skymasters configured for photographic, COMINT and ELINT reconnaissance roles. In August 1950 the squadron moved to Wiesbaden AB, bringing it closer to the centre of the USAFE organisation, and to the Berlin Corridors. In 1955, the 7499th Support Group (7499 SG) was formed from the 7499 SS at Wiesbaden AB with the 7405th, 7406th and 7407th Support Squadrons as subordinate units, each having its own distinctive role. The Group's operational remit has aptly been described as 'a cloak that drew tight over many matters'. Its operational area of interest stretched from the Baltic Sea to the Caspian and Black seas as well as Berlin Corridor and BCZ activity. The Group disbanded in March 1972, the 7406 SS having deactivated in June 1974 and the 7407 SS in 1959. The remaining squadron, 7405 SS, moved to Rhein-Main AB (Frankfurt) on 1 January 1975 and was renamed the 7405 Operations Squadron (7405 OS), remaining there until it disbanded on 23 January 1991.

Before flying operations ended in 1990 there were several changes of unit designation that attempted to align US 'Special Forces' in Europe operations with the 7405 OS flights and the work of the newly created Electronic Security Command (ESC). The 7580th Operations Squadron (7580 OS) was activated on 28 February 1983 and was responsible for providing specialist mission crews and 'maintenance personnel with the specialist skills' to look after its dedicated C-130Es reconnaissance equipment. The 7405 OS and 7580 OS were subordinate to the 7575th Operations Group (7575 OG) at Rhein-Main AB, formed on 1 July 1977. The Group also included the 7th Special Operation Squadron (7 SOS) based at Rhein-Main AB for a time, but it left the group in March 1983. The 7575 OG disbanded on 31 March 1991 following the deactivation in January 1991 of 7405 OS and 7580 OS.

The US Air Force Security Service (USAFSS)

Following its formation in 1947, the USAFSS, and later ESC, operated from many European locations for the duration of the Cold War. In Germany (and Berlin) it had a number of listening posts that monitored Soviet and East German radio transmissions and communication activities. It also provided 'back-end crew' (operators, linguists, analysts) for the peripheral COMINT collection missions flown by the 7406 SS 1956–74.[1] When the 7405 OS received a COMINT mission for its C-130Es in 1976, ESC's 6911 Electronic Security Squadron (6911 ESS) provided the specialised COMINT support needed. After 1982 that support was provided by Det 1, 6910 Electronic Security Wing (ESW), first from Hahn AB and then from Wiesbaden, until the 7405 OS ended collection missions in September 1990.

Early Post-Second World War Operations

In 1945, the Allies started a joint US–UK imagery collection programme over their respective occupation zones in Germany to update mapping, to help assess the needs of economic reconstruction and as a contingency against possible future military hostilities. Aware that post-war relations with the Soviets were going to be difficult, both were concerned that they lacked the necessary detailed targeting information about Europe that might be required in the event of a future global conflict.

In November 1945, the US 45 RS based at Fürth AB, near Nürnberg began to use its P-51D Mustangs and F-6Ks (the photographic reconnaissance version of the P-51 Mustang) to collect photographs over Germany. Details of these sorties are sparse, but by summer 1946 the squadron's 'Flight X' had flown a small number of camera-equipped A-26 Invaders on occasional covert Corridor reconnaissance missions. Former USAF major Roger Rhodarmer, then a captain, and an experienced A-26 pilot, was sent to Germany to join 10 RG for photographic reconnaissance duties, of which he had no experience. Once there he was shown a modified A-26 that had a carefully concealed, forward-facing oblique K-18 camera with a 24in lens installed in the nose for Corridor flights. Most of the two units' photographic reconnaissance tasks were not Corridor related, but involved flying between eighty and ninety hours a month on Project Birdseye, to photograph industrial and infrastructure 'targets' all over Europe at low level. The project was terminated in late 1946.[2] In March 1947, 45 RS moved to Fürstenfeldbruck AB. It was not just the A-26s that flew such missions. In June 1946 a handful of camera-equipped RB-17s of 10 PCS based at Fürth AB started flying Project Casey Jones flights. This was a series of photo-survey sorties to update maps covering significant areas all over Europe.

In 1947, Detachment 'A' of 10 PCS took on an ELINT collection role, following serious incidents in the Austrian–Yugoslav border areas. On 9 August 1946 a USAAF C-47 Skytrain had departed Tulln Airfield in Austria bound for Rome, via Venice, on a routine scheduled courier flight. It encountered adverse weather and unwittingly strayed into Yugoslav airspace where it was intercepted and shot down by Yugoslavian Yak-3 fighters. Fortunately all on board survived the subsequent crash-landing and were eventually released after being briefly interned. This sparked a series of sharp diplomatic exchanges between the US and Yugoslavian governments. Ten days later another C-47 was brought down in the same area by Yugoslav fighters. This time there were no survivors.

At HQ USAFE in Wiesbaden the question was – how could the Yugoslavs intercept the C-47s so effectively, especially in bad weather? The belief was that they possessed some form of radar fighter control capability, but hard evidence was lacking. To find the answer, two RB-17s were quickly fitted with intercept receivers and direction-finding antennae to equip them as 'ferret' or ELINT aircraft. On the first flight, along the Austrian–Yugoslav border, close to where the C-47s had been intercepted, transmissions from a familiar Second World War vintage German 'Würzburg' radar were detected, emanating from the site of a former German wartime radar school.[3] The mission's success encouraged USAFE to undertake further 'ferret' flights close to Soviet-occupied territory.

The Cold War

During the 1948–49 Berlin Airlift, the RB-17s would occasionally fly as part of a normal C-54 airlift 'block' along the Berlin Corridors. They only flew at night and never landed at Tempelhof because this would have compromised their true identity and mission. To avoid landing in Berlin, they would declare an 'emergency' that, under the strictly enforced airlift operating procedures, necessitated an immediate return to the Western Zones. Whilst the flights were attributed with detecting new radars, they did not discover any new equipment types.[4] A US Air Force report on the airlift indirectly identifies how the ELINT B-17s were covertly inserted into the airlift traffic flow under the guise of meteorological reconnaissance flights normally flown by the 7169th Weather Reconnaissance Squadron (7169 WRS). The squadron used 'weather' B-17s and flew from Wiesbaden AB too. Inserting an ELINT RB-17 into the night traffic flows, instead of a weather reconnaissance B-17, would not have been difficult. The report explains how the meteorological B-17 flights were intended to work:

> More difficult was keeping track of the fast-changing weather conditions along the Corridors and relaying that data back to the originating bases. General Smith began the process on 9 July by arranging for a B-17 from Wiesbaden to fly the Frankfurt to Berlin Corridor above the cargo aircraft to watch for thunderstorms and to provide immediate reports on bad weather. The first of these flights took place late that evening. In early August, Tunner's operations section concluded that two aircraft in every block should report the weather back to airlift headquarters, thus avoiding unnecessary use of radio facilities in the Corridor.[5]

Like Germany, occupied Austria was divided into British, French, Soviet and US zones, governed by the Allied Commission for Austria in an analogous way to arrangements for Berlin. Vienna was surrounded by the Soviet Zone and the air corridors gave Western Allies access to the city in the same way as the Corridors did for Berlin. They remained in place until May 1955. US aircraft, particularly RB-26s, prowled along the Austrian corridors monitoring Soviet installations and emissions until the end of the Austrian occupation. Donald Gardner, a 'Raven' with the 7405 SS between 1955 and 1959, described how the RB-26s flew down the corridor with 'a black box', a receiver where 'you just turn on the thing and record everything you get, up and back: air traffic control, or fire control, and stuff like that'.[6]

The number and range of airborne intelligence operations based in Germany grew continuously after the airlift. Frequent organisational and equipment changes were necessary to accommodate the plethora of relatively short-term, sometimes unique, projects that took place. Many were important in their own right, as part of the wider intelligence collection effort, but some overlapped with what were fast becoming more 'routine' Corridor and BCZ missions. These latter flights had overall approval from the JCS, later the Secretary of Defence and the White House, with day-to-day authorisation and execution being carried out in Germany. Aircraft generally flew twice daily, mostly on weekdays, but this was subject to the vagaries of equipment and weather that can hinder successful reconnaissance operations.

7405th Support Squadron (7405 SS)

Operating from Wiesbaden AB, the squadron's main responsibility was SIGINT and photographic reconnaissance flights in the Corridors and BCZ, but it also flew some peripheral missions along the Baltic coastline, the IGB and the FRG-Czechoslovak border. The unit was always very busy and frequently in a state of flux. New items of equipment were constantly being installed in the various aircraft types, operated in non-standard and often unique configurations. There were also temporary attachments of personnel and equipment for 'special' or short-term operations. These operations were mostly conducted in great secrecy, which means that finding the exact introduction and withdrawal dates for a particular aircraft and its associated projects and operations is difficult.

The squadron was initially divided into three flights:

'A' Flight: Flew predominantly peripheral ELINT missions using two ELINT equipped C-54D's between about 1955 and 1963 on Project Pretty Girl.

'B' Flight: Concentrated on photographic reconnaissance using four RB-26 Invaders, until they left service in 1958, and three C-47s until 1960. In addition, 'B Flight' also had a single C-54D (43–17248) Project Hot Pepper that arrived in 1950 and left in 1958.

'C' Flight: Responsible for military and diplomatic courier flights throughout Europe, North Africa and the Middle East and operated three C-118 (DC-6) aircraft on these duties until September 1965.

Finally there was the mysterious, but officially unconfirmed 'D' Flight. According to some sources this was rumoured to be a front for CIA-sponsored operations. Chris Pocock suggests that 'D' Flight aircraft were crewed by Polish exiles for CIA operations behind the Iron Curtain. It appears to have been disbanded in 1959 when there was a big reduction in the CIA's covert air operations.[7] In 1961, 'D' flight was recreated for the photo-equipped C-97Gs operation until 1965, when it became 'C' flight.

The Aircraft

Particularly in the early post-war years, the USA operated an eclectic mix of aircraft on Corridor and BCZ operations, including 'combat' types. After the 1953 unilaterally imposed Soviet ban on 'combat' aircraft in the Corridors and BCZ, usage became restricted to unarmed transport and trainer aircraft – though by practice not explicit agreement. Even when these 'permitted' types were used, clandestine photographic and SIGINT missions were conducted as discreetly as possible. The tell-tale bulges and aerials generally associated with SIGINT aircraft had to be minimised, made retractable, or disguised as much as possible. Cameras had to be hidden behind retractable hatches and covers. Despite such countermeasures, a close and knowledgeable observer would soon realise that these were not standard transport aircraft.

The 'designations' of the US aircraft types involved in the Corridor flights are often debatable. Various publications use designations such as EC-47, RC-54D, EC-97, RC-97, RC-130, C-130E-II amongst others, to describe them. Some designations were official, although they were not always applicable to the variants used in Germany, some were assumed, and others simply made up. Documentation, and those who worked on the aircraft often generally referred to them as C-97 or C-130, etc., identifying an individual aircraft by its tail number. It all helped maintain the external fiction, however thin at times, that these were just 'ordinary' transport and communication aircraft going about their daily trade.

Mustangs, Invaders and Fortresses

In 1945, 45 RS operated a mixture of P-51D Mustangs and F-6Ks (photographic reconnaissance Mustangs). There is some anecdotal evidence that they were used in the Corridors until their withdrawal in 1948.

'Flight X' of the 45 RS was established with A-26 Invaders. They used a carefully concealed forward-looking oblique K-18 camera with a 24in lens installed for Corridor flights. In 1948, the A-26s were redesignated RB-26s and served from 1946 until 1958. Using the call sign 'Slot', up to nine aircraft operated with the squadron, although usually only four aircraft were on strength at any one time. During this period there were two losses: on 30 July 1952 one crashed in a valley near Roith, Austria, and although there were no crew fatalities, several sustained major injuries. The following month another aircraft crashed just south-west of Wiesbaden following an engine fire, resulting in the loss of two crew members.[8] The RB-26's main camera fit was vertically mounted in the aircraft bomb bay and consisted of one K-17 with a 12in lens and a K-22 with a 24in lens, producing 9 × 9in images. A K-18 with a 24in lens, producing 9 × 18in images, was in a forward-facing oblique mount. Like the RB-17s they suffered from Soviet protests about 'combat types' but USAFE's response was that they were not on the strength of a combat unit and were used for fast courier flights to Berlin and as VIP transports.

After their adoption of the ELINT role in 1947, the Detachment 'A' RB-17s of 10 RG flew peripheral and Corridor missions. These aircraft were transferred to the 7499 SS in November 1948 and remained there until 1953. In their latter days the Soviets objected to the use of the RB-17, considering them to be 'combat types'. Their withdrawal was probably hastened by these protests. Up to eight RB-17s were used at various times during this period.

C-47 Skytrain

Between 1948 and 1960 up to eight C-47s passed through the unit, but only three were on the unit's strength at any one time. Some carried the markings of the 7167 Transport Squadron (7167 TS) then based at Wiesbaden. They used the call signs 'Willy' or 'WWA' under Project Red Owl. The cameras were installed beneath the cargo hold floor, which allowed the carriage of cargo and passengers to give an appearance of 'respectability' but made access to the cameras difficult. The C-47s are known to have carried a K-17 with a 12in lens and a vertically mounted K-22 with a 24in lens. Another three K-17s with 12in lenses mounted in a trimetrogen arrangement gave horizon-to-horizon cover. All the cameras produced 9 × 9in format images but there are unconfirmed reports of a camera being fitted that produced 9 × 18in format images.

In the early years visual reconnaissance was frequently practised. Sergeant Fordham of the USAFSS recalls that in 1953 he was tasked with standing in for his boss, Lieutenant Pearsall, on the weekly C-47 courier flight taking SIGINT material from Berlin to Wiesbaden. After take-off from Tempelhof, he was taken to the flight deck and as they overflew airfields along the Corridor, he and the flight crew noted the numbers and types of aircraft at each airfield. The flight crew had simply expected him to do this as Lieutenant Pearsall usually did so when he was on the weekly run.[9]

C-54 Skymaster

From 1950 ELINT and camera configured C-54s, of various models, flew from Wiesbaden on Corridor and peripheral missions, replacing the RB-17s. A total of ten aircraft passed through the squadron before they were replaced by C-97s in 1963.[10] Two ELINT equipped C-54D's served from 1955 until 1963 on Project Pretty Girl, although they had been Wiesbaden residents since 1951. On ELINT missions they carried a crew of thirteen that included seven electronic warfare officers. The onboard equipment included AN/APR-4 direction-finding receivers and an AN/APR-2 'panoramic receiver'. These aircraft had a very visible under-fuselage ELINT antennae, until a 1960 modification programme, and were employed on peripheral missions rather than Corridor flights.

A single C-54D (43–17248) arrived in 1949–50 to be employed on Project Hot Pepper. The aircraft was dual-role ELINT and photographic reconnaissance, though primarily used for the latter.[11] It carried a battery of cameras hidden behind pneumatically operated doors and hatches that were intended to be externally invisible. The main camera was a K-30 fitted with a 100in lens that produced 18 × 9in images. This was positioned directly behind the flight deck, used an electrically powered mounting, designed to allow it to take oblique images from each side of the aircraft. There were also three K-17s fitted with 6in lenses in a trimetrogen mount, located just behind the nosewheel housing, for mapping and survey work.[12] In 1957 'Hot Pepper' returned to the USA for an updating programme that installed a covert, removable ELINT capability by fitting: an AN/APR-9 receiver, AN/ALA-5 pulse analyser and AN/ANQ-1A recorder. The displays and operators' positions were hidden as much as possible by fake panels when on the ground. In 1958 another upgrade incorporated the AN/APR-9 system's antenna into the fin, removing the obvious bulge on the fuselage underside which made it more externally resemble a standard cargo C-54. The aircraft was withdrawn from USAFE by March 1962.

Another C-54D and two C-54Es were used for Project Sara Jane. Furnished with VIP interiors, they were equipped with fourteen concealed Fairchild P2 cameras installed in fuel-tight compartments in the wings, hidden by pneumatically operated doors. The cameras could be operated discreetly from the flight deck without any passengers being aware of it. The aircraft may have been used for courier flights to US embassies in Eastern Europe, providing additional opportunities for covert photography.[13]

One C-54D (42–72685) served with the squadron from December 1955 to November 1962. It was modified to carry photographic and infrared equipment to support the Automatic Terrain Recognition and Navigation (ATRAN) programme under Project Lulu Belle. The ATRAN programme is described more fully later in this chapter.

CT-29 Carol Ann/Ocean Gem

The CT-29A was a conversion of the T-29 navigator training aircraft that was itself based on the Convair 240/340 civil airliner. The first of four that served with the 7405th SS arrived in September 1959 to replace the C-47s that flew their final missions in May 1960. One aircraft (49–1917) was lost after crashing at Breckenheim near Wiesbaden on 9 February 1967 following an engine failure after take-off. By August 1968 the three remaining aircraft had left the 7405 SS to be modified and transferred to the Pacific Theatre for Project Ocean Gem.[14]

The cover role for the CT-29 was the operation of the Berlin air courier service and, according to a 1960 document, they flew about twelve missions per month.[15] The reconnaissance equipment was separated from the main compartment by a false bulkhead at the rear of the aircraft, so that passengers and cargo could be carried to maintain the cover story. Behind the bulkhead the camera compartment contained a trimetrogen arrangement of KA-1 cameras in a roll-stabilised mount, the operator, his console and stored film.[16] In 1962 an oblique camera with a 40in focal-length lens looking out through the aft escape hatches on a more flexible mount was installed. When the aircraft was on the ground the camera was hidden behind a false shipping crate. In 1963, the aircraft was redesignated Ocean Gem.

All the CT-29s had suffered from poor maintenance prior to their conversion and by 1965 the three remaining aircraft had their severely corroded wing spars replaced. The weight of the onboard equipment was becoming a major safety issue because the aircraft was unable to sustain flight on a single engine. This was the primary cause of the 1967 crash.

C-97G Stratofreighter

Nine C-97s, of various types, were used over the years, seven of which were uniquely configured for the reconnaissance role. They were the mainstay of US Corridor (Creek Flush) and peripheral missions from 1962 to 1975 when they were replaced by the C-130 Hercules. The squadron had, on average, five C-97s on the strength of which three were fitted primarily for the SIGINT role and two for photographic reconnaissance operations.

The C-97G's sensor fits frequently changed as camera and reconnaissance technology advanced. During the 1960s camera fits used a range of 48, 66 and 100in lenses. All the cameras produced 18 × 9in images as hard copy paper prints. After 1969 the camera fit changed to one that recorded images on 5in wide film that was viewed in positive film format. The fit became a KA-82A panoramic camera with a 12in lens mounted vertically, producing 5 × 24in images, and a KA-82A panoramic camera with a 48in lens in an oblique mount, known as the 'H-Pan'. The H-Pan KA-82A images were 5in by up to 48in in full-frame mode, although it could also be set to image a more selective field of view. RS-10 infrared cameras were also added later.

One C-97G (52–2724) was modified under Project Side Kick from late 1961 and delivered to the 7405th SS in June 1962. It soon went back to the USA for depot-level maintenance and upgrading before moving to the Pacific Theatre until 1968. It returned to Germany in late 1969, equipped with a KA-81A camera fitted with a 48in lens and a KA-82A fitted with a 12in lens as well as an RS-10 infrared device. Known as Rivet Giant, the aircraft remained until 1975.[17]

C-97G (52–2687) joined 7405 SS in October 1961, serving until December 1975. It was a combined photographic and ELINT aircraft, known as Flint Stone. With camera and ELINT equipment hidden from sight, it was still possible to maintain the fiction of being a 'courier and internal USAFE transport aircraft'.[18] Although mainly undertaking Corridor missions, it flew peripheral flights too. Depot maintenance in 1969 installed new camera equipment (KA-81A with a 48in lens, KA-82 with a 12in lens and RS-10 infrared) and the project was renamed Rivet Stem.

The other camera-equipped aircraft (52–2688 Eager Beaver) joined the 7405 SS in July 1963. It carried a 66in lens oblique camera and a KA-82 with a 12in lens. Returned from modification and upgrading in the USA during 1967, it carried a Fairchild KS-96A panoramic camera and an RS-10 infrared being redesignated as Rivet Box. In late 1969 the aircraft left Germany for the MASDC, later AMARC, at Davis Monthan Air Force Base (AFB).[19]

There were two ELINT equipped C-97s (52–2639 and 52–2686) used exclusively on peripheral missions because their large, distinctive under-fuselage ELINT 'canoes' were too obvious, making them unsuitable for Corridor and BCZ missions. The aircraft flew the IGB, Baltic, Adriatic, Black Sea and Mediterranean missions. Little Guy, the code name for 52–2639, arrived in early 1963 and carried eight ELINT operators on the main deck of the aircraft. It stayed at Rhein-Main until January 1969, when it returned to Fort Worth and subsequently passed to Israel.[20] 52–2686 left service in 1969.

The unit had a C-97 (52–2678) used as a 'front-end crew trainer', retaining the dual navigator position like the mission aircraft. Delivered in 1967, it was also used as a cargo aircraft. It only stayed until July 1969 and operated under the designation of Rivet Tub.[21] A single standard KC-97F (51–0246) was briefly used for support work and crew training between 1963 and 1964.[22]

C-97 53–0306 was Project Rivet Flare. Assigned to 7405 SS in mid 1969, it remained on strength until the last C-97s were withdrawn from Germany in 1975. Primarily engaged in photographic reconnaissance operations, it had the post-1969 panoramic camera fit installed.

The gradual rundown of the C-97 fleet started in December 1969 and was completed by December 1975. By then the 7405 SS's peripheral electronic reconnaissance tasks had been taken over by SAC RC-135s, mainly operating from the UK and Greece. Besides the 7405 SS C-97s there were two other aircraft that operated in the Corridors, BCZ and peripheral regions.

Project Pie Face

C-97A 49–2952 was the first C-97 to arrive at Rhein-Main. It had been converted to a photographic reconnaissance configuration in 1952 and assigned to the 7499 SS in the summer of 1953. The giant K-42 main camera, known as Big Bertha (and later as Daisy Mae), was fitted with a 240in lens, in a left-facing oblique mount, and was generally known by the project name Pie Face. The camera was over 6ft tall and weighed around 6,500lb, reputedly being the largest airborne camera ever built. It produced 36 × 18in negatives, known as 'Texas postcards' by the Photographic Interpreters (PI). The camera could see 30 to 40 miles and in ideal conditions could allegedly see the proverbial golf ball from 45,000ft. Besides the Pie Face camera there was also a K-30 with a 100in lens in an oblique mount and three K-17s, probably in a trimetrogen mount. These latter cameras were synchronised to operate with Big Bertha.[23]

The gestation period for Pie Face began in 1948 when the USAF experimented with very long focal-length oblique cameras to gather imagery of airfields in the Chukotski area of Siberia.[24] The missions often involved remaining in 'international airspace' but flying sufficiently close to the coast to acquire photographs of the area. But even the large 40in to 100in focal-length cameras produced imagery that was inadequate to identify previously undetected installations when standing 10 to 20 miles offshore. They were also incapable of imaging already identified installations in sufficient detail to satisfy USAF planners' requirements.[25] They were, however, a driver for the development of larger lenses.

The Big Bertha K-42s were designed at the Air Force Optical Research Center at Boston University in 1951. The cameras, with their massive 240in lenses, were fitted into an RB-36D Peacemaker aircraft and were said to be able to image installations up to 80 miles away.[26] However, the RB-36s could not be used along the Corridors, because of the restrictions. Incidentally, use of the giant RB-36 Peacemaker was regarded even too provocative to be used on many peripheral missions. So another platform had to be found if the camera was to be used in Germany. One K-42 was operated experimentally for six weeks in an early prototype YC-97 airframe and flown from Rhein-Main. Although the airframe's performance was poorer than the newer KC-97 versions, the trial proved the camera's value.[27] In April 1953, Brigadier General Ackerman of the

USAF Directorate of Intelligence sent a memo to AVM Francis Fressanges RAF in London advising him of the imminent arrival in Europe that summer of a new 200in lens camera. It was the precursor to sharing Pie Face imagery with the British.

The short runway at Wiesbaden AB meant that Pie Face C-97A initially had to operate from Rhein-Main (Frankfurt) AB, where it was known as 'Det 1, 7499 SS'. The camera's best results were achieved from around 30,000ft, but this was not possible because of the Corridors' 10,000ft upper limit and often unsuitable north-west European weather conditions. Cloud was the most obvious weather factor, but thermal currents, airborne pollution and particles, and varying temperatures contributed to image distortions. The camera also suffered from airframe vibrations caused by being mounted in the piston-engined C-97. Nevertheless, Pie Face was used on around twelve Corridor and peripheral flights per month.[28] On the peripheral flights the optimum 30,000ft was a more usual operating altitude. In 1962, retired from Europe, Pie Face had a brief reprieve during the Cuban Missile Crisis when it flew from Florida to image the island.[29]

The value of operational images acquired by Pie Face, where conditions were rarely ideal for such long-range photography, is somewhat disputed. In the early days there were difficulties with the camera's shutter design.[30] Although many praised Pie Face's operational performance, there were critics and Dino Brugioni recalls that the camera was:

> plagued with problems that caused it to vibrate and produce smearing on the newspaper size images so that photo interpreters would see several smeared frames together with several clear ones.[31]

Project Wine Sap

One C-97 used in Corridor operations (53–0106) was a very special aircraft indeed. Known as Wine Sap, it was modified during 1965 as an ELINT aircraft. It also carried a T-11 vertical camera to enable the aircraft's geographic position to be correlated with the collected ELINT data. Previously operated by the CIA, it used the 'Precision Parameter Measurements System' (PPMS) developed to collect missile data – see later in this chapter. The aircraft was assigned to Project Creek Flea, collecting information on emitters along the Corridors, particularly the SA-2 Guideline SAM (Soviet name: S-75 Dvina). This had been a high-priority intelligence target since the late 1950s when it was deployed in large numbers across the Soviet Union and close to Berlin. The data collected by Creek Flea was used to develop countermeasures to the SA-2 system that was proving so effective over North Vietnam and the aircraft was occasionally deployed for periods of work against Vietnamese SA-2 systems. After a 1967–68 equipment refit it was retitled Rivet Stock. The aircraft stayed with 7405th SS until 1975, by which time the emphasis had moved onto monitoring SA-3 Goa and SA-4 Ganef associated radars.[32]

The Sixties Peak

Lieutenant Colonel John Bessette USAF (Retired) was a C-97 navigator with secondary intelligence officer duties with the 7499 SG at Wiesbaden from September 1963 until January 1968. As a navigator he carried the responsibility during missions for ensuring that the flight remained within the Corridor airspace or, on peripheral flights, at a sufficient stand-off distance from borders and coasts. Vance Mitchell, also a retired US Air Force Lieutenant Colonel, flew three year periods in both the 1960s and mid 1970s. He too was a navigator in the 7405 SS flying Convair CT-29s and Boeing C-97s on Corridor and BCZ missions from Wiesbaden AB. He later went on to manage the programme at Headquarters USAFE at Ramstein AB for a further two years. Both men's experiences were during the heyday of CT-29 and C-97 operations. Their observations give a revealing insight into the conduct of operational missions in the 1960s.

Vance Mitchell explained many procedural aspects of the operational missions. Daily activity began at the 7405 SS at about 07.00 when the Intelligence Duty Officer began work on that day's requirements. As over 400 targets were observable from the Corridors and BCZ, there was always something going on. The more important ones – large troop movements, major training areas, airfields, and the introduction of new military equipment – required coverage ranging from daily to weekly. As Mitchell points out, less important targets were imaged anywhere from monthly to annually:

> There were also two types of 'specials'. The very rare 'Priority A' specials required that aircraft launch against them immediately unless safety of flight issues were involved. 'Priority B' specials did not mandate launches, but did have precedence over other targets if the mission aircraft flew that Corridor. The Intelligence Duty Officer melded priorities with more routine targets which needed imaging and any last minute intelligence to gain a better understanding of the outstanding requirements.

The result was the day's target list and thus the Corridors to be flown. If requirements dictated, multiple missions involving as many as four aircraft were mounted. Aircraft commanders could alter the routes into and out of Berlin for reasons of flight safety, usually to avoid severe weather. The main briefing followed at 08.15, involving the whole crew, covering topics such as: aircraft availability, maintenance issues, weather, targets, flight altitudes for best photographic coverage and so on.

Having filed necessary flight plans (including one with the BASC), departures were often between 09.30 and 10.30 hours, though this could be changed for weather or Soviet activities and to suit light angles and seasonal conditions like mist that might affect the target areas. The aircraft, at this time, used their tail numbers as call signs so the Soviets were always aware of which CT-29 or C-97 was approaching the Corridor. Once in the selected Corridor the aircraft would often change course frequently. Whilst this was necessary to capture the selected targets on film, it adversely affected the work of the ELINT operators, who needed good steady courses to be maintained, with minimal changes, to help their equipment perform at its best. So combined sensor missions, with a photographic priority, almost inevitably meant that the quality of the ELINT data collected would suffer.

When ready for departure, the CT-29s taxied to Base Operations to take on any passengers bound for Berlin. The aircraft had a number of airliner-type seats to enhance its cover as a 'courier' mission, Mitchell explains:

> The four 24-inch vertical and short range oblique cameras and two Special Equipment Operators (SEOs) occupied a tiny compartment in the rear of the aircraft behind a false bulkhead. The SEOs on all aircraft performed in-flight maintenance, activated cameras on command, and changed film magazines.

The flight deck navigator used a 'modified A-17 viewfinder' and a remote autopilot to fly a stable line of flight to ensure good-quality photography.[33] The key intelligence specialists were the 'Aircraft Observers' (AOs), who were frequently PIs, often with a detailed knowledge of some, or all, of the priority targets being covered by the flight. Their task was to look out of the observation blisters on each side of the aircraft for targets of opportunity and any items of special interest.

The C-97s rarely carried passengers on their flights. This left the main deck free for some freight to be positioned, which added a little substance to the 'regular transport' cover. Below the main cargo deck was where the real action was happening. For example, C-97 '22687', the most complex of the 7405 SS C-97 fleet, carried a 100in long-range oblique camera, four 24in vertical and short-range oblique cameras, an infrared scanner, and a four-position electronic intercept suite. The cameras and at least three SEOs occupied a relatively spacious below-deck compartment forward of the wings. There were two navigators on the C-97. The forward navigator sat in the window behind either the pilot or co-pilot with a sighting and control device to activate the long-range oblique camera. The radar navigator directed the aircraft and had responsibility for vertical and short-range targets. As in the CT-29s, any crew member could activate cameras to image targets of opportunity. In terms of the non-optical sensors Vance Mitchell explained that:

> Electronic Warfare Officers (EWOs) manned the aircraft's two-position electronic collection suite in a tiny, claustrophobic compartment below the main deck and aft of the wings. Small retractable antennae protruding from the wing and horizontal stabilizer intercepted signals, and a retractable dome, called 'the tub', extending below the fuselage, housed the direction finding antenna. The photo mission always had priority, but electronic collection proved valuable enough to remain part of the mission.

He also described for us the steps taken aboard flights to keep the aircraft looking like standard C-97s whenever necessary:

Keeping the real purpose of the aircraft covert required vigilance, cleverly designed systems and good sheet metal work. Whenever a crew member spotted another aircraft in the near vicinity, he would alert the crew to 'clean up' the aircraft by saying 'pull the tub'. That was the signal to retract antennae, close camera doors, and within two seconds make it look externally like any other C-97. Crew members used the same command on all C-97s, whether they had an electronic mission or not. The crew also cleaned up when the aircraft descended below 3,500ft for landing, instead using the command 'put everything to bed'.

On arrival at Wiesbaden the exposed film was developed to enable a quick intelligence assessment. The photos and electronic intercept tapes were then couriered to the 497 RTG at nearby Schierstein for more complete exploitation.

Following the loss of a T-39 aircraft and an RB-66 in 1964, John Bessette told us that the operating rules for Corridor aircraft became even more cautious, in an attempt to reduce unnecessary losses. Crews were instructed to fly no closer than 4 miles to the Corridors' edge and no closer than 1 mile from the BCZ boundary.

C-130 Hercules and Rhein-Main AB

Following the rundown of the C-97 fleet in late 1975, 7405 SS moved to Rhein-Main AB and was renamed the 7405 Operations Squadron (7405 OS). By December 1975 it had taken delivery of the first of three highly modified C-130Es under Project Creek Flush for Corridor, BCZ and peripheral missions along the Baltic coast, IGB and Czech–German border. The three aircraft selected for modification (62–1819, 62–1822 and 62–1828) had previously been employed on a covert photographic role in 1966 as part of the Witch Doctor programme. Externally the aircraft looked similar to standard C-130Es but a locked compartment, under the main cargo deck, concealed a single KA-82 panoramic camera that was used on covert missions until 1973.[34] In a similar way, Project Rivet Duke was intended to keep the C-130s looking like standard transports, although their equipment fit was much more sophisticated for use in the Corridors and BCZ.

The aircrafts' large holds were filled with sophisticated and specialised sensors for the 7405 OS mission and the extensive modifications made these C-130s possibly the most expensive ever built (at least until the introduction of the C-130J variants) with an estimated cost of around $75 million (£52.7 million) each at 1986 prices. Besides the specialist sensor equipment, the aircraft were also fitted, after 1985, with the wing modifications and Allison T56-A-15 engines of the C-130H. The aircraft were known by a number of designations over the years with C-130E-II being the most commonly used by outside observers; 7405 OS personnel generally referred to them as C-130Es and sometimes after the 1985 upgrade as C-130 Super Es.

Normally only two of the aircraft were with the unit at any one time, with the third being in the USA for deep maintenance, new equipment installation, or updating and repainting. Each aircraft carried cameras and COMINT/ELINT stations to monitor communications and electronic emissions, as well as additional

UHF/VHF radios. The equipment fits were similar on each aircraft but never identical. Aircraft were repainted every three years. This was not a matter of military pride, but maintaining the paintwork in the best condition possible was vital in helping to conceal the many sensor doors and hatches that would have been revealed by paintwork in a poor condition. They were also repainted to have their camouflage conform to the standards of the normal airlift C-130s among which they were parked.

There were two optical cameras. The first was a panoramic KA-82 fitted with a 12in lens that used a 2,000ft canister of 5in-wide film producing 24in-long negatives. The camera was mounted aft of the C-130's nosewheel bay in the area normally occupied by the cargo winch. When the nosewheel was down, its door covered the KA-82's hatch. The second camera was the KA-81A panoramic camera, fitted with a 48in lens that used a 2,000ft film canister of 5in-wide film, producing 48in-long negatives. The framing settings on this camera could be adjusted to produce shorter negatives. Operated in the oblique mode, it was known as the 'H-Pan'. It was mounted on a standard C-130 cargo pallet and weighed about one and a half tons. It was frequently referred to as the 'Big Item' by the crews.[35] The camera was mounted behind the main flight deck area and used a rigid cradle frame that conformed to the fuselage contours. This arrangement allowed the camera to be electrically repositioned to face either the left-hand or the right-hand side of the aircraft as required. On the forward fuselage of cargo C-130Es there are three small circular portholes. In the modified aircraft the middle one was false, being part of a larger, hidden, 18 × 30in door that could be retracted into the aircraft, exposing a 2in-thick optical glass aperture that allowed the 'Big Item' to take photographs whilst the aircraft remained pressurised. The KA-81A H-Pan could be set to produce either a 12 per cent or 56 per cent overlap to provide stereoscopic pictures.

Aligned with the leading edge of the wing root and on the aircraft's underside was an AAD-5 infrared linescan sensor for use at night or in restricted visibility. This was switched on whilst in the Corridors and BCZ to provide a continuous flight record and was regarded as especially important for resolving any later disputes about the aircraft's position and track. The device was covered by a protective door when not in use.

Very advanced for its time was the Texas Instruments SPF-1 Forward Looking Infra Red (FLIR) mounted in a ball in the rear of the left main undercarriage well. The SPF-1 control panel was situated on the cargo ramps of 62–1819 and 62–1822 and just aft of the 'Big Item' on 62–1828. If the aircraft was intercepted by fighters, the co-pilot activated a red toggle switch on the redundant JATO control panel, which retracted the FLIR ball and closed all the 'secret' doors in just eight seconds.

The 62–1819 had a large cargo container (24ft long by 8ft wide and 8ft high) with equipment and positions for up to seven personnel. This included the Phase Stability Measurement System (PSMS) and PPMS, made by ITT, developed for the Creek Flea missions many years previously by the CIA. Other positions included two for COMINT collection, two Electronic Warfare Operator (EWO) seats for collecting scientific and technical intelligence and finally a 'Tactical Co-ordinator' or 'Collection

Crew Leader' position. The size of the container required a redesign of the FLIR installation to accommodate it and this became known as Rivet Kit.[36] This combination of equipment gave 62–1819 a SIGINT and optical photographic capability, and after further modification in 1980 (Creek Victor) it was capable of verifying Radar Warning Receiver (RWR) performance against Soviet radars and ensuring that the RWR library was as up to date as possible.

The rear troop doors of the aircraft had their secrets too. The two Aerial Observers (AOs) could access a false panel in the doors and replace them with observation blisters and portable seats. This allowed the AOs a much better view out of the aircraft when looking for targets of opportunity. The blisters would be installed just after take-off, as the aircraft climbed, and removed during the descent, immediately before landing when the aircraft was unpressurised.

In May/June 1985, 62–1822 returned from the USA after an extensive overhaul and upgrade. Part of this involved replacing the old KA-81A camera with the new KA-116 Surface Reach Imagery System (SRIS) manufactured by Fairchild Wesson, fitted with a 72in lens. The camera was radically different from the KA-81A. Firstly, it was mounted on a centreline gimbal instead of in the old frame. The camera used three mirrors, each of which was said to cost $1 million (£700,000) at 1986 prices! This combination of optical technology enabled the camera to produce results of extraordinary quality that were regularly at the upper end of the National Image Interpretability Rating Scale (NIIRS), compared to the mid-range scores achieved by the previous cameras. This change significantly improved the squadron's photographic capabilities.

The PIs also saw the benefits of this radical new sensor. Chris Hughes, a British PI, remembers that the KA-116 SRIS produced excellent imagery that allowed the PI community to look into areas that were normally only accessible to 'other systems'. An additional, unofficial and very non-PC, use of the system was to image the naturist colonies and beaches along the Wannsee Lake near Berlin. The very high-quality imagery produced some 'interesting' results!

During its time in refit the aircraft was given other modifications besides the SRIS. There was a new container that carried the two FLIR positions and an upgraded COMINT collection known as '8660', which was a major advance on the previous equipment. Three EWO positions were dedicated to the collection of Radiation Intelligence (RADINT) – the unintentional electrical radiation emitted by concentrations of cables, power grids and computers – although it is believed that this was not particularly successful. Other equipment installed in the refit included a MIL-STD 1553 data bus, AN/YUK-18 mission recorders, an SKN 2443 dual Inertial Navigation System (INS) and new communications equipment. 'Dash 15' engines replaced the earlier models. Inevitably this new configuration led to its redesignation as Rivet Acorn.[37]

An unintended problem was caused by the mandatory installation and use of in-flight voice recorders, to the whole C-130 fleet. These had to be switched on at all times during flight and presented a particular problem for Berlin operations.

When on Corridor missions the circuit breakers were deactivated to prevent the recorders from doing their job. This was done to deny the Soviets any prima facie evidence of their clandestine activities if one of the aircraft crashed or force-landed in the GDR.[38]

Flying the Corridor with the C-130E

Robert Zoucha joined the USAF in July 1981 at Lackland AFB, where he underwent basic training. After completing his Combat Cameraman course he was assigned to Goodfellow AFB. In 1984, he accepted an assignment to fly with the 7575 OG on Corridor missions in Rhein-Main and he served as an SEO from July 1984 to September 1986 and flew 206 Corridor missions.

During this time the programme was known as Creek Flush, with the imagery known as Creek Misty. The intelligence activities were managed by the 7575 OG, consisting of two squadrons: the 7405 OS operated the aircraft and provided the aircrew, including loadmasters and engineers, and the 7580 OS provided the 'back-end' EWOs who operated most of the specialist equipment and the maintenance technicians who repaired the sensors. The programme was surrounded by a great deal of secrecy, even though much of it took place in plain sight on the busy Rhein-Main ramp, which was a combined military airbase and civilian airport.

The main external distinguishing feature of the 7405 OS aircraft was a third HF wire antennae that ran from the tail to the fuselage, instead of the usual two on a standard C-130E. The three externally similar 7405 OS aircraft shared the same flight line as the resident 435th Tactical Airlift Wing (435 TAW) C-130s. They were maintained by specially cleared personnel from the 435 Organisational Maintenance Squadron (435 OMS), which allowed them to work on 7405 OS aircraft. Access to the aircraft was limited to those wearing special discreetly marked flight line badges. Additionally, the individual aircraft were kept locked and were fitted with an alarm system that had to be deactivated before entry. The aircraft were closely monitored by the Base Security Forces. Failure to turn the alarm off would see lots of Security Police rapidly descend on the aircraft and, as Robert said, 'things could turn nasty very quickly'.

Knowledge of the 7405 OS mission was kept very secret at Rhein-Main. As Robert commented, this 'seemed rather ironic because the Soviets knew exactly what we were doing. We were just keeping it secret from our own people.' The Base Commander knew the mission they undertook, as did the Chief of Maintenance. 'The crew chiefs obviously knew our aircraft were different but were expected not to ask questions.' Similarly, many of the technicians, especially those responsible for some of the special equipment, would have known part of the story too. Passengers were not allowed to fly on the aircraft and special permission had to be obtained for non-crew personnel to fly on the aircraft. This even applied to the 4-star CINCUSAFE, General Donnelly, when he wanted to fly on a Corridor C-130.

Mission preparation started about three hours before take-off. The flight plans were created by the navigators and the AOs with the consent of the Aircraft Commander. Between them they created the target pack for the flight, Robert explains:

> We could fly them pretty much in the order the pilot wanted, with the major constraint that it was not possible to turn back once inside the Corridor – a fact that meant that on two occasions our aircraft was struck by lightning because we were unable to turn back in bad weather.

There were two sorts of targets: routine targets were covered on a daily/weekly/ monthly basis as required and where slippage would make little difference. 'Special' targets were often urgent, temporary and time sensitive. They were covered when the squadron was instructed to do so. Whilst the flight planning was in process, the other crew members would collect the materials necessary for their duties. The aircraft was pre-flighted by the aircrew, but everyone else on board had specific tasks for take-off and landing too. The squadron used the call sign 'Herky' as used by standard C-130 transports for training missions and 'Ask' for operational missions.

Single flights were the norm but multiple missions for an individual aircraft, and multiple aircraft missions by both night and day, were not uncommon. Aircraft could be tasked at short notice to fly additional trips and sometimes an aircraft could return from one mission, be retasked, turned round and sent off again. To allow for such contingencies the aircraft carried sufficient film canisters for two consecutive flights as standard procedure.

The crew then assembled for the pre-flight safety briefing. Crews were large, consisting of two pilots, two navigators and the loadmaster at the front with the SEOs, and up to seven ELINT operators in the back. There were also two AOs and two FLIR operators. The AOs and FLIR operators were from the 497 RTG and always wore USAF uniform, although some came from the US Army and US Marine Corps. There were no formally constituted crews; each was simply made up from available personnel. Besides normal safety aspects the briefing included actions in case of forced landing in the GDR. In such circumstances the crew were to destroy the aircraft using flares and hydraulic fluid once on the ground. There were also instructions on how to expose all the film and destroy the aircraft in flight, whilst the crew were bailing out.

After departing from Rhein-Main, the SEOs would take special aiming sights to the flight deck and place them on mounts behind and adjacent to the pilots' positions. They were described as being rather like the 'head-up displays' used in many modern military aircraft, and were used by one of the two navigators. One was responsible for the critical, accurate navigation needed whilst flying the Corridor and the other for monitoring progress and targets en route as well as operating the 'Big Item'. Soon after take-off, whilst the aircraft was unpressurised, the sensors would be uncovered and prepared for use by the crew.

The C-130 would route to its assigned Corridor, defined by the targets on the flight plan. However, this could be changed at short notice if unexpected opportunities arose. As the aircraft approached the IGB, the infrared camera would be turned on. The aircraft flew at between 3,000 and 10,000ft when in the Corridors – depending on the weather and ground activities. The 7405 OS aircraft were the only US aircraft responsible for their own navigation when in the Corridors. They flew irregular courses to take in the installations and activities on their target list. The flights used the cover story that they were just standard 'trash haulers', though this would have been barely credible to anyone regularly observing their comings and goings from the fences at Tempelhof. In later years the cover story was modified to state just that the aircraft were 'exercising their rights under treaty' to fly the Corridors.

Cameras were activated as the aircraft approached its target, with the forward navigator calling 'camera right' or 'camera left' to the SEO so he could move the camera to the appropriate side of the aircraft. The vertical panoramic camera was operated to meet the target plan, but any crew member could call for it to be activated, so that targets of opportunity, or areas of interest, could be captured for later exploitation.

There were around seven positions onboard, two of which were occupied by Russian and German linguists for COMINT operators – with the remainder being occupied by ELINT operators – who listened out for Soviet and East German military activity. They were particularly interested in Soviet and East German air defence network communications and the operators on the C-130s would provide real-time warnings to the their crew members if they believed the aircraft might be under threat. The rear crew would also communicate with US listening stations monitoring US and opposition aircraft activities.

The aircraft were regularly tracked by Soviet/GDR radars and sometimes locked onto by their SAM systems that were in, or close to, the Corridors. Coded messages would be passed between the C-130 and US ground stations, some genuine, some false, to keep the Soviets guessing. Messages prefixed 'Sky King' meant 'all aircraft copy' and could include warnings. If the ground stations, or the crew, believed the aircraft was about to be intercepted, all the sensors would be closed down and hidden as quickly as possible. On average the C-130s were intercepted about once a month, although Robert Zoucha recalls that on one flight his aircraft was shadowed by a MiG-23 Flogger, a MiG-21 Fishbed and a MiG-25 Foxbat in very rapid succession. Shortly before this the aircraft had received a 'Sky King' warning, so they simply packed up and returned to base, not really knowing why the intercepts had taken place.

Flights would normally take around two hours to go in and out of Berlin, to which another forty minutes each way could be added if using the Northern Corridor. Once over Berlin, the aircraft would fly for another thirty minutes to cover BCZ targets before landing at Tempelhof AB, almost never anywhere else. Before the aircraft landed it was 'normalised' – all the sensors were hidden and the observation blisters replaced with standard hatches. After landing the crew would disembark – up to twenty-three of them – and stop to have a lunch break of between an hour and one hour and twenty minutes. During the break one of the AOs would contact the Tempelhof intelligence unit (then the 6912th Electronic Security Group) to check for any urgent changes to the return leg of their flight plan. This inevitably led to the crews being described as the 'Berlin for Lunch Bunch' or BFLB by parts of the USAFE community and C-130 personnel in general.

On returning to Rhein-Main, the SEOs would put the exposed film in canisters and leave them onboard to be taken by the AOs to the 497 RTG for processing and exploitation. Robert recalls that there was little feedback on the results of individual missions, although the AOs would occasionally say that they had some 'good shots'. Given the frequency of the flights, there was probably little time to provide feedback.

On rare occasions the aircraft encountered sensor problems – such as being unable to close camera hatches or retract the FLIR ball. In such instances it was considered impossible for the aircraft to return to Rhein-Main as this would unacceptably expose it to public view. Instead the aircraft would divert to Ramstein AB where a special C-130-sized hangar was kept empty for such contingencies. After passing the message 'Maggie's drawers are down' the aircraft would divert to Ramstein AB and land and taxi directly into the hangar before shutting down the engines whilst the hangar doors were quickly closed behind it.

One of the 7405 OSs unusual tasks was in the aftermath of USMLM Major Nicholson's shooting on 24 March 1985 at Ludwigslust. He was shot dead by a sentry with Soviet military authorities alleging that he had been climbing a fence to gain access to the installation. The day after the shooting a 7405 OS C-130E was tasked to photograph the incident site. The resulting imagery revealed that not only was there no fence, but the fence Nicholson was supposed to have been climbing when shot was being frantically erected by Soviet troops.

US Corridor missions were flown until 29 September 1990, just a few days before the formal German unification and the disappearance of the Air Corridors. When US flights halted, they had flown 'more than 10,000 missions patrolling the Berlin Corridors and siphoning vital information from the very heart of the Soviet presence in Europe'.[39]

Other Operations

In addition to the 7405 OS's Corridor missions, other missions were being flown by the CIA, SAC and other squadrons from the 7499 OG.

The CIA Connection

Besides US Air Force operations the 7405 SS appears to have had close connections with the CIA, although discovering the extent of this relationship is still not easy. For example, Chris Pocock records the deployment of Agency RB-69A (Lockheed Neptune) Project Cherry aircraft to Wiesbaden in 1957 for low-level reconnaissance operations.[40] Tart and Keefe have also provided a more detailed account of other CIA operations conducted by 'C Flight' alongside 7405 SS 'Special Project' activities. 'C Flight', flew up to three C-118As from Wiesbaden on 'diplomatic courier flights' to US embassies in Europe, North Africa and the Middle East. Two of the aircraft were allegedly used to provide regular, non-scheduled support flights for some of the CIA's extensive operations in Europe and the Middle East.[41] The aircraft were administratively and logistically subordinate to the 7405 SS but operationally they answered to an element in Headquarters USAFE.

Two aircraft are known to have carried 'bogus' tail numbers for a time: 51–3823 was allocated '51–3842' in July 1965 but reverted to its original tail number when it returned to the USA in October 1965; similarly 51–3825 was allocated the false serial '51–3846' in June 1965, reverting to 51–3825 on return to the USA also in October 1965. There is speculation that these aircraft were used in support of CIA operations.

One of these C-118s was involved in an incident that illustrated how closely connected USAF and CIA operations could be. On 27 June 1958, C-118A (51–3822), came down in Soviet Armenia. The aircraft was in regular military transport aircraft markings and had left Wiesbaden AB bound for Karachi in Pakistan, routing via Wheelus AFB in Libya and RAF Nicosia in Cyprus. It left Cyprus for Tehran using the civilian airway that passed through Turkey about 50 miles south of the Soviet border. The C-118 appears either to have become genuinely lost or to have been 'spoofed' into straying into Soviet airspace. The aircraft was intercepted and engaged by Soviet fighters when about 100 miles inside the Soviet Union. It finally force-landed on a very short, partially finished runway in a remote part of Azerbaijan around 50 miles from the Iranian border and was totally destroyed in the post-crash fire. All nine occupants escaped serious injury, five having abandoned the aircraft by parachute as it had descended. All the occupants were taken into Soviet military custody. The US State Department statement said that the aircraft was on an 'embassy courier run'. Michael Beschloss has described the flight as transporting CIA personnel, sensitive documents and other items to the various locations en route. Some of the documents are alleged to have related to CIA-sponsored U-2 operations in the Middle East, and to other governments' participation in the U-2 programme.[42] In the face of strong US diplomatic representations and the lack of any incriminating evidence, the Soviets were unable to significantly disprove the US cover story, so accepted the US version of events that the aircraft was lost. Ten days later, the personnel were handed over to the US Attaché from the Tehran Embassy at the Iran–Azerbaijan border.

Precision Parameter Measurements System

Another CIA operation, mounted in the Corridors, involved collecting ELINT data under a programme originally sanctioned in 1954. This programme involved the CIA developing a 'Precision Parameter Measurements System' (PPMS) to collect high-quality ELINT data. The intention was to measure very accurately radar signal parameters to determine their detection capabilities and tracking characteristics. The first serious attempt to measure these for intelligence purposes in this way was in 1958 against the Soviet P-35 Saturn (NATO Code name: Bar Lock) early warning radar. This was being deployed to a number of locations to detect and track US U-2s as they began deep-penetration flights over the Soviet Union. CIA managers demanded definitive information on the Bar Lock's power output, radiation pattern coverage and detection and tracking capabilities to more precisely assess this threat to the U-2 programme. A set of power-measurement equipment, although crude by modern standards, was installed in the hold of a C-119 (Boxcar) aircraft. With little advance testing, a series of flights was undertaken along the Berlin Corridors where the Bar Lock signals could be easily intercepted. Although the experiment was not entirely successful in its power measurement, it suggested some possible solutions for additional collection and the development of new measuring equipment.[43] These were incorporated into the successful follow-on Project Wine Sap C-97G.

The ATRAN Programme

In 1956 two squadrons of the 7499 SG were involved in a short-lived task to provide support for the ATRAN system that guided the TM-76A Mace and TM-61B Matador nuclear-capable 'cruise missiles' to their targets. The TM-61B version of the missile had a maximum range of around 700 miles and would fly at below 1,000ft. The missile's guidance system compared the actual in-flight radar terrain scan with that of a pre-loaded 35mm filmstrip radar reconnaissance map and then made any necessary course corrections. The film was produced from actual and simulated radar images marked with the route's key topographical and other features.

The 7406 SS's task was to collect the required radar imagery for the targeting film strips as part of Project Aunt Sue. They flew three specially modified RB-50D aircraft (Project Half Track) along the IGB, collecting a combination of modified navigation radar and optical camera imagery. Between June 1956 and 19 October 1956, 'A' Flight flew 52 RB-50D ATRAN missions. These missions terminated almost a year before the first successful airborne ATRAN test was completed in late September 1957.[44]

The 7405 SS flew a modified C-54D (Project Lulu Belle) to collect photographic and radar imagery in the Corridors and along the IGB. The aircraft flew forty-three ATRAN missions between December 1955 and autumn 1956 when the project was halted and the associated equipment removed. The modifications included installations of a stabilised 'thermal reconnaissance device', an APS-27 radar and the Goodyear AN/DPQ-4 ATRAN system. To make the necessary space for the electronic equipment, the auxiliary fuel tank area was reconfigured and false bulkheads were installed to hide the classified equipment from non-cleared passengers and observers.[45] There is some debate about why both the RB-50Ds and the Lulu Belle C-54D were used. A possibility is that the latter may have been an interim platform pending arrival of the Half Track RB-50Ds or was used to provide a 'quick reaction capability'.[46] More likely, the Lulu Belle C-54D could be flown in the Corridors without provoking an adverse Soviet reaction, which the RB-50s couldn't. Whilst the terrain and routing for the missiles in West Germany and close to the IGB and in the Corridors could be mapped accurately, once they were in East Germany beyond that view, the filmstrip had to be created using sand box terrain models.

USAFE Reconnaissance Operations outside the Corridors

USAFE's wide area of interest meant that it conducted ICFs outside the Berlin Corridors and BCZ. Initially these missions were flown by B-17s of Det 'A' 10 RG, which soon expanded USAFE 'ferret' flights further afield to include the border of the Soviet Zone with West Germany, Austria and the Baltic Sea area.

7406th Support Squadron (7406 SS)

From its formation in 1955 until disbandment on 30 June 1974, the 7406 SS flew peripheral, predominantly COMINT, missions from the Baltic in the north to the Black and Caspian seas in the south. The Baltic missions ceased in June 1973 as the emphasis moved to the Mediterranean area, with increasing numbers of operational missions flown from Hellinikon near Athens. During its nineteen-year existence the 7406 SS mainly operated from Rhein-Main AB and although the squadron was a USAFE asset, the USAF Security Service (USAFSS) together with the NSA controlled much of its tasking.[47] For operational missions, the 7406 SS provided the flight crews and aircraft, but specialist crew members (sensor operators) in the back of the aircraft, known as 'Sailors,' came from Detachment 1 of the 6911th (later the 6916th) Radio Squadron Mobile that was part of the USAFSS. The 7406 SS missions ended when the SAC RC-135s, flying out of RAF Mildenhall in Suffolk, UK, took over the missions and the squadron disbanded on 30 June 1974.

Aircraft of the 7406th SS

The 7406 SS initially received seven RB-50s, including four Boeing RB-50 Dreamboats assigned to 'B' Flight and three for the ATRAN mission. The first arrived on 11 December 1956 but operational missions did not start until January 1957 because of security and training problems. The RB-50s were notoriously difficult to keep airworthy because their unreliable R4360 engines, similar to those in the C-97 Stratofreighter, which required constant maintenance and frequent changes. The maintenance personnel believed that if a RB-50 or C-97 arrived at its destination with all four engines running, something was wrong!

The Dreamboat era did not last long and in June 1958 the squadron began conversion to ten C-130A-IIs (Projects Sun Valley I / Rivet Victor I). The aircraft had a second navigator position installed on the flight deck. The rear cargo door was sealed and the main cargo deck had three bays containing ten intercept positions. At the rear of the cargo deck there was an electronics maintenance station. Crew comfort was a considerable improvement over the standard C-130 with four 'airline-type' seats at the rear of the main cargo deck, a galley with oven to provide hot meals and drinks and an airline-type toilet. As with previous aircraft the flight crew were drawn from the 7406 SS and the ten sensor operators from the USAFSS.[48] In October 1971 the C-130A-IIs were replaced by C-130B-IIs (Projects Sun Valley II / Rivet Victor II), which remained on strength until the 7406 SS disbanded.

7406 SS Flight Profiles and Modus Operandi

Missions were flown at around 24,000ft and often lasted for between twelve and fourteen hours. Their patrol areas included: over the Baltic Sea between Finland and Sweden; over West Germany to monitor the IGB and the Czech–German border areas. Another route from Rhein-Main, skirted the Balkans and ended at Incirlik in Turkey. Finally, there was a route from Incirlik to Lake Trabzon and Lake Van to the south and east of Turkey. Numerous missions were also flown over the Eastern Mediterranean – especially during the various Arab-Israeli crises. From 1956 to 1964 the squadron established its Detachment 2 (Det 2) at Bodø in Norway for forward operations, although aircraft were never permanently stationed there.[49]

By October 1971, Sun Valley C-130s regularly used Hellenikon in Greece from where over half of the missions originated. They covered NATO's southern flank by operating from Greece, Italy, Turkey, Sigonella in Sicily, Rota in Spain and Tehran in Iran.[50] The move to the Mediterranean bases was justified by the growing military importance of the area, especially the volatile Eastern Mediterranean.

On 2 September 1958 the squadron suffered a catastrophic loss when seventeen personnel were killed after their C-130A-II was shot down close to the Armenian capital of Yerevan after straying over the Soviet border. The details of this loss only fully emerged into the public domain in the 1990s. The story was a heady mixture of espionage, deception, secrecy and denial that typified the Cold War.[51]

7407th Support Squadron (7407 SS)

Perhaps the most exotic unit was the 7407 SS, which conducted high-altitude imagery collection overflights of Czechoslovakia, East Germany, Hungary and Poland. President Eisenhower had authorised the continuation of high-level over-flights of denied territory in July 1953 under the 'Sensitive Intelligence Programme' (SENSINT). The squadron implemented part of this directive. Operating from Bitburg and Rhein-Main AB's it participated in some relatively short-duration programmes, the best known of these being projects Slick Chick and Heart Throb. These programmes were interim solutions until the U-2 entered service.

Project Slick Chick

In 1955 Detachment 1 of 7407 SS was established at Bitburg AB, operating three camera-equipped variants of the F-100A Super Sabre called the RF-100A Slick Chicks. The front fuselage below the cockpit was modified to accept a combination of cameras: two split-pair vertical K-38 with 36in lens; two oblique K-17 that imaged via a mirror arrangement; a single vertical K-17C with 6, 12 or 24in lenses; and three K-17s with 6, 12 or 24in lenses in a trimetrogen installation.

The aircraft were shipped by sea to Belfast, from where they were flown to Bitburg, arriving there on 16 May 1955. Between then and mid 1956 they flew around six penetration missions in Europe covering Bulgaria, Czechoslovakia, the GDR, Hungary and Poland, with the major targets being the national capitals, industrial cities, Soviet military installations and exercises.[52] Although the flights were tracked by larger than expected numbers of radars, the Soviets and East Germans were unable to engage them. The detachment flew no more overflights after mid 1956 and was disbanded on 1 July 1958. During Slick Chick's time in Europe, one aircraft was lost in a training accident.[53]

Project Heart Throb

The Martin B-57, a licence-built version of the English Electric Canberra, was a workhorse airframe for a large number of special reconnaissance projects. Many passed through Rhein-Main at some time, either as part of 7407 SS or for periods of temporary duty for other short-term or 'special' operations tasked directly from the United States.[54]

The first RB-57A arrived at Rhein-Main in May 1955 for Project Sharp Cut. The modified aircraft carried a camera with a 240in lens, similar to Pie Face, designed by Boston University Optical Research Laboratory and installed in the aircraft's bomb bay. The camera used 'folded optics' and was able to image between 65 and 75 miles into denied territory.[55] It was also used on peripheral missions along the IGB, to Kaliningrad in the Baltic and Albania in the Adriatic. It remained in Germany until November 1960.

In the summer of 1955, five more RB-57As arrived at Rhein-Main. They were designed to acquire vertical photography under Project Heart Throb. Their overall black colour scheme made them look like 'regular' B-57s. Internally they had been subjected to a ruthless weight reduction programme that entailed removing the navigator's seat and associated equipment, armour and the rotating bomb door with its associated hydraulics. The bomb bay was then skinned over. An optical periscope and pilot-operated intervalometer were fitted to allow the single pilot to sight and operate the cameras. As the aircraft were expected to operate at such high altitudes, a pressure suit ventilation system was installed. Besides the Boston optical lab-designed camera, the Heart Throb aircraft are known to have carried two oblique-mounted K-38 cameras with 36in lenses and a single vertical T-11 camera with a 6in lens for mapping and tracking. The 'Heart Throb' aircraft had a 900-mile radius of action. The average flight time was about three and a half hours, which allowed just over an hour's coverage of target areas.[56]

After crew training and aircraft preparation, the pilots arrived at Rhein-Main on 23 August 1955. Captain (later Major General) Gerald Cooke, a Heart Throb pilot, believes that they flew some fifteen to nineteen overflights between November 1955 and August 1956.[57] Navigation was by deduced (dead) reckoning using only visual fixes. Radio silence was imposed from take-off to landing. Penetrating hostile airspace above 50,000ft, as fuel burned off the aircraft gradually climbed to between 62,000ft and 68,000ft and as far as 400 miles away from Rhein-Main. The return was largely on idle power as the aircraft flew a very gentle extended descent.

There is little verifiable information available about the areas covered by Heart Throb missions but Captain Cooke's three flights were close to Brno and Bratislava in Czechoslovakia, Budapest in Hungary and parts of northern Yugoslavia. He believes that other missions flew along the Baltic coast across Poland and into the Kaliningrad

Oblast.[58] Targets included cities, large airports, industrial centres and sometimes road and rail junctions. About six to twelve photographs were taken of each target.

The Heart Throb programme stopped in August 1956 because of the growing level of risk, exacerbated by the escalating tensions in Eastern Europe. The risks now outweighed the benefits and the missions were believed to be insufficiently productive to justify their continuation.[59] Although Heart Throb did not formally end until sometime later, the halting of European flights in summer 1956 dovetails fairly neatly with the start of U-2 flights from Wiesbaden.[60]

Other 7407 SS Operations

In June 1959, six 'big wing' RB-57Ds were delivered to the 7407 SS from 4025 Strategic Reconnaissance Squadron (4025 SRS), which had been operating them on detached duty at Rhein-Main for some time on peripheral flights under the code name Operation Bordertown. The RB-57D was a USAF project that never met the U-2's altitude goals and so was considered unsuitable for deep-penetration overflights, so it was restricted to peripheral missions in Europe.[61] The RB-57Ds came in two versions: five single-seat RB-57D-0s that carried four cameras (two K-38s with 24in lens and a 390ft film magazine in a split-pair configuration and two KC-1Bs with 6in lenses for precision mapping, fitted in the space where the back-seat crewman would usually have been. The camera's coverage overlapped to give high-quality, horizon-to-horizon coverage). A single-seat RB-57D-1 (53–3963) was equipped with the AN/APQ-56 high-resolution side-looking radar for all-weather radar mapping reconnaissance with the aircraft nose radome covered the antenna for the AN/APN-107 system.[62] The aircraft served in Germany until 1964 when wing fatigue problems became apparent.[63]

The RB-57F, another 'big wing' version, arrived in Germany in early April 1965. They carried the 'HTAC' high-altitude camera, weighing almost 2,000kg (4,400lb), used for acquiring oblique photography at up to 60 nautical miles range from the aircraft. ELINT/SIGINT equipment was also carried. On 14 December 1965 7407 SS lost an RB-57F over the Black Sea. It had departed from Incirlik in Turkey and, despite very extensive searches by Soviet and NATO units, no bodies or significant wreckage, was ever recovered.[64] The two remaining RB-57Fs, and a trainer aircraft, continued operations until the 7407 SS was deactivated on 1 October 1968.[65]

Conclusions

US airborne intelligence collection operations in Germany and covering NATO's northern and southern flanks during the Cold War were comprehensive and very complex. What began in Europe amidst the uncertainty following the end of the Second World War, developed to become a critical part of a worldwide intelligence-gathering effort. For the duration of the Cold War, USAFE had a very wide-ranging intelligence-gathering remit, although sometimes there was a duplication of effort caused by inter-agency rivalries and lack of communication. These operations gave the USA almost daily coverage of what could have been the flashpoints for conflict in Europe. Whilst the US reconnaissance programmes developed worldwide, Berlin, the Air Corridors and the periphery, remained at the forefront of intelligence gathering on the large Soviet and East German forces located in the GDR. The intelligence collected often had strategic significance that rippled well beyond the confines of the European theatre. The US operation's products were exchanged with other Allies, especially the British, and contributed significantly to producing a comprehensive intelligence picture of the Cold War Soviet Union and its Warsaw Pact allies.

Notes

1   L. Tart (2013), *History of the US Air Force Security Service (USAFSS)*, Vol. 2 (West Conshohocken, PA: Infinity Publishing).
2   Rhodarmer (2003), in Cargill Hall and Laurie (2003a), pp. 15–16.
3   J. Bessette, http://creekmisty.fatcow.com/bflb/27443/index.html.
4   P. Lashmar (1996), *Spy Flights of the Cold War* (Stroud: Sutton Publishing), p. 33, Note 16.
5   Miller (1998), p. 70.
6   W.E. Burrows (2001), *By Any Means Necessary: America's Secret Air War* (London: Arrow Books), p. 193.
7   C. Pocock and Clarence Fu (2010), *The Black Bats: CIA Spy Flights over China from Taiwan 1951–1969* (Atglen, PA: Schiffer Publishing), pp. 37 and 50. See also Lashmar (1996), p. 160.
8   J. van Waarde (2010), *Target Iron Curtain*, p. 2. Available at: http://www.16va.be/TargetIronCurtain-JanvanWaarde2010.pdf.
9   Tart (2010), pp. 594–5.
10 Grimes (2014), pp. 19–20.
11 Ibid., pp. 17–18.
12 Ibid.
13 Ibid., pp. 21–2.
14 Ibid., p. 28.
15 www.eisenhower.archives.gov/research/online_documents/aerial_intelligence/Summer_1960.pdf.
16 Grimes (2014), pp. 27–8.
17 Ibid., p. 36.
18 Ibid.
19 Ibid., pp. 37–8.
20 Ibid., p. 38.
21 Ibid., pp. 41–2.
22 van Waarde (2010), p. 7.
23 Grimes (2014), p. 13.
24 J. Richelson (1987), *American Espionage and the Soviet Target* (New York: William Morrow Inc.), pp. 102–4.
25 Cargill Hall and Laurie (2003b), Doc 4–1, p. 413.
26 Grimes (2014), pp. 10–12 and Cargill Hall and Laurie (2003b), Doc 35–1, p. 473.
27 Ibid., p. 12.
28 www.eisenhower.archives.gov/research/online_documents/ aerial_intelligence/Summer_1960.pdf Accessed 21 August 2014.
29 Lashmar (1996), p. 192.
30 Grimes (2014), p. 14.

31 Ibid., and Brugioni (2010), p. 75.
32 Grimes (2014), pp. 39–40.
33 Ibid., p. 27.
34 Ibid., pp. 253–4.
35 The term 'Big Item' was the name used by many crews over the duration of Corridor operations simply to refer to the primary large camera carried on their particular aircraft.
36 Grimes (2014), pp. 276–7.
37 Ibid., p. 278.
38 Robert Zoucha interview.
39 Boyne (2012).
40 Pocock and Fu (2010), pp. 37–8.
41 Tart and Keefe (2001), *The Price of Vigilance* (New York: Ballantine), pp. 550–1.
42 Beschloss (1986), pp. 158–9.
43 https://www.cia.gov/library/center-for-the-study-of-intelligence/kent-csi/vol12i2/html/v12i2a02p_0001.htm Accessed 21 August 2014.
44 G. Mindling and R. Bolton (2011), *US Air Force Tactical Missiles 1949–1969* (Morrisville, NC: Lulu.com publishing), p. 177.
45 Grimes (2014), p. 23.
46 Ibid.
47 Tart and Keefe (2001), pp. 246–7.
48 Grimes (2014), pp. 115–17.
49 van Waarde (2010), p. 13.
50 Tart and Keefe (2001), p. 256.
51 Ibid., pp. 301–510.
52 Brugioni (2010), pp. 75–6.
53 C.H. Rigsby, 'Project Slick Chick Overflights in Europe: 1955–1956', in Cargill Hall and Laurie (2003a), pp. 178–9.
54 Grimes (2014), pp. 85–7. There is still considerable detail to be unravelled concerning precise equipment fit and individual airframes involved in RB-57 operations in Germany – especially among some 'big wing aircraft'.
55 G. Cooke (2003a), *Early Cold War Overflights 1950–1956: Symposium Proceedings*, Vol. 1: *Memoirs* (Washington DC: Office of the Historian, National Reconnaissance Office), p. 193.
56 Ibid., pp. 203–4.
57 Ibid., p. 194.
58 Ibid., p. 202.
59 Ibid., p. 204.
60 Pedlow and Welzenbach (1992), p. 100.
61 In contrast to operations from Alaska which overflew Soviet territory.
62 van Waarde (2010), p. 20.
63 Grimes (2014), pp. 32–3.
64 Tart and Keefe (2001), pp. 163–5.
65 van Waarde (2010), p. 21.

4

British Corridor Flights and European Reconnaissance Operations

Knowledge of the British political background and approval processes for their Corridor flights is useful to better understand the experiences of those who flew the missions. The British effort was very modest when compared to the American. For example, in 1962 the RAF flew something like fifty corridor missions compared to over 500 flown by the USAF.[1] Even so it represented a significant effort by the RAF and British Army for over forty years. The operation was classified as 'TOP SECRET – UK/US Eyes Only' for its entire duration. It was so secret that its participants over the years were warned of 'career limiting effects' and other dire consequences that would result from unauthorised disclosure – 'The Tower, keys and throw away' often featured in these threats even long after individuals' involvement with the operation had ended.

It was only in 2011, over twenty years after the flights ended, that the curtain began to be lifted. The security classification of Corridor operations meant that most RAF and British Army records relating to them were destroyed shortly after its 1990 termination.[2] Those remaining are generally fragmentary, but offer a fascinating glimpse into the operation from the prime minister down to the dangers faced by the men flying the missions and those supporting them. The majority of information available about the flights today, certainly the operational aspects, now only resides in the memories of those former RAF and BAOR personnel involved in them.

Early Post-War Years in Germany

The use of British military aircraft on photographic operations in Germany required political approval. In the early years that control was only lightly exercised. Between 1945 and 1955 political control in the British Occupied Zone (BOZ) of Germany rested with the British Military Government (BMG), even after the formation of the West German government in 1949. During that time the Foreign Office (FO) in London took the view that diplomatic matters in the BOZ were the preserve of the BMG, a de facto extension of the UK government, having little direct regard to German-led administrative arrangements. The FO considered that the Air Ministry to War Office were the lead departments in any approval process for photographic flights. Locating official information on these early operations has proved elusive. So trying to establish the early approval processes is really educated guesswork. Until 1955 any submission probably started at HQ BAFO or HQ 2TAF, which probably made representations to the Air Ministry in London for their endorsement and approval to undertake the missions, with the relevant ministers being kept informed. In essence there was probably little direct political control exercised from London, as the British felt it was an 'internal issue'.

The US forces had begun a photographic survey in their zone of Germany, and the British followed suit under Operation Nostril from autumn 1952. The operation was flown by camera-equipped Lancasters of 82 Squadron, then being withdrawn from their Middle East Air Force commitment, to RAF Benson in Oxfordshire.[3] Four aircraft were detached to Germany to carry out the task – a 1: 20,000-scale photographic survey of the BOZ – due for completion prior to 82 Squadron re-equipping with Canberra PR-3s. The task was a high priority one, second only to the 'European Targeting Programme' (Operation Dimple). Indeed the task was considered so urgent that PR Mosquitoes from 58 and 540 squadrons were later drafted in to help complete it.[4] A pause, caused by the shooting down of the RAF Lincoln on 12 March 1953, resulted in a self-imposed ban on being within 10 miles of the SOZ boundary, but this had to be relaxed for Operation Nostril.[5] The operation was finally completed in 1954.

In the 1945 to 1947 period an eclectic mix of aircraft were used for photography in the Corridors, starting with a Mosquito using a forward-facing F.52 camera in 1945 and 1946. The Mosquito's replacement, until 1947, was the C-in-C's personal Dakota with a hand-held F.24 camera pointed out of the co-pilot's window. The Dakota was abandoned as a platform because the C-in-C became concerned about the compromise of 'his' aircraft that he used when he represented British forces on the Continent and the rather unsatisfactory view from the Dakota's flight deck.

In 1947 the Avro Anson was selected for Corridor flights for two reasons. First, the type was in widespread use in Britain and mainland Europe as a communications aircraft and so was a common sight. Secondly, some Ansons had already been modified for photographic reconnaissance work and used to update urban mapping of the UK to assist with post-Second World War reconstruction plans. The Ansons used on Corridor operations initially had a single vertically mounted US-origin K-17 camera with a 6in lens and a single vertically mounted F.24 both of which were mounted on the right hand side aft of the main wing spar that looked out through two holes in the cabin floor. When not in use these camera apertures were covered inside by two sheets of plywood, which were then hidden by the carpet. In 1953 or 1954 this antediluvian arrangement was replaced by a split-pair of F.52 cameras with either 14in or 20in lenses and a single port (left) facing oblique with a 36in lens. This camera fit remained extant until replaced by Pembrokes from 1956, although some Ansons soldiered on until 1957. During the Anson-era the crew consisted of the pilot, navigator, an Intelligence Corps major from the APIU (BAOR) and a SAC photographer. The photographer was responsible for operating the cameras under the direction of the major who wore other regimental titles when he was on the flights.[6]

The only purpose-built PR aircraft used in the Corridors were the Spitfire PR.XIXs of II (AC) Squadron operating from Bückeberg for a short time from 1950. They were used on 'unofficial' flights to photograph Soviet Zone airfields for indications of any build-up of aircraft that could be a precursor to a further Berlin blockade. The Spitfires operated with a split-pair of F.52 cameras with 36in lenses sometimes used in an oblique mode by banking the aircraft. Often flown above 10,000ft, the Spitfires were not part of the British Corridor programme but assigned for that specific task.

2TAF Communications Squadron and its predecessors were based at RAF Bückeberg until 1954 when the squadron moved to RAF Wildenrath and became heavily involved in British Corridor operations. In 1955 it possessed approximately twelve Anson Mk.12/19s and 21s, a Valetta, a Devon, a Prentice and some Vampires. From January 1956, the Ansons were gradually replaced by Percival Pembrokes. The three Pembrokes initially operated CASEVAC missions between Germany and England. On 1 January 1959, 2TAF Communications Squadron was renamed the 'Royal Air Force Germany Communications Squadron' (RAFG Comms Sqn) with Pembrokes, a Devon, a Heron and a Valetta used by the C-in-C RAF Germany. On 4 February 1969 it became 60 Squadron RAF.[7]

Stronger Political Controls

Following the 1956 Crabb affair, PM Anthony Eden had instigated an urgent review of UK intelligence operations. A key outcome of the review was greater direct exercise of political control over all future British intelligence operations.[8] Another issue was the agreement between the naval and air intelligence staffs with diplomats made in July 1955 on 'Political Approval for Certain Intelligence Operations', which essentially gave the services blanket approval for activities against 'opportunity targets', with the main restrictions being on aircraft and ships not entering the territorial waters (or airspace) of another state and 'taking reasonable precautions to avoid incidents'. The review suggested that these procedures be significantly tightened by requiring more detailed scheduling, the necessity for individual mission approvals from senior military and government-level officials, coupled with the introduction of greater safety distances.[9]

In 1955 Federal Germany became a sovereign state and the three Allies' military governments were withdrawn. Formal diplomatic relations with Germany now centred on Bonn, designated as the West German capital until some future unspecified reunification. This normalisation of diplomatic relations required formal changes to the approval procedures for Corridor and BCZ operations. The Foreign and

Commonwealth Office (FCO) became more actively involved in the policy and approval processes as London took over responsibility for them. Berlin continued to be treated somewhat differently as it officially remained under four-power occupation status until 1990.

The submission to government for general approval to mount regular air photographic operations in the Air Corridors and BCZ was initiated by the Air Reconnaissance Sub-Committee of the Joint Air Reconnaissance Intelligence Board (JARIB) and 'Ops Recce', RAF, at the Air Ministry/MoD in London. The submission always included the term 'Overflight Clearance' and included a Defence Intelligence Staff (DIS) Risk Assessment. These submissions were regularly updated and reviewed on a biannual and later annual basis for the duration of operations. The submission was led by the MoD at two-star (air vice-marshal) level and incorporated FCO views and advice. The agreed combined submission would then be sent to the JIC in London for its recommendation. It was the JIC's responsibility to place the proposal before a Cabinet sub-committee comprising the prime minister, Foreign Secretary, Secretary of State for Defence and Secretary of State for Air with the Chairman of JIC London in attendance. They would give the final broad approval for the continuance of operations and specified the ministerial rules under which they would operate. The approval also specified the annual maximum number of flights for both Corridor and BCZ operations. The high level of political approval required shows how sensitive the operation was considered.

This broad political approval was kept under constant review to capture changes to the political or military situation in Germany and internationally. This sometimes required modification to the devolved authorisation or the curtailment, or suspension, of individual operations for short periods. Such decisions would usually be approved by the Cabinet sub-committee acting on the JIC's recommendation. International tensions with the Soviets affected the programmes, with constraints probably being at their most severe between 1960 and 1962.[10]

Following the loss of Powers' U-2 on 1 May 1960, the British immediately suspended all photographic collection flights in the Berlin Corridors and BCZ, although normal Pembroke transport and Chipmunk training flights continued. By the autumn of 1960 pressure was building for the resumption of UK photo missions along both Corridors and inside the BCZ – especially to gather more information on what was viewed as the burgeoning SA-2 Guideline threat.[11] On 14 December 1960 a ministerial meeting, chaired by PM Macmillan, agreed to the cautious resumption of sorties with two Corridor and two BCZ sorties which were to be completed by the end of February 1961. As one note records, the 'photographs were well received by the US intelligence agencies', with whom the British shared their imagery.[12] Similar requests for flights continued to be submitted on a regular basis through 1961, and although nineteen corridor flights were authorised, only nine were completed because of time, technical and weather constraints. For the Americans, although U-2 and other overflights were under Administration control, Corridor and BCZ flights were regarded more as 'routine operations' and had continued largely unaffected. Following the 1960

U-2 and RB-47 shootdowns, successive British Cabinets were much more cautious than the Americans, and were prepared to cancel missions to avoid even the slightest possibility of potentially embarrassing incidents.[13]

The August 1961 construction of the Berlin Wall resulted in the serious curtailment of some intelligence sources and the complete loss of others, especially HUMINT ones. As a result the Corridor and BCZ Chipmunk programmes assumed a greater importance in intelligence collection. Requests for further flights took on a new imperative, particularly when some unsubstantiated reports were received of East German forces being present in East Berlin and troops deployed from mainland Russia rumoured to be gathering east of the city. This time there was to be no step back. The USA itself had ramped up Corridor and IGB flights as the tensions rose but these revealed no massing of Soviet forces preparing to take West Berlin.[14] Requests for the continuance of reconnaissance flights increased as the crisis in Berlin spiked during late October 1961, with US and Soviet tanks facing each other at Checkpoint Charlie. However, the tensions persisted; in February 1962 the Soviets attempted to restrict airspace resulting in the activation of the 'Jack Pine' HQ for some time to sustain the Allied presence in the Corridors.[15]

The Easing of Controls

The direct political control of individual flight authorisations gradually eased during 1961, passing to the General Officer Commanding (GOC) Berlin for Chipmunk BCZ flights and C-in-C RAFG for Pembroke Corridor and BCZ missions. This was formalised in a minute from Sir Norman Brook in April 1962, specifying a maximum limit of two Chipmunk and one Pembroke flights per week, and detailing where and how they were to be conducted.[16] Local discretion over the number of flights was soon extended to allow both GOC Berlin and C-in-C RAFG to authorise additional missions if local circumstances warranted it.[17] The flights went ahead successfully, although not everyone in government was happy about them. Harold Watkinson, then Defence Minister, commented on one early request, 'I doubt myself whether the risk is worth taking. Using the Corridor for spy flights would be a good card for the Russians.'[18]

In April 1962 a blanket clearance was granted for one Pembroke and two BRIXMIS Chipmunk flights per week that could be authorised by C-in-C RAFG and GOC (Berlin) respectively with no further recourse to London. By August 1962 this had changed and the C-in-C RAFG was permitted to authorise up to two additional Pembroke flights per week providing the situation warranted it, again without further authority.[19] Before an individual flight was authorised in Germany the relevant diplomatic sections at the British Embassy in Bonn and/or BMG in Berlin had to be consulted. This mechanism of London controlling overall approval for the annual numbers of flights remained in place, with periodic modification, until the cessation of operations in 1990. Besides political nervousness, there were also some worries at senior command levels over who would be held responsible if something went wrong with a flight. This served to colour decisions which perhaps became over-cautious at times.

The experiences of the Crabb and 1960 U-2 incidents became firmly entrenched in the British political psyche and approval processes for Corridor and BCZ operations. In subsequent years the approach was generally cautious. Short suspensions were often made on either side of senior British ministerial or state visits to and from Germany, the Soviet Union and Warsaw Pact states. British flights were often suspended for a few days during US presidential visits and elections at American request, and British flights were curtailed during General Election campaigns for fear of an incident. They would be quietly resumed after the new government had come into office in London and had been informed of the overflight programmes and given assent to their continuation.

RAF Pembroke Operations

Our account of RAF Corridor operations really starts from around 1960 when the accepted norm was that only transport and training aircraft were allowed to use the Corridors and BCZ airspace. The Pembroke clearly met those requirements. According to a 1969 JIC paper the Pembroke was primarily 'selected for clandestine photography because it is in current use as a communications aircraft in RAF Germany'.[20] Operating from RAF Wildenrath, these venerable Percival Pembrokes led a 'dual existence', flying very different types of mission. Some were configured as VIP and communications aircraft, shuttling equipment, senior officers and military personnel around Western Europe. Three Pembrokes led the more clandestine existence of regularly prowling along the Air Corridors and around the BCZ, photographing Soviet and East German targets. Intertwining overt and covert tasks in the same unit meant it was possible to disguise, to a certain extent, the true role of the camera-equipped aircraft.

Photo-Equipped Pembrokes

Six Pembrokes were originally built for photographic duties in the Far East. They flew with 81 Squadron, a specialist photo-reconnaissance unit used mainly for survey work. The unit based at Seletar in Singapore, with detachments to Labuan, Butterworth and Kai Tak, operated its Pembrokes between December 1955 and August 1960. Ray Dadswell was a photographer responsible for fitting and loading cameras in Pembrokes and Meteors with 81 Squadron between 1957 and 1959. He recalls that at that time the aircraft usually carried either F.24, or two F.52 cameras and sometimes an F.49 for survey work. The F.52s were usually fitted amidships as a split-pair. One camera pointed a few degrees to port and the other a few degrees to starboard. The optical flats through which images were taken were covered by manually operated twin doors.[21] A further two (XL953 and XL954) were converted from C1 airframes to C(PR)1 versions on the production line.

Everything about the use of the Pembroke for Corridor photographic operations was a compromise. Political caution, together with financial parsimony, meant a different aircraft type was unlikely to be procured for use in Germany for a very long time. Perhaps the Hallmark programme even extended the life of the communications Pembrokes as the RAF delayed replacement of the camera-equipped aircraft in Germany? As the airframes approached the end of their lives and spares became difficult to source, the Pembroke was finally retired and the Andover replaced it in RAF Germany firstly in the VIP role.

The original equipment 'fit' for the photo-reconnaissance Pembrokes in Germany was similar to those of the Ansons they replaced:

- A port-facing F.52 with either a 36in or 48in lens
- A split-pair of two F.52s with 14in or 20in lenses
- A vertical F.49 'mapping camera' with a 6in lens.

The fit did not produce the quality of imagery that many sought – achieving satisfactory results only as far as 2 to 6 miles from the aircraft and not the desired 10-plus miles. Among the National Archive files, one very detailed paper, and accompanying technical commentary, illustrates the shortcomings of the original Pembroke camera fit. Problems included the lack of 'image motion compensation' for the F.52s, which limited the conditions in which they could be used at low level in good weather conditions, and even then the resolution was not high. Equally there were concerns that camera vibration would be a significant issue in achieving high-quality imagery. It recommended improvements that could be made without having to move to a new aircraft type.[22]

RAF post-Second World War aircraft camera development had concentrated on equipment suited to either extremely high-level or low-level flying. Cameras optimised for the Corridor operating altitudes (3,500–10,000ft) were largely neglected. The document recommended a number of short-term solutions pending the procurement of a more suitable aircraft. The recommendation was to fit five F.96 cameras mounted in a special frame anchored to the aircraft's floor and ceiling. Three of the F.96s, with 12in lenses, were to be in a 'fan' configuration and two F.96s with 48in lenses in oblique mounts. This F.96 camera fit was originally developed and flown in a Hastings of 51 Squadron. The Hastings had been proposed as a Pembroke replacement but the programme was cancelled during an early 1960s Defence Review. In the Pembroke the oblique cameras looked out of the cabin windows – third from the front on the port side and second from the front on the starboard side – and this necessitated the replacement of the standard windows by very expensive 'quartz' windows to minimise distortion. To operate the cameras, appropriate control panels and some wiring changes also had to be made. The cameras were fitted with 250ft and 500ft film magazines. The weight of the F.96 camera fit plus the crew and fuel brought the Pembroke close to its maximum take-off weight, which limited its range, especially during hot weather. Consequently some flights to Berlin could require an interim refuelling stop, at RAF Gütersloh for Northern Corridor and at the USAF Bitburg or Rhein-Main ABs for Southern Corridor missions. As more flying restrictions (weight increases and age) were imposed on the Pembroke, one of the oblique cameras, usually the left-facing one, was removed during the summer months. This may have allowed the aircraft to fly direct to Berlin without a fuel stop.[23]

To improve imagery quality, special camera mountings that minimised airframe vibration were essential. The Pembroke had a very low ground clearance so sliding camera hatches were installed on the fuselage underside to preserve an element of secrecy and protected the lenses. The equipment choices were all compromises, based on what was readily available in RAF equipment stocks and could fit into the narrow confines of the Pembroke's cabin.[24] In addition to these 'short-term' measures, a long-term solution to replace the Pembroke with a Vickers Varsity was discussed, although soon rejected on cost grounds and the availability of airframes for conversion.[25]

The RAE suggested a total modification cost of £150,000 for three aircraft, which pales into insignificance compared to the US investment in its Corridor operations. The Pembrokes clearly lacked the capabilities of the highly specialised US platforms, but as an investment in 'aerial espionage', they generated a good political and military return for many years. In the original case for updating the Pembroke camera fit, one argument was that modification would improve the UK's contribution to imagery collection, thus enabling the Americans to justify their continued exchanges with the British. However, the JIC made the point that because US–UK armed forces and intelligence agency relationships were so strong, the UK contribution of Corridor material probably made little difference in influencing the continued supply of US Corridor imagery to the British.[26]

On 10 January 1963, the modification programme was approved in principle. The most important part of the project was the design and installation of the special vibration-reducing camera mountings. That task was given to Fairey Air Survey Limited, which had the appropriate security clearances and was also involved on the secret camera fits for the 'V' bomber force.[27] The modification of the three aircraft was to be carried out under a contract issued in support of 'Modification 614'. Work began at the end of 1963 to modify three Pembrokes – XF799, XL953 and XL954 – for photographic work. These Pembrokes would become known in Germany as the 'in fit' aircraft. An additional aircraft – XF796 – flew in the role until 1975, but with the less capable original camera fit.

The modification programme had problems. The development and installation of fixed aircraft attachment points for the removable elements of the frames was a key task. Because the Pembrokes had been hand-built, rather than jig-built, each aircraft was unique, so each set had to be custom-built. This meant it was impossible to construct a standardised, interchangeable set of components until the differences between the three aircraft were properly identified. The construction of the frame for the third aircraft was only started after these problems had been overcome on the first two aircraft, which considerably delayed the programme. Company representatives had to visit Germany in September 1965 before there was much progress. The third aircraft was so different from the other two, that the fixed fittings were unlikely to be compatible with the removable ones. The original intention to have just two sets of removable fittings to keep two aircraft available was abandoned and a third set was purchased.[28] The delays were so long that one aircraft in the 'old' camera fit (inaccurately listed as WV796) was retained in service until the third 'fit' aircraft became available.[29] In late 1966, financial approval for a third 'new' fit aircraft (XF799) was granted and what should have been a relatively straightforward modification programme turned into a tortuous one that lasted over four years.[30]

Another major problem was designing an electrically activated 'fogging' device. Development of this modification and manufacture of the 250 and 500ft magazines was by Williamsons and managed by Faireys. The intention was that, in an emergency, the switches would be thrown and the exposed film rewound over a light source to completely over-expose the imagery, rendering it totally useless. This was expected to take some four minutes for a 250ft magazine and seven minutes for the 500ft one. Difficulties in resolving these problems significantly delayed the entry into service of the new camera fit. Missions with the new F.96 installation began on 23 November 1964, but without the oblique cameras. The 'fan' cameras could be used because they had a manual fogging device and used shorter film magazines in the interim. It was not until 1967 that the Pembrokes began to fly with the full F.96 fit.[31]

Squadron Leader Phil Chaney, 60 Squadron navigator and later CO (1988–90), explained:

> around 1980, more modern camera equipment became available to us – similar to that then used on the U-2 which gave us true horizon to horizon coverage. The resolution on those cameras was much higher and therefore more susceptible to the effects of vibration.

That became a problem on one particular aircraft – XL953. This had constant vibration problems which affected the aircraft's photographic performance. Despite many efforts the vibration was never really rectified, although it was ultimately solved in a rather drastic way:

> On 16 May 1980, the aircraft was being prepared for deep maintenance at RAF Wildenrath. A static charge ignited some remaining fuel being drained from it and the resulting fire saw the hangar roof damaged and half of XL953 burnt out.

The story has since become part of squadron folklore. Later that day the new CO, Squadron Leader Andy Spanner, was greeted on his return to Wildenrath reportedly with: 'Boss, good news is we've managed to sort out the vibration problem on '953. Bad news is the aircraft is burnt out!'[32]

Flying the Corridor

Flight Lieutenant David Clark, who had previously flown Pembrokes with 152 Squadron in the Middle East during the mid 1960s, was posted to 60 Squadron for a second Pembroke tour in May 1975:

I remember on my arrival at Wildenrath, we were shown around an aircraft in the hangar by the Boss. Being experienced on the type I noticed all sorts of funny pipes and things on the inside of it, so I asked what they were. The Boss casually said 'just ignore it', which I did. I had no idea that we were doing the reconnaissance flights until some months later when I was introduced to the role. The reconnaissance side of the operation was never spoken about. One began to think that something funny was going on because the aircraft 'in fit' was always parked directly outside the squadron – on the first slot. Only that aircraft was allowed to park there and with its door always facing the hangar. The curtains were always drawn and it was kept locked.

Brian King's first experiences were a little different:

I knew nothing about the reconnaissance role. But then you noticed aircrews whom you didn't know or have any idea what they were doing. That there was an aircraft that always has closed curtains, always kept in the hangar when not flying, never just parked outside. People were careful who was around when it was out and no visitors allowed near it.

He said that the Boss introduced him to the role 'with a very brief, briefing'. 'Very few on the Station knew what we did. But people did notice the oddities of your behaviour.' 'We always had ad hoc crews. We would get the programme about a month ahead and so would know roughly when we would be on standby, a scheduled trip and so on.'

Within 60 Squadron, certainly not all the air and ground crews knew what the 'fit' aircraft and their crews were doing. Phil Chaney told us, 'knowledge of Operation Hallmark was kept very closely guarded with only a very small number of people on the Station having full knowledge.' At that time there would be only thirty-four people with full access to the details of the programme: fifteen on the squadron, the Station Commander, Station Intelligence Officer and OC Ops Wing, C-in-C RAFG, his deputy with the rest in London in the prime minister's Office, Secretary of State for Defence and Cabinet Office. Operation Hallmark was also kept closely guarded at HQ RAF Germany and HQ BAOR at Rheindahlen; official knowledge of the 'clandestine photography' flights was restricted to those RAF and Intelligence Corps personnel analysing the imagery itself, senior staff officers and others involved in their duties within the Reconnaissance Section. There was also a wider grouping at Rheindahlen and Wildenrath aware of at least elements of the tasking – even if not officially briefed on the full operation. This would have included photographic technicians, maintenance crews and some members of BRIXMIS.

A number of select personnel at RAF Gatow also knew the purpose of the 'special fit' Pembrokes visiting the airfield. Peter Kirkpatrick of the Aircraft Servicing Flight (ASF) was one of those, serving at RAF Gatow and completing his tour in January 1988:

The ASF always had good advance warning of flight arrivals, nobody was going to carry out an emergency diversion 100+ miles up the corridor, after all! The only real exception to this was 'that' Pembroke which was known to us as 'The Unsched'.

We could use this term in front of other people if necessary without giving much away. To cover the short notice availability, we were on call and carried a pager, which normally frightened the hell out of us if it actually went off.

Over the years the photographic reconnaissance sorties developed into a stable routine. Aircraft usually flew to Berlin down one Corridor and exited via a different one. The journey time on Southern and Central routes was two to two and a half hours, considerably longer on the Northern Corridor. Once in the Corridor the aircraft generally flew at 3,500ft, if cloud conditions allowed. The exact route and altitude would depend on the targets for the flight and flying conditions. The Pembrokes' flight path down the Corridor was a very erratic one, unlike most regular Corridor traffic that strictly adhered to the centreline, following it rigidly all the way in and out. Crews were acutely aware of the dangers involved in flying Corridor missions, when very minor mistakes in navigation could result in tragedy. If a photographic Pembroke had ever come down in GDR territory, the British would have tried to deny that the mission's task was photographic.

Crews were generally assigned to flying the Corridor for a week, usually completing one round trip during that time, sometimes two. On the Monday they were told the outline flying plan for the week. This was matched with the weather forecasts, clearly crucial for successful missions. Likely flight days might be vague – depending on expected Soviet military activity levels. Dave Clark again:

> the Navigator got the prescribed route from HQ RAFG at Rheindahlen. We would generally take off by about 10.00 and use a standard routing to a Corridor entrance. Once in the Corridor it was down to the navigator how close we went to the edge of it. One navigator was up front, next to the pilot and the other down the back operating the equipment.

Paul Hickley, a 60 Squadron navigator, explained their two different roles:

> The front-seater was responsible for all of the route navigation, including preparing both the navigation flight plan and the Air Traffic flight plan notification. The rear-seat navigator could not see forwards and so, for vertical shots, had to rely entirely on the front seat navigator (or occasionally the pilot) for information on when to switch the vertical cameras on. However, he did have a vertical sight, a drift-sight, rather like a downward-pointing telescope, that could act as a track indicator. If the initial line-up was less than ideal, the navigator could 'talk' the pilot onto the right line once he saw the target. The pilot would then use coarse (indeed, rather agricultural) applications of rudder, whilst trying to keep the wings level, because a gentle turn with bank would have displaced the target from the centre.
>
> Most important of all, the front seat navigator was to ensure that the aircraft stayed within the Corridors. These only extended 10 miles each side of the centre-line and some of our vertical targets lay very near indeed to the Corridor edge. We were

always advised that we faced the possibility of being shot down if we strayed outside. Watching the Pembrokes on their radars, this would sometimes make the air traffic controllers in the BARTCC rather nervous until they got the message that the Pembrokes were best left alone to go about their business. Most bona fide air traffic in the Berlin Air Corridors hugged the centre-line, as we did ourselves when not on Hallmark missions, because they knew the risks of not doing so. Our job required us to go to the edges, and it concentrated the mind.

Brian King added that:

we had some ridiculous stories to justify what we are doing – such as a navigator on a 'chop ride' trying to pass the course so don't push us back. Then someone would realise that they should leave us alone. Inside the BCZ, ATC would sometimes give you vectors away from edges. So you would ask, 'are you giving me a mandatory vector to fly?' and again we would try to subtly remind ATC that we were doing something different.

Paul Hickley:

Many of the targets were 10 to 15 miles outside the corridors and were perfectly open to photography if the visibility was good enough. The F.96 oblique cameras had a sight-line that could be varied by a manual spring balance adjustment from the horizontal to about 15 degrees depression angle. If the rear-seat navigator saw the target out of the side windows in good time, he could adjust the camera down to the correct depression angle by visual estimation. Once the camera was in line, he could squint down the barrel (the lens assembly looked like a telescope and filled much of the cabin's width) and ask the pilot to make any final adjustment required by a combination of bank and rudder, which kept the wing down the right amount but didn't change heading. If he picked it up late, the whole aiming process would have to be done by talking the pilot on to the right angle of bank, because the camera angle motors were quite slow. The pilot needed to keep the aircraft as steady as possible to enable cameras to function properly without blur and on target.

Brian King pointed out:

Each flight had routine and unique elements, but were rarely identical. We might be briefed on a mission to overfly what was likely to be a training exercise outside of the normal pattern. That might be a precursor to a deployment taking place at a given time and location. Then when we actually got there we would find just a caravan obviously pushing out transmissions and spoof material. We had a standing brief not to miss targets of opportunity. Some were at limits of visibility – so what they actually got from it I am not sure. Training areas stood out particularly clearly from the air. Most things stood out because of the differences around them. Particularly in GDR, if something was neat and tidy it normally meant it was important. Sometimes we would go and photograph a point even if nothing was visible to us. Pilots rarely got to see the pictures. I always tried to take something on a flight to get a smile from the guys in PR. I once took a picture of a hot air balloon in mid-flight by lifting the Pembroke's wing and they later sent me a copy of the picture which I still have.

On approach to RAF Gatow the crew would switch off the equipment and close the curtains. After landing they would always park in the same place with the door opposite the hangar so that the East German Border Guards, in the nearby watch towers, could not see into the aircraft. Outdoors crews had to be careful in conversation as directional microphones were used by some watchtowers. Brian King, as many other pilots did, had a high opinion of the ground handling in Berlin:

> At RAF Gatow, the ground crew from the ASF were responsible for the Chipmunks but also for us. They were selected as being above average guys, so the aircraft would be turned round as quickly as possible – one of the best pre- and post-flight services you could get. These guys were highly motivated and were very good at their job. Then we were ready to go off on a local sortie when told to do so.

Off the flightline, 'in fit' crews had access to a secure room, from where they could talk more freely. Peter Kirkpatrick explained:

> It must be said, the Pembroke crew were more chatty about where they had been, than the Chipmunk crews. They would mention where and who they had been looking at, sometimes pointing stuff out on our wall map. I must be clear that this was not an operational briefing, more a 'bit busy round there' sort of chat over a brew. Also, we could normally tell from the amount of urgency in the crew if they had been 'busy'. After most flights they would saunter around and have a cuppa with us. But some days there was a bit more urgency, wanting to get fuelled up and in the air again for either a 'local' or a return flight.

The pilot would create a fictitious 'snag' on the aircraft, always something relatively minor, but requiring an air test after 'rectification'. Dave Clark elaborated:

> the fault on the RAF 'Form 700' was never declared to ground crew. So when I put a snag in the sheet I also removed it from the '700' afterwards and destroyed it, so to all intents nothing was ever wrong. For the overnight stays the aircraft would be fuelled, locked and left with the film on board. We tended to keep away from the Gatow mess because we might be asked questions, so we would often stay down town at the Edinburgh House military hotel. At Gatow, on the following morning, we would speak to Rheindahlen on the secure phone to check our outbound route.[33]

Brian King took up the account:

> the airtest generally took place in the afternoon, or perhaps the following day if
> weather, or planning, required it. The flight would usually necessitate flying around
> the BCZ – particularly close to its edge with the cameras working at from 2,000 to
> 3,500ft. Often in winter we were limited by weather windows, so we would have
> to be flexible as to when flights would take place. We would then return to RAF
> Gatow to stay overnight. Being able to stay in Berlin was one of the good parts of
> the job, being able to have a good meal and a few beers.

Whilst the Pembroke crews may have been enjoying time off in Berlin, the ASF
were responsible for the aircraft while it was on the ground at RAF Gatow. Peter
Kirpatrick described:

> The 'Unsched' was kept closed and locked at all times when it was with us. The
> door locks must have been sourced from the same place as Austin-Morris got theirs.
> If I remember correctly my old Morris Thousand boot key fitted it! The only thing
> that was taken off it outside would be that lovely big wooden crate they called a
> 'lunch box'. If anything needed to be removed from the aircraft we would push it
> in to the hanger and close the doors first. The curtains were still kept drawn inside,
> but at least we could then remove the large 'briefcase' which contained a very nice
> high-speed hand-held camera (kept locked in a separate cabinet). Other than that
> we didn't really have anything to do with the 'special fit' aircraft.

Generally the following day, with 'fault' cleared, the Pembroke departed, repeating the
inbound procedure in reverse. It was standard practice that flights in and out of Berlin
were flown along different corridors so as to maximise target coverage. Peter added
that 'we never flew outside the permitted boundaries. We would have been mortified
to do so, because it would have meant our navigation was inaccurate.'

On arrival at RAF Wildenrath the Pembroke would be towed into the hangar
and the film quickly removed. The crew would be debriefed at Rheindahlen and the
films processed as a high priority at the Photographic Reconnaissance Unit (PRU),
often within a couple of hours. Once printed the images were examined by PIs from
the co-located RAF Photographic Interpretation/Intelligence Department (PID)
and BAOR's 6 Intelligence Company.

The attempts to hide the true role of the camera-equipped Pembrokes saw them
operating alongside the squadron's 'standard' communications and VIP transport aircraft. As part of their extended cover, the camera-equipped aircraft also regularly took
photographs of British bases and training locations in Germany to maintain up-to-date
photography and justify their special configuration.[34] If anybody asked why the aircraft
were camera-equipped, the explanation given was that they were taking photographs
of training areas to verify farmers' compensation claims for military damage. Another
story was that they were flying an urgent spare part into Berlin and were using the

only available aircraft that just happened to be in camera fit. Aircrew kept flight time logged in their individual logbooks, where the Corridor reconnaissance flights are simply, if misleadingly, listed as 'training', 'flight checks' or other innocuous activities.[35]

If a Pembroke had ever been forced to land in the GDR, a prepared cover story was to be used. However, it was unlikely to last much longer than the time it took to recount. An Appendix to the 1962 'Operations Instruction' illustrates this. Providing the aircraft lands intact, it starts with the admission that 'the aircraft is used for aerial photography on legitimate occasions'. They instruct that the purpose of the flight was to 'bring up to date the survey of Gatow airfield', and that any exposed 'operational' film magazines are to be 'fogged' and exchanged with 'cover' ones by the crew. The cover magazines contained either unexposed film or footage of RAF Gatow.[36] The crews were also told that they could set fire to the aircraft, but quite how this was to be done was not made clear. In National Archive material, ministerial and official exchanges often express the view that the possibility of losing a Pembroke due to engine problems was relatively insignificant because it was a twin-engined aircraft.[37] However, the aircrews themselves often mention the Pembroke's abysmal single-engined performance, especially when operating at close to maximum take-off weight as the 'in fit' aircraft did.

The operation code name changed on numerous occasions. Sometimes changes appear to just have been routine to keep the Soviets guessing. On other occasions changes may have been in response to concern over possible security breaches. For example, until 19 April 1962 the operation was known as Fabian. A memo of that date suggests that the code word may have been compromised through possible discussion of operational details on an insecure line, so sometime before 13 June it was renamed Operation Tokay.[38] Around the 25 May 1965, it was renamed Ladbrook after another mis-communication over the operations security classification.[39] A JIC Report of October 1969 names the operation Remote.[40]

A Unique View of UK Corridor Operations

In the history of British Corridor operations, retired Air Vice-Marshal Mike Jackson is uniquely qualified to comment on them. He served as OC 60 Squadron between 1975 and 1977, commanded the Joint Air Reconnaissance Intelligence Centre (JARIC) in 1987 and was later the Director General Intelligence and Geographic Resources on the Defence Intelligence Staff. He joined the RAF in 1960 and by 1967 was a navigator, flying Beverly aircraft with 30 Squadron in Bahrain, supporting counter-insurgency operations in Dhofar and the Radfan. This was his first introduction to the world of intelligence-related work.

Following completion of a staff course in 1974, Mike's first contact with 60 Squadron was when he was posted to RAF Wildenrath in late June 1975 to become its next OC. Even at that stage he did not know that the unit flew Corridor reconnaissance missions and admitted to it initially being a bit of a disappointment:

nobody knew what the squadron was doing. The role of 60 Squadron was really kept quiet, well-guarded, all the way through to the end of the Cold War and I find it quite extraordinary that on a busy station like RAF Wildenrath it remained such a secret. A number of things struck me when I arrived. I was virtually the youngest guy on the squadron [and there were] quite a lot of elderly navigators and a number of them came from Canberras. Without anything really sinking in, I just thought this was a rather strange squadron. It wasn't until I got a handover from my predecessor, Ronnie Thomas, that I discovered what our primary role was. That took me back into old roles and I fitted into it pretty comfortably.

For Hallmark operations the OC ensured the whole process worked smoothly. He had to be certain that these flights got the priority and resources needed within the squadron, without giving too much away. When it came to the details of mission planning, Mike was told of the date, time and main target areas but otherwise was not generally involved in the detailed mission planning. During his tenure as OC, Mike Jackson also flew occasional Corridor flights with crews to ensure he remained familiar with operations and procedures. On a crew's return from a Corridor trip he often took part in the debrief – especially if there were notable sightings or an incident. There were generally around twelve aircrews assigned to the squadron at the time. About half the aircrew were assigned to Hallmark operations at any one time and sometimes referred to themselves as the 'Black Hand Gang'.

The ground crew component of the squadron was quite large, numbering around ninety personnel. These included significant numbers of specialist photographic and camera technicians engaged in Hallmark-related work. Mike said he was very proud of the many ground crews who were well trained in cross-servicing other countries' aircraft types under the NATO Ample Gain arrangements. He recalls frequent aircraft visits from other NATO states – especially Norwegian and Danish F-104 Starfighters. If they turned up rather unexpectedly and an 'in fit' Pembroke was parked up outside the squadron, there would be a sudden discreet rush to get it back into a hangar before the visitors could see too much.

The mid 1970s is often regarded by political observers of the Cold War as the 'height' of détente, when relations between the protagonists were generally at their most relaxed. However, Mike Jackson explained that the military held a rather different view. Leonid Brezhnev was just about at the zenith of his power; 'the "Brezhnev Doctrine" was at its height' and he had managed to accumulate all the key positions of the Soviet State. Not only was he CPSU General Secretary and president, he had appointed himself as Chairman of the Defence Council, was Marshal of the Soviet Union and in 1977 C-in-C of the Soviet Armed Forces, so consolidating his sole grip on power. Many in NATO were very concerned how Brezhnev might exercise this accumulated power, so looking for aggressive manifestations of that grip was a priority. In the end Mike's tour as CO 60 Squadron passed without major incident.

Subsequently moving on through a number of intelligence-related posts – including a tour as Defence Attaché in Poland – Mike Jackson became OC JARIC at RAF

Brampton, the British centre of excellence for PI, from 1987. As he said: 'I began to see some of the things that 60 was doing that I didn't see when I was there and on occasions just how close to the edge they really went.' 'I began to appreciate the real benefit of what Hallmark was producing.' He explained how the view on the value of Corridor operations began to change. There was hugely profound political change beginning to happen in the USSR and the rest of the Soviet bloc, even though its ultimate destination was then uncertain. Second, the imagery produced by the Pembrokes, although of good quality, was beginning to lose value. Even after the introduction of the 'Baker' camera (as used on the U-2) its imagery was qualitatively matched and surpassed by satellite material. Satellites had also become easier to re-task and the quality of their imagery, especially oblique, greatly improved. This combination of factors meant that the value of Corridor imagery was gradually declining – although the Pembroke's replacement may have somewhat redressed the balance for a while.

Latecomer: The Andover

A Pembroke replacement had been talked about since the 1960s. They were old, wearing out and their load-carrying capacity was very limited. In the 1980s it was finally agreed that their replacement would be the Andover. It was larger, more modern and far more flexible in the amount and type of equipment it could carry. Two aircraft were selected for conversion, but only one (XS596) was completed. Unsurprisingly the programme took longer than planned because of difficulties integrating the new sensor package into the airframe. It was finally delivered to 60 Squadron in the summer of 1989 but required further modification work at RAF Wildenrath, including the installation of a false bulkhead and seats in the rear of the aircraft so that, when the rear loading doors were open, all that was visible was an aircraft in passenger configuration. Operational flights began in early 1990, after the collapse of the Berlin Wall. Both Pembrokes and Andovers were flown on Hallmark missions during this overlap period, with some final Pembroke sorties being recorded into November 1989.

The Andover's camera fit was:

- A KA-95B panoramic camera with a 12in lens.
- An F.126 vertical camera with a 6in lens. This was used to produce small-scale (1: 20,000) photographs for installation (area) prints, mission tracking and maybe survey images to help map production.
- Two F.126 oblique, one left facing, one right facing. These F.126 bodies were fitted with reworked 48in lenses from F.96s.
- An Agiflite hand-held camera fitted with a 12in lens for the use of crew members to photograph anything of interest.
- A Sergeant III Thermal Imager. This was proposed but never used operationally because of security concerns about how to destroy the tapes in the event of an emergency. By the time a solution was found, the operation had ceased.

Paul Hickley described the final months of flying:

> We had virtually ceased operations by August 1990. It was not that the operation
> was officially cancelled, just that the tasking requests dried up because the operation
> had become pointless in view of impending German reunification.

Operation Hallmark was officially wound up on 30 September 1990. However, the
last full flight had one final, unexpected twist. As the then OC 60 Squadron, Phil
Chaney, described:

> Our final Hallmark flight was on 6 September 1990. Take-off was delayed because
> the Wildenrath armoury was on fire. Eventually we got off and flew to Berlin
> along the Corridor (which by now had become a formal civil airway). On our
> return we overflew the site of the armoury, which was now a roofless, smouldering
> shell, using our few remaining feet of film. Those last few feet of the final Hallmark
> film were declassified and released to the President of the Board of Inquiry into
> the fire. He was astounded to find such high-quality imagery was available to aid
> his investigation.

Open Skies

After German reunification and the demise of the Corridor mission, XS596 found
a new role, as the UK's Open Skies aircraft, operated by QinetiQ from Boscombe
Down in Wiltshire. Its prior configuration for Corridor work meant it required little
modification for use in Open Skies other than the removal of much of the previously
installed camera equipment. All sorts of similarities, and ironies, reveal themselves in
treaty operations. What was once 'Top Secret' in Corridor operations now became
absolutely 'transparent' under Open Skies. The Open Skies proposal originated,
albeit it in a different form, with President Eisenhower, although it had been quickly
rejected by the Soviets at Geneva in 1955. That rejection was viewed by Eisenhower as
one of the final triggers for approving deep-penetration U-2 overflights. From 1992
XS596 was involved in precisely the sort of photographic missions that had resulted
in Gary Powers being shot down, but which are now permitted by the treaty.

The Andover flew over 1,200 flying hours on more than seventy Open Skies-
related flights until the UK abandoned the provision of its own aircraft in 2009.[41]
XS596 was scrapped at Boscombe Down in June 2013.

British SIGINT Aircraft in the Corridors?

Unlike the French and Americans, the British do not appear to have maintained any
permanent airborne SIGINT capability for use in the Corridors. There are some

anecdotal reports of individual or small groups of aircraft – generally of Varsity and Hastings vintage – that may have undertaken one-off, or short-term operations and passed through RAF Gatow. The explanation for this is probably quite simple: the UK and USA operated large SIGINT facilities at Teufelsberg on the edge of Gatow and within RAF Gatow itself. As we have seen, the USA undertook Corridor SIGINT flights and the USAFSS and NSA were also listening in throughout West Germany and elsewhere from their facilities. Most of the information collected would have been shared with the British under the UKUSA SIGINT agreement, so a permanent British airborne Corridor SIGINT capability would probably have been a largely unnecessary luxury. Maintaining even a modest airborne SIGINT capability in Germany would not have been cost-effective, especially considering that the supporting ground infrastructure for such operations was already available in Britain only a short flight away.

British airborne SIGINT activities have always been euphemistically known as 'Radio Proving Flights' (RPFs). The RAF's airborne SIGINT capabilities were limited, scarce and expensive. They were mostly flown by 51 Squadron Canberras, Comets and later Nimrod R1s, which were always very busy. The Canberras and Nimrods could not have been flown in the Corridors because they were not 'training' or 'transport' types. However, RPF flights were conducted along the IGB, Baltic coasts, Mediterranean and beyond for much of the Cold War and these would have provided Britain with a significant SIGINT take. Historical detail of many of these flights is still currently a 'closed' topic but a 1967 National Archive file provides some details of a series of flights launched over the Baltic from RAF Laarbruch under the code names Cabana, Lorry and Martinet. Each had different objectives, involving the use of single and multiple Canberra and Comet aircraft – detached from 51 Squadron. They involved flying within 30 to 50 miles of Soviet territory to test air defence reaction times and radars. Other flights were conducted directly from RAF Wyton in Huntingdonshire, including the code names Tumby and Hockey, usually monitoring Soviet SAM and anti-aircraft artillery radars along the IGB.[42] On the monthly programmes there is also mention of regular IGB border flights:

> up to four sorties will be flown in the monthly series of border flights against targets in East Germany, which, as usual, will be the subject of a separate submission for approval by the Secretary of State Defence.[43]

These missions were co-ordinated at the monthly US–UK meetings and were signed off by four senior personnel from an Air Commodore at DIS, through ACAS (Ops), VCAS and an Under Secretary at the political level. Individual flight authorisations were normally reviewed forty-eight hours before take-off.

Conclusions

Clearly British Corridor operations were much more limited than those of the USA. However, they were still of considerable importance. To the British they represented a first-hand intelligence gathering capability, under their own control, to discover Soviet and East German activities in and around the Corridors and Berlin. For the USA, British imagery represented an additional intelligence source. Possibly, for the British the greatest significance of Corridor flights was a political one. The UK gains a great deal from its intelligence agreements with the USA that gives it access to global, wide-ranging data and information it could not hope to generate by itself. The UK was, and is, very keen to maintain that relationship. Within government the question has often been raised over the years of what contribution can 'we' (the British) make to justify the USA continuing to share the large amounts of the intelligence it gathers with us? This anxiety appears to be a much greater British preoccupation than an American one. Corridor and BCZ flights were considered an important part of the British contribution to that relationship by ministers and senior officials within the FCO, MoD, and Cabinet Office. The efficacy with which the mission was accomplished in Germany by RAFG and BAOR, with very limited resources, provides a strong testimony to their technical skills and high levels of professionalism.

Notes

1   The National Archive: PRO AIR 2/1856: CMS.4123/62 21 August 1962.
2   The British Corridor reconnaissance flights, known as Operation Hallmark for much of the period under discussion here; other operational code names were also used over the years, including Tokay, Fabian, Ladbrook, Plainsman, Remote and Venton.
3   The National Archive: PRO AIR 14/3995 Air Ministry to Bomber Command: Air Survey Photography – British Zone of Germany, 26 August 1952.
4   The National Archive: PRO C.50169/DDOPS(Photo), 26 and 29 August 1952.
5   The National Archive: PRO C.50169, 10 August 1953.
6   Memories of Walter Drew, SAC photographer at Buckeberg and Wildenrath 1953 to 1955
7   http://www.rafwildenrath.de/staffeln-squadrons/2ataf-rafg-communications-sqn/.
8   Aldrich (2011), pp. 140–2.
9   Ibid., pp. 525–6.
10 The National Archive: PRO AIR 2/18561 Reconnaissance Operations: RAF Germany 1962–1967 Folio 114A, 117A and 118A.
11 Information about the SA-2 was regarded as so important that the USA dedicated a specialist aircraft (project CREEK FLEA) to gather data relating to it around Berlin.
12 The National Archive: PRO FO 371/160623, 30 May 1961, minute Sir Norman Brook to PM.
13 Aldrich (2001), p. 541.
14 Brugioni (2010), p. 338.
15 W. Taylor (2003), *Royal Air Force Germany since 1945* (Hinckley: Midland Publishing), p. 97.
16 The National Archive: PRO FO 371/160623, minute to PM, 24 April 1962.
17 The National Archive: PRO FO 371/160623, minute to PM, 24 April 1962.
18 The National Archive: PRO FO 371/160623, minute to PM, 3 September 1961.
19 The National Archive: PRO AIR 2/18561 minute Brook to PM, 22 August 1962.

20 The National Archive: PRO CAB 191/2 '*The Joint BAOR/RAF Germany Air Reconnaissance Requirement Covering East Germany*', JIC (Germany) (69)24 Final, 31 October 1969, para 27.

21 Kevin Wright, personal communication, Ray Dadswell, 81 Squadron photographer.

22 The National Archive: PRO AIR 2/18561 RAFG/TS.1247/OPS, 17 July 1962.

23 Peter Jefferies, personal communication, Stewart Ross, 60 Sqdn, December 1973 to November 1976.

24 The National Archive: PRO AIR 2/18561: 1 RAFG/TS.1247/OPS, 17 July 1962, p. 5.

25 The National Archive: PRO AIR 2/18561: CMS.4123/62, 21 August 1962.

26 The National Archive: PRO AIR 2/18561: RAFG/TB675/65/OPS, 29 February 1965.

27 The National Archive: PRO AIR 2/18561: CMS.4123/D.D. OPs. (Recce) B & R 136, 10 January 1963.

28 The National Archive: PRO AIR 2/18561: MoD Air to RAFG, MoD Signal Message Form, 29 July 1966.

29 The National Archive: PRO AIR 2/18561: KFM 55569/ops HQ RAFG to MoD AIR, 15 September 1966.

30 The National Archive: PRO AIR 2/18561, D/365/2/641 AVM Hodges to RAFG, 19 April 1966.

31 The National Archive: PRO AIR 2/18561, Loose memo, HQ RAFG to MoD AIR, 1 February 1967.

32 K. Wright (2011), 'The Photo Pembrokes', *Aircraft*, Vol. 44, No. 3, p. 24.

33 Interview with David Clark.

34 The National Archive: The National PRO AIR 2/18561, RAFG/TS1247/OPS, 29 January 1962, Para 7e.

35 Aircrew logbooks are personal documents which record details of aircraft types flown, duration of mission, reason for flight, destinations, etc. They are regularly countersigned by the pilots'/navigators' commanding officer. Details of security classified or other 'sensitive' missions are normally omitted or disguised in some way.

36 The National Archive: PRO AIR 2/18561, Appendix 'A', to HQ RAFG (2nd TAF) Operation Instruction No. 2/62, 29 January 1962.

37 The National Archive: PRO FO 371/160623, Cabinet Secretary to PM, 1 September 1961, p. 2.

38 The National Archive: PRO AIR 2/18561, minutes 19 April and 13 June 1962.

39 The National Archive: PRO AIR 2/18561, minutes 19 April and 13 June 1962.

40 National Archives: PRO CAB 191/2 '*The Joint BAOR/RAF Germany Air Reconnaissance Requirement Covering East Germany*', JIC (Germany) (69)24 Final, 31 October 1969, para 6.

41 K. Wright (2009), 'Opening the Skies: The Fascinating World of Open Skies Overflights', *Aircraft Illustrated*, Vol. 42, No. 5, pp. 60–4.

42 The National Archive: PRO AIR 20/12133 TS4042/DD Ops(Recce) RAF Doc. 49.

43 The National Archive: PRO AIR 20/12133, 19 June 1967.

5

THE FRENCH CONNECTION: THE ALLIES' 'EARS'

As the Americans and British did, the French Air Force (Armée de l'Air – AdlA), also conducted covert reconnaissance operations along the Berlin Corridors and Baltic coast. They did so in considerable secrecy and, until recently, most of the details remained outside the public domain. Approaches to the French authorities to examine official documents have been unsuccessful. However, in 2009 some participants in these operations produced an account of their experiences in a book, *Les avions de Renseignement Électronique*, published under the auspices of L'Association Guerrelec.[1] This and Hugo Mambour's extensive and authoritative website, Red Stars over Germany, which covers much detail of the Soviet military presence in the GDR, the AMLMs work and Allied Corridor flights has enabled the assembly of a credible account of AdlA Corridor and BCZ operations.[2]

The AdlA used specialist units, aircraft and crews together with dedicated ground stations to collect SIGINT to establish and continually update the Soviets' and Warsaw Pact's Electronic Order of Battle (EOB). SIGINT flights made up by far the highest proportion of French missions with photographic flights being of secondary importance. The numbers of AdlA photographic missions were much smaller than those of the British, let alone the United States. The AdlA also expended considerable air effort monitoring the Baltic coast and IGB areas. After 1969 the assets used on Corridor missions were also deployed outside Europe, to support operations and exercises around the Mediterranean and parts of Francophone Africa.

French SIGINT flights adopted the name 'Gabriel', although the origins of its use are unclear. One possibility is that in the French armed forces, Gabriel is the patron saint of signals personnel. It could also be an acronym of the Groupement Aérien de BRouillage et d'Interception ÉLectronique (Air Jamming and Electronic Interception Group) who were responsible for early SIGINT operations. The designators Gabriel I, Gabriel II, etc., refers to the generations of onboard SIGINT equipment, rather than the aircraft type into which it was fitted. Gabriel I–IV referred to the equipment fitted on the C-47, Gabriel V on the Nord N2501 Noratlas and Gabriel VI on the C-160G Transall. Day-to-day operational sorties were frequently referred to as COmmunications ÉLectroniques (Electronic Communications – COMEL) flights.

French Berlin Corridor operations started in 1957, although the details remain unclear, the main platform for these early Comel flights being the ubiquitous C-47 Dakota. Gabriel I or IV C-47s of Escadrille de Liaison Aérienne 55 (Air Liaison Squadron 55 – ELA 55) flew intelligence missions in the Berlin Corridors from 1957 until the aircraft's withdrawal in 1963. ELA 55 was based at Lahr-Hugsweier (Lahr) in Germany, alongside the nuclear strike capable F-100 Super Sabres of Escadrons de Chasse 1/3 Navarre and 2/3 Champagne.

On 1 January 1964 a unit reorganisation transferred the three initial Noratlas Gabriel V aircraft from ELA 55 to Escadrille Électronique 54 (Electronic Squadron 54 – EÉ 54) at Lahr on 31 October 1963. Aircraft and crews now reported to COmmandement du Transport Aérien Militaire (Military Air Transport Command – COTAM). The 1,000th Comel mission milestone was achieved on 14 January 1964, with the 2,000th flight some four years later on 8 November 1968.[3]

In August 1964, EÉ 54 was named, following French Air Force tradition, after the commune of Dunkerque in northern France. EÉ 54's aircraft were distinctive from other units because they generally did not carry unit markings, or codes. The only known exception appears to have been the Noratlas cargo variant, No. 49.

France's withdrawal from NATO's Integrated Command Structure in 1966 caused considerable upheaval amongst its allies. The subsequent departure of US and Canadian forces resulted in significantly reduced intelligence sharing. This was especially noticeable in the co-ordination of activities centred on Berlin. Whilst the Americans and British continued regular intelligence exchange, the French became all but excluded, apart from material covered by the AMLM Tri-Mission agreement.

Withdrawal from NATO brought significant changes to Corridor flight operations too. The unit moved from Lahr to Metz-Frescaty in north-east France, with a final mission from Lahr on 15 June 1966. The Groupement Électronique 30.450 (Electronic Group 30.450 – GÉ 30.450) and the renamed Escadre Électronique 54 (Electronic Squadron 54 – EÉ 54) moved to Metz, in the same month, flying their first mission on 2 August 1966. On 1 July 1966 GÉ 30.450 had become Groupement Électronique 35.351 (Electronic Group 35.351 – GÉ 35.351), a numbering it retained until becoming the Groupement Électronique Tactique (Tactical Electronic Group 30.341 – GÉT 30.341) on 1 September 1971. Finally it was renamed Escadre Électronique Tactique 54 (Tactical Electronic Wing 54 – EÉT 00.054) on 1 January 1988. That change saw EÉT 54 take control of both airborne and ground-based electronic warfare units. Meanwhile, the Electronic Flight of EÉ 54 was redesignated Escadron Électronique 1/54 (1 Flight/Electronic Squadron 54 – EÉ 1/54).[4]

The French military regarded the Gabriel aircraft as a 'national reconnaissance asset' rather than a theatre-level one, so they were liable to be deployed elsewhere in the world when wider French interests took priority. Gabriel III C-47s are known to have operated COMINT missions during the 1959 to 1962 Franco-Algerian war but may have been involved earlier. During Algerian operations the aircraft usually carried nine crew members: two pilots, a flight mechanic, a radio navigator, an Arab linguist, three intercept operators and a team leader.[5]

N2501 Noratlas Operations

The arrival of the first Noratlas Gabriel V in late 1962 started the type's long association with the French Corridor operations, which continued until 1989.[6] The first Noratlas modified to Gabriel V configuration appears have been in 1960 but ELA 55 did not receive its first aircraft until autumn 1962, flying its first mission on 29 October. Other modified airframes soon followed. During this transition period, the C-47s probably flew alongside the Noratlas until the latter became fully operational.

A total of eight Noratlas were eventually modified to Gabriel V standard – Nos 25, 28, 33, 36, 39, 41, 42 and 66. By 1968 seven were configured for electronic reconnaissance work and the eighth (No. 36) was mainly used to trial the Furet (Ferret) SIGINT systems. The actual number of Gabriel aircraft in the squadron's service at any one time varied over the years with the addition of a small number of standard transport versions for training and support duties.

On 1 April 1963, GÉ 30.450 took up residence at Lahr. It was responsible for four fixed ground intercept sites in West Germany that listened to Soviet radio communications and, in conjunction with the Gabriel flights, monitored Soviet and East German VHF/UHF aircraft and ground transmissions.[7] Much of the Noratlas equipment was initially US Second World War technology and its limitations soon became apparent. Its relative simplicity and lack of precision meant that it was largely inadequate for the complex operations the Noratlas was called upon to perform. US equipment was soon superseded with that made by French companies CSF, Thomson and Dassault. They produced 'S' and 'X' band receivers in 1962 for Furet I (Ferret I), 'L' and 'C' bands in 1964 for Furet II (Ferret II) and 125–1000 MHz equipment for Furet III (Ferret III) in 1967. These programmes produced enhanced receivers that were more suited to the aircraft's role.[8]

Much of the new equipment was frequently installed first on Noratlas No. 36, used as the unit's flying test bed from 1966 onwards. Initial testing involved the competitive evaluation of prototype Belette (Weasel) and Furet ELINT systems. Weasel was promptly abandoned in favour of the more promising Furet II. In 1969 operational trials were launched from Metz that involved no fewer than fifty flights in one month from Metz along the IGB. After further modifications, a further series of flights took place along the Air Corridors in 1970 and 1971. A 1964 photograph of No. 36 at Berlin-Tegel by photographer Peter Seemann shows that by then it had acquired wingtip pods housing the interferometry antennae of the Ferret III system.[9] By 1977 No. 36's experimental days were largely over and it was converted back to a standard transport aircraft, but the external scars left by the installation and removal of equipment over the years were still clearly visible.

Whilst the aircraft were primarily configured for SIGINT operations, they were capable of photographic reconnaissance. The earliest camera assembly was fitted to the aircraft's cabin roof with the lens pointing out of the windows in the rear clamshell cargo doors and looked like something designed by Roland Emmett. This arrangement proved generally unsatisfactory and produced sub-optimal quality, which perhaps explains why photographic missions were regarded as a lower priority. Later, some of EÉ 54's Noratlas cargo aircraft had cameras mounted on a removable floor cradle that probably used an underside hatch to expose the lens. Noratlas camera configurations included a Omera 40 panoramic camera with a 75mm (3in) lens and a fan of three Omera 36 cameras with 600mm (24in) lens in a three camera installation – one vertical and two oblique – to produce horizon-to-horizon coverage.[10] Production of consistently high-quality imagery was not fully resolved until the C-160G Transall entered service in 1989.

Gabriel V crewing

The front-end crew of a Noratlas comprised a pilot, co-pilot, engineer and two navigators/radio-navigators from EÉ 54. The mission commander was usually a pilot or radio navigator. The back-end equipment operators, in the cargo hold, came from Groupe Électronique GÉ 30.450.

The layout in the rear cabin changed over the years but the following provides a representative picture of crew positions. Behind the flight deck on the starboard (right-hand) side was the flight mechanic, adjacent to the externally mounted APU turbine. He was responsible for the APU, the sole power source for all the onboard electronic equipment. The original APU, fitted to the first three aircraft, was a modified Peugeot 403 car engine installed at the rear of the cargo hold. From around 1968 an externally mounted 'Air Research' 25 kVA 115 Volt/400 Hz gas turbine replaced the Peugeot APU.[11] Before the turbine APU was fitted on Gabriel aircraft, the flight times on each route could be up to an hour longer. The 'Team Leader', responsible for all the rear cabin personnel and compiling the mission summary report, sat close to the flight mechanic.

Two crew positions concentrated on detecting, locating and analysing radar signals in the 50–10,750 MHz range using the AN/ALR 8 equipment. This determined a signal's relative bearing to the aircraft by using two rotating antennae housed in two black rounded fairings mounted under the fuselage centreline. These were the Gabriel V's main external distinguishing feature. Two intercept and recording positions monitored VHF transmissions in the 30–300 MHz range using ESM 180 and 300 receivers and a QHAE4A magnetic tape recorder stored the intercepts for further exploitation. One position intercepted and recorded UHF emissions using an ED80 receiver and tape recorder. Another position intercepted MF signals using an NR/AN 8 radio compass and recorder. The ADF receiver would be used to home in on the various VHF beacons located along the air routes and at airports.[12] This was the only piece of equipment that did not undergo significant modification over the years, although its analytic and recording interfaces were replaced by French ones compatible with the Smyrne system. One crew position undertook immediate operational analysis of signals.[13]

All the positions were manned by trade specialists from GÉ or the Centre d'Exploitation du Renseignement Tactique (Tactical Intelligence Operations Centre – CERT):

L'Analyse Technique: These men were responsible for intercepting, locating, analysing and identifying all electronic signals originating from Soviet aircraft and ground stations.

L'Analyse Phonie Graphie: Operators responsible for locating, identifying and analysing transmissions from aircraft and air-related ground stations. They were all linguists who understood the procedures and operational techniques employed by Soviet and East German forces.

L'Interception: Linguists proficient in Russian, Czech and German with specific knowledge of aviation-related vocabulary who listened in to all air-related transmissions on a wide range of frequencies. The more experienced were able to recognise individual pilots by their voice intonations, even when they used throat microphones.

Les Intercepteurs Graphie: These operators worked the lower end of the HF band monitoring the Morse networks. They continuously transcribed the stream of information into text for immediate analysis.

Les Décodurs: 'Decoders' de-cyphered tens of metres of teletype printout, looking for Soviet code keys. [14]

In addition there was the radio mechanic whose role was to rectify any technical faults with the equipment that developed during the mission. The final crew position was at the rear of the aircraft and was isolated from the rest of the crew by a curtain. This seat was occasionally used by a coder-decoder, photographer or other 'passengers', including MMFL members who sometimes used it as an opportunity for intelligence collection on selected targets. The total crew of a Noratlas Gabriel was around seventeen, although this number fluctuated as aircraft equipment fits changed. [15]

The long duration and high altitude of Gabriel operations required the fitting of additional specialist equipment to try to improve the crew's operating environment and almost non-existent comforts. Besides the APU, there was soundproofing and a strengthened cargo floor and all the workstations were fitted with an oxygen outlet. An electric oven was installed to provide hot in-flight meals, managed by the turbine mechanic. Despite the very basic operating conditions, the aircraft engine noise, the permanent turbine whistle when the APU was operating, air turbulence and the need to use portable oxygen equipment when moving around, the operators had considerable success intercepting and translating enemy radio communications.

The Noratlas, especially in its later years, experienced frequent unserviceabilities, especially engine failures. These frequently caused missions to be aborted and diverted, although no aircraft was ever lost. Because of an engine shortage and the lack of skilled maintenance personnel, it became very difficult to achieve a 70 per cent aircraft availability rate in the 1970s, so maintenance operations were

staggered to achieve maximum aircraft availability.[16] On one flight, a Noratlas returning from a Baltic mission destined for Berlin-Tegel, experienced an engine failure
as it approached the entrance to the Northern Corridor. The aircraft commander
decided to divert to the West German Luftwaffe base at Wunstorf, near Hannover, and
asked the Team Leader to send a coded message to the Metz Command Post advising
them of the diversion. The Team Leader delegated the task to a young and inexperi-
enced analyst who informed Metz that the aircraft had a damaged engine and would
be making an emergency landing at Wünsdorf, south of Berlin and very close to
HQ GSFG itself! The reactions in Metz, HQ Force Aérienne Tactique (Tactical Air
Force – FATac) and elsewhere must have been interesting. Whilst nobody probably
thought for a moment that the now single-engined aircraft might attempt to land in
the GDR, it may have momentarily increased a few heart rates.[17]

By 1987, EÉ 54 had only four operational aircraft – Nos 28, 41, 42 and 66. The first
to retire was No. 42 in January 1988, followed by the remainder between January
and October 1989. The last Noratlas Gabriel V flight by EÉ 1/54 was by No. 66 on
26 October 1989 after twenty-seven years' service with the unit. It was also the final
French Air Force Noratlas flight. By the time of the Noratlas' withdrawal the whole
SIGINT effort involved around 800 people including the flight crews, ground crews,
listening station personnel, operations centre and CERT.[18]

Mission Planning and Operations

French Noratlas Corridor operations developed into a well-established routine that
started with mission planning. Tasking for individual flights came from the Bureau
de Guerre Électronique (Electronic Warfare Office – BGÉ) of the 1st Commandant
Aérienne Tactique (1st Tactical Air Command – CATac, later FATac). They planned
missions based on data from the CERT. BGÉ sent the orders, including date, timings,
route, targets, etc., to the Joint Operations Centres of the GÉ and EÉ at Metz.

The Gabriel aircraft's main mission was intercepting and analysing electromagnetic
emissions from Warsaw Pact Air Forces in the GDR, Czechoslovakia and Poland.
Their targets were radars, radio beacons, air-to-air and air-to-ground radio communications, data link transfer systems, etc. They noted frequencies, call signs and
operational procedures. Radars of all types were located and their function determined and classified, including airborne radars and those of air-to-air missiles. It was
essentially about 'hoovering up' as many transmissions as possible to establish the
Soviet and Warsaw Pact EOB. After each Soviet conscript troop rotation, most radio
frequencies, call signs and operators were changed, so out-of-date information had
to be updated as quickly as possible. During these periods all the staff would be very
busy and the Gabriel aircraft would often fly multiple missions daily, with additional
aircraft on standby, until the EOB had been re-established and verified.

Missions were generally carried out during daylight, but this routine would
change during Warsaw Pact exercises, periods of unusual activity, or in times of crisis.
A Gabriel that left Metz between 0900 and 1000 would arrive at Tegel and spend the
night there. But timetables could vary depending on the briefed mission and other

contingencies, so the aircraft might return to Metz on the same day. Mission reports would be sent to Metz via the Berlin-Tegel ground monitoring station.

Gabriel missions from Metz followed three main routes:

RE1: Inner German Border: The route ran from Metz to Frankfurt-am-Main and then to Würzburg adjacent to the Czech-GDR border. It then turned north to Lichenau, Leine, Hamburg and, finally, to Michaelsdorf, a tiny village close to the North German coast, before returning to Metz.

RE2: Czechoslovakian border: This followed RE1 to Würzburg covering areas between the Czech-GDR border including passing close to, or over, Nuremberg and towns like Bayreuth, Allesburg and Straubing before returning to Metz.

RE3: Berlin Corridor flights: From Metz the route headed towards the entrance of the selected Corridor – South, Central or North – then to Berlin, followed by a night stop at Berlin-Tegel before returning to Metz.[19]

The latter mission profile was sometimes called a 'Baltic' when, after departing Berlin-Tegel, the aircraft would route through the North Corridor, head for Hamburg and then towards Malmö in Sweden. It would fly in international airspace, over the Baltic Sea, flying parallel to the edge of Polish and Soviet-controlled airspace. After leaving the Baltic area it would return to Berlin-Tegel after an approximately six-hour flight. Baltic missions were only flown during the winter because in hot weather the Noratlas had insufficient range to complete the mission. Flying close to the Swedish, Polish and Soviet borders regularly triggered a reaction from the Swedish air defence forces, which sent J-35 Draaken or J-37 Viggen fighters to intercept the 'intruder'. The Soviets too regularly launched interceptors to have a closer look at the Gabriels and photograph them.

Michel Adam, pilot and Commander of EÉ 54 between 1970 and 1972, describes the unit's flights as being undertaken during the Soviet and East German forces' 'normal working hours' and occasional night-flying periods. Flights along the IGB and Czechoslovak borders were flown at altitudes between 10,000 and 15,000ft, at a speed of around 160 knots, and lasted around six and a half hours. Flying at such altitudes meant that the Gabriels on Corridor missions were able to collect emissions well beyond the GDR into Poland.

The NATO ADIZ along the IGB meant that there was little risk of accidental border penetration, but navigation needed special attention. Corridor missions required more careful flying and there was always heightened tension onboard. Flights were generally flown under Instrument Flight Rules (IFR) keeping to the Corridor centreline. The lack of pressurisation, the noise level in the cargo hold, and the inability to avoid bad weather often made flights challenging. In winter, icing added to the difficulties and in summer there were often strong stormy conditions – especially over the Bavarian mountains, whilst in the north there was often considerable air turbulence.[20]

The Noratlas would remain outside the Inner German ADIZ that ran parallel to the GDR and Czechoslovakian borders. Because they flew close to the ADIZ the aircraft were sometimes intercepted by NATO fighters. When this happened the Gabriel crews would occasionally play games with them by gradually reducing their airspeed to see how long the escorting interceptor could stay with them until it either stalled or had to break away. Corridor flights were limited to the agreed maximum ceiling of 10,000ft, but more normally flown between 7,500 and 8,500ft and much lower when on occasional photographic tasks.

Accurate navigation was of paramount importance in the Corridors and depended mainly on the radio navigator's skill. For most of the flight, pilots flew the aircraft manually. The interception of messages from Soviet radars and fighter aircraft on the other side of the border would soon indicate that the Gabriel had been identified. The Gabriels were easily tracked by Soviet air defence radars, who named them 'Lobsters'. They knew the difference between a standard Noratlas and a Gabriel variant. Fighters sent to provide visual identification would sometimes position themselves below and adjacent to the Gabriel to check for the presence of the two tell-tale ventral radomes and, if they were present, would report 'it's a male'.[21] The Soviets regularly used the Gabriels as training targets for their fighter pilots and SAM operators, but this was a double-edged sword because by doing so they provided the French listening crews with a valuable source of information. Like their British and US counterparts, Gabriels were sometimes subjected to 'meaconing' that retransmitted false radio beacon signals on genuine frequencies to try to lure the aircraft outside the Corridor. The Gabriel's onboard operators could determine, with a few minutes' delay, their aircraft's position as it was seen on the Soviet's own radar scopes, using the intercepted signals passed between the radar sites and their command centre.

EÉ 54 aircraft also worked in conjunction with MMFL ground tours. Having detected a 'new' emission from an unknown location, they would ask the MMFL to investigate the site, if possible, to visually confirm what was there. The absence of a robust French photographic capability meant that this was often the only way to verify visually the physical presence of equipment at a particular location.

A Typical Corridor Comel Mission

A few hours before a mission, the flight engineer, sometimes with a deputy, would thoroughly check the aircraft in the hangar, including activating all the electronic equipment to ensure it was functioning correctly. If all was well, the aircraft was available for flight barring any sudden aircraft, or engine, unserviceabilities. The flight crew and equipment operators would assemble in the briefing room together with the meteorologist, who would detail expected weather conditions. The GÉ's night shift supervisor would advise of any incidents or events from the previous day's flight that could affect the mission's conduct. The BGÉ's 2ème Bureau (intelligence) representative would brief the crew on new sightings, air and ground unit dispositions and any activity that might be important, or affect operations. The mission commander briefed the crew on the mission, its objectives, route, ETD, general safety and personal equipment.

After briefing, the crew boarded the aircraft, with flight crew using the main cabin door and the 'back-end' team the rear door. Crew members would take their work station, preparing flight and personal equipment which usually included a parachute on Corridor flights. On reaching the assigned flight level, the 'Team Leader' ordered the turbine to be started so the operators could test their electronic equipment. The linguists would start working almost as soon as they passed over Frankfurt-am-Main, but the radar interceptors could only get to work as they entered the Corridor close to Mansbach when radar signals became sufficiently reliable.

The Noratlas had no modern navigation aids, so the navigator would plot the aircraft's course onto a map. The operators began looking for emissions based on the pre-briefed priorities. If a signal of interest was detected, it would be isolated and then subjected to an initial analysis that recorded essential details such as frequency and modulation. The precise identification of transmission locations became easier as signals became stronger. Once a target was fully identified the operators would move onto the next. Details of each intercept were passed to the 'Team Leader' who ensured the relevant information was transmitted back to base in summary form. If anything particularly new, or interesting, was revealed then the flight could be changed to try to capture it again on the return. After landing the aircraft commander would conduct a 'hot debrief' and all the COMINT and ELINT 'take' would be removed for further in-depth analysis and reporting up the chain of command.[22] After the stop at Berlin-Tegel, often involving a night stay, the Gabriel would either depart to Metz or head north if a 'Baltic' was tasked.

What would have happened if a Gabriel had been force-landed in the GDR? The French crews' instructions were very similar to those for the British and American crews. All documents and maps were to be torn into small pieces and ejected from the aircraft using the marker flare ejector chute on the side of the aircraft. Once on the ground, the last man to leave the plane was to open the fuel drain taps inside the fuselage and discharge an emergency flare to set the aircraft ablaze.

A Gabriel Photo Flight

A regular transport Noratlas fitted with photographic equipment left Metz to fly the Southern Corridor, tasked to photograph a Soviet SAM site located on its southern edge.[23] The Captain was one of the most skilled on the squadron, being EÉ 54's Chief Pilot. The mission was flown, apparently without incident, and landed at Berlin-Tegel in the late morning as normal. The Commander of GÉT 30.351, Colonel Michel Danthon – a former Mirage III reconnaissance pilot and commander of 33 Escadre de Reconnaissance – received a phone call warning him that the Chief American Controller at the BASC was filing an 'airspace violation' against the aircraft for leaving the Corridor. His first reaction was 'what difference does it make to the Americans?' He believed that the Americans were probably concerned about the Soviet reaction to the alleged incident and so, to take the 'heat' out of the situation and pre-empt any Soviet indignation, decided to report it themselves. Danthon called the crew in Berlin and asked the pilot about the flight and the weather at the time. He was told that the flight was normal, weather excellent and there was nothing to report. The Soviets had still said nothing.

At Metz the situation escalated and the Commander FATac called Danthon to tell him that the alleged incident had now reached diplomatic levels and the Quay d'Orsay was involved. Danthon was summoned to the Chief's office to explain the situation. There was still no Soviet reaction. Before reporting to the General at FATac for an expected 'one way chat show', he consulted other unit members to try to find an alternative explanation for the alleged offence. At that time the Soviets were transmitting data from their radars in duplicate, via both microwave and HF radio. The French ground intercept stations had detected and recorded the Soviet radar information as the photo flight progressed along the Corridor. The unit's analysts and linguists reconstructed the mission, seeing exactly the same picture that the Soviet controllers had seen – and plotted the results on a map. They saw the aircraft approach the edge of the Corridor to photograph the SAM site but never leave it. The French view became that 'the Americans had, once again, over reacted'. Colonel Danthon reported the findings to his CO and was confident that there had been no violation. He delivered the details showing that the Soviet's own radar information indicated that the aircraft never left the Corridor. As far as Danthon was concerned that was the end of the affair.

When the Noratlas returned from Berlin the incident was discussed with the crew and it became very clear that the aircraft never left the Corridor's lateral boundaries. However, in order to acquire larger-scale, higher-quality photography they had descended to around 2,500ft, which was below the Corridor's lower limit. The American radar had detected this breach but the Soviet radar apparently had not, perhaps pointing to a potential limitation of Soviet radar capability that they did not want to expose.[24] An alternative explanation might have been simply that the Soviets were well aware of the breach but chose not to make an issue of it on that occasion for reasons of their own.

Listening to the Listeners

On 10 March 1964, the French monitoring services had a front seat when they recorded the loss of a USAF RB-66B electronic reconnaissance aircraft from the 19 Tactical Reconnaissance Squadron (19 TRS) based at Toul-Rosières in France. USMLM's 1964 Annual Report describes the flight as 'local training flight'. The US account states that the aircraft was seen on radar approaching the Soviet Zone of Germany. The plane disappeared from the radar screen after it had reached the vicinity of Gardelegen in the GDR, north-east of Helmstedt.[25] That official account gives little away about the real drama being played out. Doug Gordon's description of the incident indicates that the aircraft was about 120 miles off course and well into GDR airspace. Four MiG-19s intercepted the aircraft and fatally damaged it with gunfire, forcing the crew to bail out.[26] The rescued crew were treated for their injuries and handed back to the US military a few weeks later without further conditions, although it caused a diplomatic spat between the two nations. The USA has always stuck to the 'navigational error' story, whilst the Soviets insisted that it was a 'provocation' flight to test their air defences. Some accounts suggest that the aircraft was operating inside one of the Corridors but this is unlikely because of the ban on their use by 'combat aircraft' and the necessity to file a flight plan with the BASC prior to any Corridor flight.

The French account of the incident offers a somewhat different perspective. It suggests that the RB-66 was operating near the entrance to the Central Corridor, where it was believed to be attempting to identify a new Soviet radar. The aircraft's position was supported by the last radar trace being close to Gardelegen on the northern edge of the Centre Corridor and close to the Letzlinger Heide major training area. A Noratlas Gabriel V, flying in the Southern Corridor at the time, and the listening post at Berlin-Tegel recorded the RB-66 flying towards the IGB and then being downed by the MiGs. The intercepted radio conversations and exchanges were simultaneously translated and recorded by the Gabriel V and the ground station. Between them they were able to triangulate the position where the aircraft had come down.[27]

The SA-10 Grumble Saga

In 1977 a French Corridor mission intercepted Soviet radar emissions on new frequencies which stopped when the Gabriel aircraft approached their source. It was thought that these signals emanated from the new SA-10 Grumble (S-300) SAM system that had not been seen outside the Soviet Union at that time.

To gather more information on this potentially important target, a 'trap' was organised using a photographic configured Noratlas cargo aircraft and a Gabriel operating in concert. The photo aircraft flew though the Central Corridor where the new SAM system's signals had been detected in the area of the Letzlinger Heide training area, north-west of Magdeburg. The Gabriel flew along the Northern Corridor listening for transmissions. The Gabriel informed the photo Noratlas that the suspect emissions were being received. As the photo Noratlas overflew the training range, the emissions ceased but the aircraft activated its cameras anyway. The run of stereoscopic photographs revealed the radar vehicle in the process of retracting its antenna, which was an added bonus, and the Gabriel verified the system's frequencies – a good day all round. The 'trap' produced the first aerial photography of the SA-10 Grumble system, which had hitherto only been operated under cloud cover to escape the prying view of American satellites.[28]

Watching Us Watching You

The co-ordination of ground stations' activities with the Gabriels gave the French a unique capability. One ground station that collected HF transmissions, used an ingenious device that captured emissions from Soviet air defence systems. It consisted of an 'automatic reader' which intercepted the transmissions and then, using software installed on a PC, decoded the messages and displayed the track's positions on a screen. This allowed the French to observe the position of 'targets of interest' to the Soviet air defence system at almost the same time as the Soviets themselves were looking at them. Denis Aubert describes the satisfaction it gave the French to view US Air Force SR-71 Blackbird flights operating far away over the Baltic Sea, using the Soviet radar picture to see them.[29]

Fencer Arrives

The first Soviet SU-24 Fencer fighter-bombers appeared in East Germany during late 1986 and early 1987, flying 'racetrack' patterns with another SU-24 pursuing and joining them. The communications interceptors picked up voice transmissions from the Fencers saying 'contact' and 'separation' as aircraft joined up and then broke away. The conclusion was that the aircraft were probably undertaking air-to-air refuelling (AAR) operations, but decodes of the Fencers' IFF transmissions made it clear that no fuel transfer took place because the pilots were in the early stages of their AAR training. Later, the first live fuel transfer was recorded.[30]

C-160 Transall Gabriel VI

In 1984, the French Defence Department began searching for a modern SIGINT aircraft to replace the obsolescent Noratlas. A number of options were considered, with the C-160NG selected in March 1986 after multiple evaluations. Two standard C-160NG airframes, F-216 (G-1) and F-221 (G-2), were chosen for conversion to Gabriel VI configuration, both fresh from a recent overhaul and equipped with refuelling probes. Sogema was the prime contractor for the conversions, the key part of the new aircraft's sensor suite being the Analyseur Superhétérodyne TACtique (ASTAC) ELINT system. This provided a quantum leap in reconnaissance capabilities over previous generations of equipment in the Noratlas. The C-160G Gabriel VI was distinguishable from a standard transport Transalls by the belly radome which contained the SPRUCE SIGINT equipment, two wingtip pods containing the ASTAC system and four antennae on top of the fuselage.

F-216 was delivered to Metz in June 1989 and was joined by F-221 on 2 July. G-1 flew the first Berlin Corridor mission on 3 July 1989 – less than twenty-four hours after the two aircraft were officially declared operational. Corridor monitoring was their primary task but as the Cold War ended in 1990 so did the flights, although the two aircraft continue to support French SIGINT interests across the globe.

For Corridor flights C-160Gs flight crew consisted of two pilots, a radio navigator and an engineer. The modified cargo hold, with the rear ramp welded permanently shut, was occupied by eight personnel comprising up to three ELINT, three COMINT and one HF operator plus a systems engineer and Team Leader. The ASTAC system sensor, mounted in wingtip pods, worked in conjunction with ground stations, tracking up to twenty emitters a second and immediately processing the information.

The data collected was managed by the mobile ground-based Organisation Système d'Intégration du Renseignement et des Informations SIGINT system (OSIRIS). The airborne component processed information and recorded data, producing emitter location maps.[31] The OSIRIS ground station received the information by data link, completing the initial on-aircraft processing to produce an overall situation picture.

In Metz the Intégration du Renseignement et des Informations SIGINT (IRIS) computer produced a more comprehensive picture of the collected data.

The C-160G Transall Gabriel VI met a long-standing photographic capability requirement that had never been adequately fulfilled by the Noratlas. For photographic tasks the C-160G carried two Omera 51 panoramic cameras, mounted in tear drop shaped fairings on each side of the fuselage. A protective, sliding cover opened to allow photography. This fit solved the difficulties of previous generations of Gabriel aircraft and the conflicting needs of photographic and SIGINT equipment. The SIGINT community wanted to fly as high as possible so that their receivers could capture the maximum number of emitters. The PHOTINT community wanted to fly as low as possible to collect large-scale, high-quality photography. The Gabriel VI solved this problem by having cameras capable of producing good-quality imagery at high altitude.

The external configuration of the C-160G Transall made it an obvious SIGINT aircraft and its function would have been very clear when used in the Corridors. There was no great attempt to conceal its true purpose, which speaks volumes for the changing political climate in Germany by 1989.

Beyond the Corridors

Besides the Gabriel Corridor and peripheral missions conducted using 'tactical intelligence' platforms, other aircraft also mounted flights along the IGB and over the Baltic Sea. These included the DC-8 Système Aéroporté de Recueil des Informations de Guerre Électronique Sarigue (Opossum) 'strategic' reconnaissance aircraft and the SA-330 Puma Hélicoptère Électronique Technique (HÉT) that operated along the IGB.

The DC-8–33 Sarigue

A DC-8–33 (F-RAFE 45570/134) that was already serving with the AdlA was converted to the electronic intelligence role and entered service in July 1976. Escadre Électronique 00.051 (Electronics Squadron 00.051 – EÉ 00.051 Aubrac) was specifically created to operate this aircraft that was declared operational on 1 June 1977, initially flying from Brétigny before moving to Evreux in December of that year. The aircraft retained the same external colour scheme as other AdlA DC-8 transports but the plethora of bulges and aerials quickly revealed its true purpose. Like the Gabriels, the Sarigue was primarily a SIGINT platform but was also photo-capable.

The COMINT suite included VHF/UHF radios that could intercept frequencies between 20 and 500 MHz. The ELINT equipment intercepted radar emissions between 30 and 125 MHz and could intercept and locate radars using frequencies between 125 and 18,000 MHz, using interferometry antennae, mounted in wingtip fairings. The ventral radome housed antennae targeted at frequencies above 1 GHz. Photographic equipment consisted of three Omera 36 cameras in a trimetrogen mount (one vertical and two oblique) to give horizon-to-horizon coverage.[32]

The Sarigue's flight deck crew consisted of two pilots; one or two radio-navigators and a flight engineer. Depending on the type of mission, the numbers of the SIGINT team could vary significantly. For European operations thirteen ELINT operators and ten COMINT operators were the usual 'back-end' crew, together with a camera operator seated in the left-hand rear of the cabin. The aircraft also operated in Africa, the Middle East and Indian Ocean before being retired in July 2001. Its successor, DC-8–72 (CF) Sarigue NG (New Generation) F-RAFD (46043/443), entered service on 12 April 2001 but operated for only just over three years before being withdrawn from service.

SA-330 Puma HÉT

The AdlA Hélicoptère Électronique Technique (HÉT) programme commenced in spring 1989 using a modified SA-330 Puma helicopter (No. 1595). It belonged to part of Escadrille 21/54 and was based at the Goslar ground listening station. The Puma had a flight crew of three: a pilot, pilot-navigator and flight engineer. The rear cabin housed a team of three: the 'Team Leader' who operated a console (similar to the Furet IV on the Sarigue) that detected and designated the signals, together with two ELINT operators. The Puma carried three retractable antennae in main cabin wells to detect Soviet electronic emissions. The detection and analytical systems carried by the Puma HÉT were fully capable of collecting and classifying the new radars then entering Soviet service. The 'Fall of the Wall' in November 1989 meant that the Puma's operational life was very short.[33] The helicopter was subsequently transferred to Mont-de-Marsan to continue operations for a while before being reconverted to a standard transport configuration.[34]

Why Not More Co-ordination and Co-operation?

The French devoted significant resources to monitoring Soviet and Warsaw Pact communications and electronic emissions throughout the Cold War. This emphasis on SIGINT allowed them to develop a full picture of the Soviet EOB. French Corridor photographic intelligence collection was of less significance. Why did the French not co-operate more extensively with the British and Americans?

The best explanation is probably a combination of domestic French politics and national interests. The creation of the Fifth Republic in 1958 brought Charles de Gaulle to a greatly strengthened presidential office. The conclusion of the Algerian war had freed up military resources that were redeployed to meet France's modest NATO commitments, which it had been unable to fulfil for some years. It allowed ELINT gathering equipment and personnel to be redeployed from North Africa to the FOZ of Germany and Berlin. De Gaulle's distrust of both the British and the Americans led him to pursue his goal of establishing a 'strong and independent France' to take its rightful place in the modern world. In particular, his ambition to create an independent French nuclear deterrent significantly changed France's future intelligence needs as a new priority became the development of reconnaissance and targeting capabilities for the embryonic Force de Frappe.

One effect of this was the cessation of Corridor imagery exchange, probably known as 'Blue Train', but this was no great loss because it never produced a significant quantity of material. From the British and US perspective the French were minor players in photographic intelligence collection mainly because their Corridor photographic sorties were so infrequent. In fact contemporary British PIs cannot remember ever having seen French Corridor imagery.[35] The supply of French BCZ imagery continued because it was subject to the formal Tri-Mission agreement covering AMLM exchanges.

Tactical and strategic aircraft provided the mainstay of the early French nuclear forces and needed to be capable of penetrating the Warsaw Pact's air defences if they were to reach their targets deep in Eastern Europe. The arrival of the Mirage IV bomber intensified the need for ELINT to enable their bombers to penetrate deep into Warsaw Pact air defences to deliver their deadly payloads. This requirement was the principal driver of French emphasis on EOB collection along the Corridors, IGB and Baltic.

There was little formal co-operation between the French and other Allies over Corridor missions. Besides interference from issues of high politics, there were simple pragmatic reasons too. British and US co-operation and co-ordination were not only facilitated at the highest national political levels but day-to-day efforts were delegated to operational theatres and individual units. British and US Corridor flight operations were in relatively close geographic proximity to each other in Germany, but French operations, from the mid 1960s, were centred on Metz-Frescaty in eastern France. This isolated them from the British and American operating locations and simply made co-operation physically more difficult.

It was mandatory to file flight plans with the BASC to operate in the airspace so potential conflicts could be identified and managed safely, but all three Allies operated differently in the Corridors and BCZ. Where possible the British operated at lower levels as their emphasis was on photographic collection. The French usually flew at higher levels to achieve better signals reception, only flying at lower levels for photographic missions. It was only the Americans, because they operated across the full altitude range available in the Corridors, who ran significant risk of collision with their 'partners in espionage'. Accounts from all three countries have not revealed any instances of systemic airspace conflicts. Certainly the comparative lack of Anglo-American co-operation with French-related operations, other than the AMLMs, throws into even clearer relief the extremely close British and American co-operation on intelligence issues.

Notes

1   'Electronic Warfare Association'.

2   Comité Historique de l'Association Guerrelec (2009), *Les Avions de Renseignement Électronique* (Panazol: Lavauzelle Graphic) and http://www.16va.be.

3   J.R. de Soultrait (2009), 'L'EE 54 "DUNKERQUE" de Lahr-Hugsweier, 1965, a Metz-Frescaty, 1967', *Renseignement Électronique*, p. 101.

4   http://www.16va.be/gabriel_part1_eng.html.

5   A. Cape (2009), 'La Guerre Électronique en Algérie', 1959–1962: des Detachments sol au C-47 Gabriel, *Renseignement Électronique*, p. 68.
6   The N2501 was also known as the '*Grise*' (grey) in the French Air Force because of its colour.
7   J. Martinot-Lagarde (2009), 'Création du Groupe Électronique 30/450, 1963–1965', *Renseignement Électronique*, pp. 79–80.
8   P. Baratault (2009), 'Les grands programmes industriels Français dans le domaine ELINT', *Renseignement Électronique*, p. 41.
9   After further development some of that equipment appeared on the AdlA's reconnaissance DC-8 Sarigue aircraft.
10 These cameras were also used on Mirage F-1CR and Mirage IVR aircraft.
11 M. Adam (2009), 'Des oreilles et des ailes ou quatre ans a l'escadrille Électronique EE 54 "DUNKERQUE", 1968–1972', *Renseignement Électronique*, p. 107.
12 P. Pallot (2009), 'Témoignage d'un opérateur ELINT sur Nord Gabriel', *Renseignement Électronique*, p. 180.
13 The various operator designations and operating positions on the Gabriel Vs changed over the years as equipment was modified or replaced. A summary of some of these changes can be found in Annex 2 to *Renseignement Électronique*, pp. 399–403.
14 Pallot (2009), pp. 162–3.
15 de Soultrait (2009), pp. 96–7.
16 M. Danthon (2009), 'Deux ans au Groupement Électronique Tactique 30/351', *Renseignement Électronique*, p. 121.
17 Pallot (2009), p. 169.
18 D. Aubert (2009), 'Du GET à la 54 Escadre Électronique Tactique et du Nord *Gabriel* au Transall *Gabriel*, 1986–1989', *Renseignement Électronique*, p. 218.
19 Adam (2009), p. 108.
20 Ibid., p. 109.
21 de Soultrait (2009), p. 103.
22 Pallot (2009), pp. 166–8.
23 Note by Peter Jefferies. This was probably the Rosslau SA-6 Gainful site which was close to the corridor edge.
24 Danthon (2009), pp. 145–8.
25 *USMLM Annual Report*, 1964, p. 15.
26 D. Gordon (2006), *Tactical Reconnaissance in the Cold War* (Barnsley: Pen & Sword Books), p. 132.
27 J. Martinot-Lagarde (2009), *Renseignement Électronique*, pp. 83–4. This account records the incident as 4 January 1964. All others record the RB-66 loss as 10 March 1964. However, a USAF T-39 aircraft was shot down on 28 January 1964 near Erfurt. In either case it demonstrates the capabilities of the French systems.
28 C. Fontaine (2009), 'Quelques souvenirs sur Nord *Gabriel*', *Renseignement Électronique*, p. 152.
29 Aubert (2009), p. 220.
30 Ibid., p. 219.
31 H. Wetzel (2009), 'Du Transall *Gabriel* au DC-8 *Sarigue NG*', *Renseignement Électronique*, p. 215.
32 Hugo Mambour, http://www.16va.be/gabriel_part1_eng.html.
33 H. de Quatrebarbes (2009), 'Le programme hélicoptére d'ELINT Technique (HÉT) sur SA330 Puma modifié', *Renseignement Électronique*, pp. 359–67.
34 Aubert (2009), p. 225.
35 Peter Jefferies in conversation with British PIs of that era.

6

ALLIED BCZ LIGHT AIRCRAFT AND HELICOPTER PHOTOGRAPHIC FLIGHTS

The Berlin Control Zone covered about 125 square miles of GDR territory, including the divided city of Berlin. Within this space several major Soviet and East German airfields, garrisons, logistic and support installations were located. Some of these were in PRAs that prevented ground observation by AMLM ground tours but could be viewed from the air and this spawned the idea that the Western Allies could use BCZ airspace to their advantage.

The 1945 agreement allowed local flights in the BCZ so that the four wartime Allies could exercise their freedom of access to this airspace. Flight safety requirements were the only restrictions to this freedom. From the outset there was disagreement between the Western Allies and the Soviets over the definition of 'local flights'. The agreement's actual wording was:

> It is desirable that, wherever possible, local flights (testing, training etc) be executed above the national sectors. However, if necessary they may be executed above the remainder of the Control Zone, subject to normal clearance by the BASC.[1]

The Soviet view was that the Western Allies could only fly over their City Sectors. The Western position was that 'local flights' encompassed the whole of the BCZ. This impasse prevailed until the end of the Cold War in 1990. The Soviet response to the Western stance was to endorse all BASC flight clearance cards for flights originating in Berlin, but not destined to terminate in West Germany, with 'safety of flight not guaranteed'. Despite this there were never any major incidents involving locally based Allied aircraft or helicopters. After the arbitrary Soviet imposition of altitude limits on the Corridors in 1953, there were concerns that the Soviets might try to extend these limitations to the BCZ airspace below 2,500ft by only recognising tracks that, whilst allowing arrivals and departures to the three West Berlin airfields, would deny the Western Allies the full freedom of flight in the BCZ.

Allied Light Aviation in Berlin

The Western Allies' light aviation assets consisted of fixed-wing aircraft and helicopters to support their field formations and national commands in the city. Helicopters were confined to flying over the city's Western Sectors, although there was no clear legal reason why they could not roam further into the BCZ. This self-imposed restriction probably reflected concerns about the range and reliability of early generation helicopters and the possible consequences if they suffered engine failures over urban areas. The fixed-wing elements were allowed to venture outside the city limits into the wider BCZ. The units' tasks included border patrols, liaison, visual and photographic reconnaissance, troop lifts and resupply of outposts.

To avoid duplication of effort and to deconflict flight paths, the AMLMs held monthly liaison meetings to co-ordinate forthcoming flights in a similar manner to the way that they co-ordinated their ground tour programmes. The meetings produced a jointly agreed programme allocating certain days and times to each mission. This generally worked well but there were some difficulties because the French and US aircraft belonged to their respective city national commands who decided when and where their aircraft would fly and their missions had no control over this. BRIXMIS, on the other hand, had the sole use of the British aircraft on a number of days each week, so they had total control over the conduct and timing of their photographic flights. These split control arrangements sometimes led to two aircraft being in the same place at the same time, causing red faces and confusion all round. By the 1980s a more professional attitude prevailed and amicable co-operation was the order of the day. Under the Tri-Mission agreement photographs taken during the flights were exchanged so no nation 'lost out'. The modus operandi for all the Allies' photographic flights were broadly similar, but we concentrate on the conduct of British flights, with some further details about American and French operations.

In mounting the BCZ light aircraft photographic flights the British led the way, starting them in 1956. The French did not base a light aircraft (a Cessna L-19 Bird Dog) in Berlin until 1960 and, although the USA had light aircraft based at Tempelhof, they did not start their photographic missions – Project Lark Spur – until 1968.

BRIXMIS Chipmunk flights

A single De Havilland Canada DHC-1 Chipmunk trainer aircraft arrived at RAF Gatow in 1954 to form the Station Flight. It had three overt roles: to provide RAF aircrew on ground tours in Berlin with continuation training to maintain their flying skills and, more importantly, retain their flying pay; to maintain the British right of access to BCZ airspace, especially below 2,500ft; and to provide assistance with public relations tasks. In April 1968, after much wrangling mainly caused by FCO concerns that the Soviets may have viewed the arrival of the additional aircraft as an 'escalation' or a 'provocative' act, a second Chipmunk was allocated to the Gatow Station Flight to ensure that at least one aircraft was available at all times to respond to any intelligence, political or tactical requirements for visual or photographic reconnaissance.[2]

In total nine Chipmunks served with the RAF Gatow Station Flight during its existence. Initially they wore an overall silver colour scheme with a black anti-glare panel on the nose and national markings on the fuselage, above and below the wings and on the fin. Serial numbers were applied to the fuselage and under wing. In the 1970s, light aircraft grey replaced the silver and this was retained until the end of operations. The individual aircraft involved were: WG303 from December 1956 until April 1968 and WK587 from November 1962 until April 1968. This pair were replaced by WP850 (left November 1975) and WP971, which departed in October 1975. WZ862 was in place from December 1974 until June 1987 and WD289 from May 1975 until June 1987. WG478 arrived in May 1987 and departed in July 1987. It returned to Berlin in 1994 to make-up a three-ship formation as part of the withdrawal ceremonies. The final two aircraft were WG486 from May 1987 together with WG466 which arrived on an unknown date, with both staying until 1994 when operations ceased. WG486 currently flies with the Battle of Britain Memorial Flight at RAF Coningsby as a trainer to familiarise new pilots with tailwheel aircraft and WG466 is displayed at the Militärhistorisches Museum der Bundeswehr at Flugplatz Berlin-Gatow. By the late 1970s the Chipmunk's age and increasing obsolescence meant that the possibility of major failure was never far from the minds of the operators. Sqaudron Leader Vince Robertson (Squadron Leader Operations) produced a paper proposing that they should be replaced by Scottish Aviation Bulldog, which was the RAF's basic trainer at that time. It had a tricycle undercarriage, better avionics and most importantly, a heater! Trials in the UK confirmed the Bulldog was a suitable platform and Vince submitted the paper to the Deputy Chief of Mission who endorsed the findings. In the finest British tradition, nothing further was heard so the venerable Chipmunk soldiered on.

The Chipmunk gave the British a unique opportunity for visual reconnaissance tours within the BCZ but the arrival of Group Captain F.G. Foot, RAF, as Deputy Chief of Mission changed this.[3] He was a former air attaché in Budapest and believed that all sightings should be photographically confirmed, giving impetus to the idea that the Chipmunk should be used to photograph Soviet and East German installations in the BCZ at low level to complement the photographic material from the Corridor and other programmes. So, in 1956 the Cabinet approved its use on clandestine low-level photographic collection operations in the BCZ under the auspices of BRIXMIS.[4] Day-to-day approval of the photographic flights was devolved to a senior Berlin-based military officer. The programme's political approval was part of the Corridor flight approval process, kept under constant review and revalidated every six months. Changes in the international political and military situation, especially where it affected Germany and Berlin, could result in the curtailment or suspension of flights and the devolved authority for short periods. Political constraints on the flights were at their most severe between 1960 and 1962.

The photographic flights were both politically and militarily sensitive. By some definitions they amounted to aerial espionage (spy flights) because their primary collection method was cameras rather than visual observation. The counter argument was that the flights were 'operated by military aircraft, crewed by uniformed personnel in airspace that we were legally allowed to use, carrying out airborne reconnaissance tours that were a logical extension of BRIXMIS ground-touring operations'.[5] However, using cameras was certainly outside the flight's stated public purposes of asserting access rights and crew continuation training. Had the Soviet authorities ever acquired prima facie evidence of photographic 'spy flights', serious diplomatic repercussions would undoubtedly have followed with the crew possibly being subjected to a 'show trial' followed by a lengthy prison term – euphemistically referred to in BRIXMIS as 'the very long Russian language course' – or worse.

Flight Approval and Authorisation

Until 1960 the individual flights were planned by the Squadron Leader (Operations) at BRIXMIS and approved by the Deputy Chief BRIXMIS, usually an RAF Group Captain. This changed dramatically after the U-2 incident in May 1960. London immediately imposed a total embargo on all photographic flights and assumed direct control. After the building of the Berlin Wall in August 1961, many intelligence sources were seriously curtailed and some completely lost. This persuaded the PM to personally approve limited resumption of a small number of photographic flights (in blocks of single figures) to be executed within a specified time frame.[6]

These restrictions were onerous, cumbersome and inefficient, and significantly slowed the Chipmunk's reaction time when events were at their most dynamic and fast moving around the city. In 1961 the PM approved twenty-eight flights, plus a small number that could be launched at the discretion of the GOC (Berlin). Only thirteen were flown because of poor weather and aircraft availability.[7] In December 1961 London relaxed the constraints slightly by approving a number of photographic flights that could be flown with approval of the GOC (Berlin), but without a time limitation.[8] In 1962 these restrictions were further relaxed and allowed the GOC (Berlin) to approve two flights in any one week.[9] By the mid 1960s London had increased the BRIXMIS flight allocation to five days per fortnight, with approval of the GOC (Berlin) after consulting with the BMG in Berlin for any political input. This approval procedure remained extant until photographic flights ended in September 1990.

Crew Selection and Training

The primary selection criteria for RAF officers posted to BRIXMIS were for them to have an intelligence background and personal qualities that enabled them to be good touring officers, which was their primary employment, capable of dealing with the rigours of mission life. Aircrew officers were told to retain their flying clothing but no reason was given for this.

Before the British services began to take intelligence matters more seriously in the 1970s, intelligence and pre-posting training for aircrew destined for BRIXMIS was minimal and mainly unsuited for the mission's role. They attended the School of Service Intelligence (SSI) course at Ashford, in Kent, that was orientated towards military attachés. It therefore did not accurately reflect the rigours and hazards of mission life because most attachés generally operated in a more civilised environment.

To rectify this deficiency the SSI introduced the Intelligence (Special Duties) Course that was tailored to meet BRIXMIS requirements. A large portion of the course was devoted to vehicle and equipment recognition. Officers and NCOs, regardless of service, had to become proficient in recognising Soviet and East German ground and Air Force equipment and the types of units that possessed them. Camera handling and operation was included in the course syllabus, but was biased towards the ground tour environment. Consequently prospective Chipmunk observers had no formal training in air-to-ground photographic techniques but were deemed to be competent for the task. The establishment of a dedicated Chipmunk crew in the 1980s, mainly on flight safety grounds, led to a more professional approach being taken to aerial photography and new observers performed one or two 'dry' missions over West Berlin to familiarise themselves with the cameras and hone their skills to enable them to get the best results from operational missions where a single pass over the target was the norm.

Until the mid 1970s most RAF pilots' initial flying training was undertaken on the Chipmunk so familiar to them. Some had considerable experience on it. The amount of Chipmunk 'refresher training' required depended on the pilot's previous experience. Pilot training for the photographic flights consisted of an 'acceptance flight' at RAF Gatow, followed by a number of 'clean' (non-photographic) route flights to familiarise pilots with the details of the BCZ. Experienced observers assisted on these familiarisation flights by 'nursing' the pilots until they were as familiar with the BCZ as the observers.

Hans Neubroch was posted to BRIXMIS as a touring officer and became first BRIXMIS Chipmunk pilot between 1956 and 1959. He already had several hundred hours on the aircraft as an instructor so his training requirement for the BRIXMIS role was minimal. Mike Neil was a Chipmunk pilot at Gatow between 1973 and 1977 and again from 1980 to 1983, when he was also Wing Commander (Operations). In 1973 his training had consisted of one flight around the 'standard BCZ route' with his predecessor followed by some additional 'clean' (non-photographic) familiarisation flights. When Mike handed over to his successor in 1977, he gave him a one-flight 'standard BCZ tour'. On his return to Gatow in 1980 he was simply given an acceptance check, after which he was considered operationally ready because of his previous experience.

The question of replacing the Chipmunk with something more modern was often discussed but progressed little beyond this stage. Retired Squadron Leader Vince Robertson, Chipmunk pilot and BRIXMIS Touring Officer from 1976–79 told us little about the efforts to replace the Chipmunks at RAF Gatow:

I was becoming increasingly aware of age of the Chipmunk and while maintained to the highest standards by the excellent groundcrew at Gatow, the possibility of a major failure was never far from the minds of the aircrew involved in the operation. I wrote a paper to the Deputy Chief Of Mission, Group Captain Mike Rayson, voicing my misgivings and proposing that we look at a replacement. I undertook to investigate the suitability of the Scottish Aviation Bulldog, then still in use as a trainer with the University Air Squadrons in the RAF. It was a modern, more comfortable machine with a few more electronic refinements and, significantly, a heater! I went to London UAS, then based at Boscombe Down, and carried out a series of trial flights with then Flight Lieutenant (later Air Commodore) David Williams as photographer. The trial was successful and we showed that the Bulldog would be a suitable platform for reconnaissance sorties in the BCZ. My paper was well received but I think the Bulldog was turned down on the basis that it would be a major change in our operations and would not sit well with the Soviets. The fact that the US Mission had changed their aircraft during my time in Berlin to the Pilatus Turbo Porter counted for nothing with the British authorities. And so the replacement saga came to an end and the worthy Chipmunk soldiered on for another 10 years, God Bless Her!

David Cockburn was the dedicated Chipmunk pilot between 1986 and 1989. Although he had only two hours' previous experience on Chipmunks he was an experienced low-level navigator and glider pilot. He attended two courses before arriving in Berlin: the Central Flying School (CFS) course to learn how to fly the Chipmunk and the Intelligence (SD) Course. Because of the secrecy surrounding the Chipmunk's activities his CFS instructor was totally unaware of the type and amount of flying his 'student' would be doing. Consequently, he spent a lot of time flying from the front seat, concentrating on obtaining an instrument rating because the aircraft would be operating in the controlled airspace of the BCZ. This was found to be really a waste of effort because BRIXMIS Chipmunk flights were always flown from the back seat and under Visual Flight Rules (VFR) conditions. The Intelligence (SD) Course introduced him to his new unit and its overall role but not the specifics of his new job – this came later. When David was told that he was the dedicated BRIXMIS Chipmunk pilot, he realised, after ten years in a training role, that he was returning to an operational flying environment.

From 1956 until 1960 the Chipmunk crew consisted of a pilot in the front seat and an observer/photographer in the rear seat. The observers were generally from the Army, but on one occasion a Royal Marine officer filled the seat. The observers were normally mission ground touring officers but occasionally RAF personnel flew, because of their service specialisation. The pilot was either a BRIXMIS member, or a Berlin-based pilot on a ground tour. The rationale behind this was to maintain the 'continuation training' cover story. As the BRIXMIS members were also ground touring officers it meant that sometimes they might have just completed a forty-eight-hour ground tour of the GDR, immediately followed by a Chipmunk sortie. Roy Marsden, an observer and Russian linguist from 1973 to 1975, remembers that in one day he flew a Chipmunk sortie in the morning, acted as interpreter for the Chief of BRIXMIS at a meeting with the Soviet External Relations Branch (SERB) in the afternoon and then went out on a ground tour in the evening![10] This concept of being touring officers as well as Chipmunk crew members gave rise to concerns that fatigue could be a contributory factor in the event of a Chipmunk accident. It speaks highly of the crews' professionalism and dedication that there never was one. In 1981 the Deputy Chief of Mission established a dedicated Chipmunk crew whose sole purpose was to plan and execute the Chipmunk flights and report their results. At the same time the 'continuation training' part of the cover story was discreetly dropped. In the event of a BRIXMIS pilot being unavailable, certain officers at RAF Gatow were aware of the flights' real purpose and would step into the breach.

The Army element at BRIXMIS made a case in the 1970s that they should permanently provide the observer because the majority of the targets were ground force orientated. The RAF pointed out that the sometimes violent manoeuvres and the peculiar flying attitudes often necessary during the flights made even the most hardened aircrew feel airsick and, in case of an emergency, a high degree of crew co-operation and airmanship was required to bring the flight to a successful conclusion. Ultimately common sense prevailed and all the photographic flights continued to be RAF crewed.

Sensors and Films

Chipmunk crews used a 35mm hand-held camera that could be fitted with a variety of lenses as standard. There is some evidence that a fixed F.95 oblique camera fitted with a 4in lens producing 70mm square format stereoscopic photography was used sometime between 1959[11] and 1961 and this is referred to in some official papers.[12] References to the fixed F.95 often infer that it was fitted and in regular use. However, the reality may have been somewhat different. Hans Neubroch is certain that it was not fitted between 1956 and 1959 when he was the Chipmunk pilot. Francis Bacon, the corporal in charge of the BRIXMIS photographic section from 1959 to 1961, said that they never handled any 70mm film and that their darkrooms were not equipped to handle that film format.[13] He recalled discussions proposing installation of a fixed camera in the Chipmunk with the lens pointing through the centre of the fuselage roundel to conceal its presence. Whilst some initial work may have been carried out, the available evidence indicates that the F.95 was either never actually fitted or done so only for a very short period. By December 1961, the JIC in London recommend that use of the F.95 should be 'discontinued' and more easily disposable hand-held cameras be substituted.[14] Certainly, the presence of a fixed F.95 would have made denying the flight's true purpose impossible if the aircraft had force-landed in the GDR or East Berlin, with consequent political and diplomatic repercussions.

The cameras went through several iterations as technology advanced. Initially, a hand-wound Leica M3 body, usually fitted with a 200mm Telyt lens, was selected. This used Kodak Panatomic-X film (rated at 64 ASA) that could be uprated to 1600 ASA by modifying exposure and processing techniques. By the 1970s two motor-drive Nikon F1 bodies were introduced. They came with a selection of Nikon lenses: 55mm for wide-angle shots, 135mm for closer shots and 500mm for really close-up shots. The 1,000mm lens was introduced during this period but it was very difficult to use in the Chipmunk's cramped cockpit with its vibrations and the 80-knot slipstream. The camera had to be held very steadily to achieve results that were not out of focus and shaky. Film used was Kodak 400 ASA monochrome and 100 ASA colour. Infrared film was occasionally used to ascertain which vehicles were painted with IR reflective or absorbent paint. By the 1980s the motor-drive equipped Nikon F3 was the standard body that could be fitted with lenses ranging from 35mm for wide-angle up to the 1,000mm for very close-up work.[15] By then Kodak colour 100 ASA and 400 ASA film was exclusively used.

Ready-use spare film was carried in the observer's flying overall pockets. By the 1980s it was carried in a brass cassette containing about 20 rolls of film (720 frames) with a further 20–30 rolls (720–1080 frames) carried in flying overall pockets in case a sortie presented a particularly large number of opportunities. The average sortie used 15–20 rolls (540–720 frames).

Although digital cameras became available in the 1980s they were never used on Chipmunk photographic flights because the digital images could still be recovered even if the memory card was damaged. The photographic film images were easily destroyed by exposure to light or fire and thus less of a challenge to 'deniability'.

Tasking and Targeting

Primary tasking for Chipmunk photographic flights was done by HQ BRIXMIS based on their intelligence requirements and local knowledge. Other tasks originated from the UK MoD in London, HQ BAOR and HQ RAFG in Rheindahlen and HQ Berlin Infantry Brigade (BIB). The various requests were all considered and incorporated into individual flight plans.

There was a plethora of Soviet and East German targets for the flights. They included two complete Soviet ground force divisions, elements of two others, a complete artillery division, 6 Motor Rifle Brigade based at Berlin-Karlshorst that formed the Soviet Berlin garrison, two major airfields (one fast jet and one helicopter), several SAM sites and significant logistic installations. The GDR had a complete army division, other army units, logistic installations and its Border Command Centre (Grenzkommando Mitte – GKM). East Berlin housed major GDR government organs, including the Headquarters of the infamous Ministerium für Staats Sicherheit (MfS), more popularly known as the 'Stasi'. On the Berlin Railway Ring the rail yards and sidings at Berlin-Karlshorst, Bernau, Döberitz, Elstal, Priort, Satzkorn and Wüstermark were used for importing and moving military equipment. Therefore there was plenty of 'trade' for the flights.

Besides photographic targets the Chipmunk was sometimes asked to carry out other forms of reconnaissance. Bob Hamilton remembers being tasked to overfly Werneuchen airfield, a MiG-25 Foxbat base. They were given special approval to overfly the base, its hangars and storage facilities whilst holding a detector connected to a sealed aluminium box, supplied by an unknown department, out of the cockpit. On the second, or third, pass a Foxbat was vectored to chase them off. The Foxbat is a big, fast aircraft and was not to be tangled with. Discretion being the better part of valour the Chipmunk made a 'tactical withdrawal' to the safety of West Berlin. They never found out what, if anything, the box had detected.

Conduct of Flights

Until 1960 there was a relaxed, almost laissez-faire attitude to the flights. They were planned at HQ BRIXMIS in the Olympic Stadium in West Berlin and the plan was approved by the Deputy Chief BRIXMIS. About two hours before departure the pilot submitted the flight plan to the BASC, so the Soviets were well informed of the flight. At RAF Gatow the pilot 'self-authorised' the flight in the authorisation book with 'Gatow – Berlin Ring Photo' entered in the Duty column, so here was another opportunity for compromise. The flights at this time were seen as a cost-effective substitute for ground tours in the BCZ area with the emphasis on the liaison and 'flag showing' part of the BRIXMIS role. The crew travelled to Gatow in whatever transport was available, including private cars, and boarded the aircraft on the pan outside the hangar. The flight was flown at between 500ft and 1,500ft. On return the crew disembarked outside the hangar and returned to BRIXMIS HQ.

This somewhat carefree world came to an end after the 1960–62 restrictions when concerns about the potential compromise of the photographic flights and crew grew significantly. The flight plan was now submitted to the GOC (Berlin) for his personal approval in writing after consulting the BMG. This approval was seen as the final opportunity to stop the flight. There was, however, a back-stop in the form of the standard RAF flight authorisation procedure. This ensured that the crew were competent to operate the aircraft, understood their brief and were aware of any limitations. So, in extremis, the RAF Gatow authorising officer – the Station Commander or Wing Commander (Operations) – as the only officers allowed to authorise the BRIXMIS flights, could be contacted to stop it. This never happened.

To maintain the cover story the conduct of all flights was the same, so there was no procedural difference between a 'clean' flight and a photographic one. The crew travelled to Gatow in ordinary service transport, not the distinctively marked BRIXMIS vehicles. They wore uniforms and flying clothing devoid of any accoutrements that identified them as BRIXMIS personnel. At Gatow the crew entered the hangar by the back door. They donned helmets and goggles before boarding the aircraft whilst still in the hangar. The aircraft was then pushed out onto the pan in front of the hangar and started.[16] Such precautions were regarded as necessary because the watchtower at the Gross Glienicke East German Border Guard installation that overlooked RAF Gatow was known to be equipped with long-lens cameras and long-range directional microphones, operated by trained personnel, to monitor airfield activity. This meant that conversations outside the hangar were restricted just to those necessary for the aircraft's operation.

It soon became apparent that the early practice of the pilot in the front and the observer in the rear limited the latter's ability to photograph targets because of the restricted view.[17] Additionally it meant that the cockpit had to be fully open when undertaking photography, which did not contribute to the crew's comfort, especially in winter. So the arrangement was reversed in the early 1960s when the observer began occupying the front seat, where he had a better view to acquire targets and carry out photography, and the pilot moved to the rear.[18] This meant that the Chipmunk's canopy needed only to be partially opened for photography, making for a slightly more comfortable environment, at least for the pilot.

Photographic flights conformed to VFR flight rules, which meant the pilot was totally responsible for collision avoidance. David Cockburn's Chipmunk training at the CFS had taught him to fly the aircraft from the front seat. He had not been trained for the 'back-seat driving' required in Berlin, so the unit's Qualified Flying Instructor (QFI) had to remedy this deficiency. The VFR regime and the low-level operating regime (1,000ft and lower) meant that his recently hard-earned instrument rating was apparently not required, although the vagaries of the Berlin weather often brought it into play to ensure a safe return to base.

Once airborne from Gatow, flights were flown in a clockwise direction and would last up to two and a half hours. Anti-clockwise flights were sometimes used depending on the weather and the individual observer's preference. Operating altitudes were normally around 800ft, with 500ft reserved for special occasions, or requirements. Routes were planned to pass over as many installations as possible. Early morning flights were often a very useful way of detecting convoys and troop movements, whose locations could then be passed on to the BRIXMIS local ground tours for further investigation.[19]

To maintain the cover story the 'clean' flights were flown in the same manner as the photographic sorties and ranged throughout the BCZ with two crew. The non-operational flights were normally flown at between 1,500 and 2,500ft with no cameras or other sensitive equipment on board. If BRIXMIS personnel formed the crew, or part of it, on non-operational flights, they were used as an excuse for navigation exercises to become familiar with the major installations and the BCZ's exact boundaries, beyond which they were not allowed to fly. If the non-operational flights had just remained in the Gatow circuit, it would have probably drawn unwanted attention to the photographic flights.

Flights were supposed to remain inside the BCZ but they sometimes operated on its fringes or just beyond. Werneuchen airfield in the north-east was half in and half out of the BCZ as was an engineer barracks and co-located SAM site at Glau in the south-west. In the late 1960s and early to mid 1970s, photographs were acquired of Finow airfield and a buried antenna that were well outside the BCZ.[20] Apart from a few such deliberately tasked sorties outside the boundary, other incursions into GDR airspace were the result of a crew 'becoming temporarily uncertain of their position' – i.e. lost! By the 1980s the BCZ boundary was regarded as sacrosanct and strictly enforced. Although installations outside the BCZ were photographed, the aircraft remained within its boundaries.

1   Tyuratam Missile Test Range, now the Baikonur Cosmodrome, a key target for U-2 deep-penetration flights. (Photo: USAF)

2   Wreckage of Powers' U-2, still displayed at the Central Armed Forces Museum in Moscow. (Photo: Kevin Wright)

3   In front of the BASC building at Kleistpark with the four national representatives
on 26 January 1989. (L to R) Major Rick Fuller (US), Wing Commander David Pollock
(Britain), Colonel Claude Favier (France) and Colonel Boris Shunin (USSR). The BASC
was one of only two Four Power institutions that functioned through the Cold War.
(Photo: USAF – CMSgt Don Sutherland)

4 BASC at work. Major Vladimir Zhurba (USSR) discusses flight information with Captain Bill Sumption (US). (Photo: USAF – CMSgt Don Sutherland)

5 The BARTCC operations room photographed in January 1987. Located at the US Tempelhof Airbase in Berlin, BARTCC controlled aircraft in the Corridors and BCZ and was exclusively manned by USAF personnel. (Photo: USAF – Thomas Farr)

6   With its defensive armament removed, RB-17G Fortress 44-8889 gathered SIGINT with the 7499th Support Squadron from April 1949 until September 1953. (Photo: USAF)

7   Douglas VC-47D Skytrain 43-48186 at Tempelhof in June 1961. C-47s performed a wide range of VIP, freight, personnel and medical transport flights, as well as reconnaissance duties along the Corridors. (Photo: Ralf Manteufel)

8   Convair CT-29A 49-1912 Carol Ann on approach to Tempelhof. Every effort was made to hide its cameras and aerials from watching Soviet and East German eyes. (Photo: Peter Seemann)

9   Boeing C-97 Stratofreighter 49-2592 Pie Face that carried a huge Boston K-42 camera with a 240in lens (see frontispiece) but externally still looked like a standard C-97 transport. (Photo: Ralf Manteufel)

10　Boeing C-97 Stratofreighter 52-2688 Eager Beaver PHOTINT aircraft served in Germany from July 1963. In later years, with the addition of new equipment, it became known as Rivet Box. Leaving in early 1970, it was retired to the Arizona desert at Davis Monthan AFB. (Photo: Ralf Manteufel)

11　Boeing C-97 Stratofreighter 53-0106 Wine Sap equipped to monitor the SA-2 Guideline missile system. Converted to the role around 1965 it is seen here taxiing out at Tempelhof on 9 August 1971. (Photo: Ralf Manteufel)

12   Boeing C-97 Stratofreighter 52-2687 Flint Stone in August 1964. Serving with the 7405th for over fourteen years, it was latterly known as Rivet Stem, a photographic aircraft, after removal of its SIGINT equipment. It was the last C-97 to leave Wiesbaden Air Base in 1975. (Photo: Ralf Manteufel)

13   Douglas C-118A Liftmaster '51-3842' at Tempelhof. Its real tail number was 51-3823. The real serial 51-3842 was allocated to a C-121 (Lockheed Constellation). It was one of four C-118s which were given false tail numbers in 1965–66, generating speculation that they were connected with CIA operations. (Photo: Ralf Manteufel)

14 Lockheed C-130E-II Hercules 62-1822 photographed on the Rhein-Main (Frankfurt) in November 1981. In 1985 the aircraft returned to Germany, after upgrading in the US, fitted with the superlative KA-116 SRIS camera. (Photo: Manfred Faber)

15 Three RF-100A Slick Chick aircraft operated from Bitburg AB in 1955–56. Their armament replaced by cameras and carrying extra external fuel tanks, they flew a small number of penetration flights over Eastern Europe. (Photo: USAF)

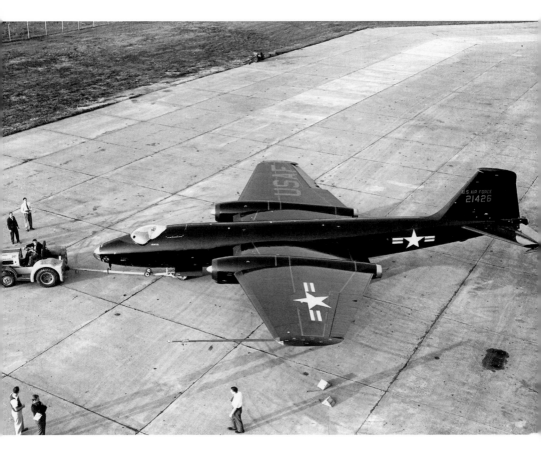

16   A licence-built version of the British Canberra, a small number of Heart Throb Martin RB-57As undertook a short series of East European overflights in 1955–56. Later, 'big wing' versions of the RB-57 continued operating in Europe until late 1968. (Photo: USAF)

17   For a short period the RAF used the C-in-C's Douglas C-47 Dakota aircraft, similar to this one, in Germany for photography in 1946 and 1947 using a hand-held F.24 camera. (Photo: Stefan Wright-Cole)

18   The Anson was a common sight in a number of roles in Europe during the 1940s and 1950s. Similar aircraft to this one were used by the British on their Corridor and BCZ photographic flights from 1948 until 1958. (Photo: Kevin Wright)

19   Pembroke C(PR)1 XL953 on approach to Tempelhof AB. The Pembroke was the mainstay of British photographic operations in Germany for over thirty years until their end in 1990. This particular aircraft was burned out in a hangar fire at Wildenrath in May 1980. (Photo: Peter Seemann)

20 Percival Pembroke C(PR)1 XL954 banks away to show the 'post-Mod 614' camera doors. The Pembroke's low ground clearance meant that camera doors were necessary to protect the lenses on the ground and to try to hide them from Soviet and East German eyes. This aircraft is currently based in Ireland. (Photo: Classic Air Force)

21 By the 1980s the Pembroke's age and the weight of its camera load were causing operating problems and one camera was removed in the summer months. This cartoon shows the PIs solution to the weight problem by boosting its take-off using a Harrier-style 'ski ramp'. (Photo: Reg Deness)

22 The East German Border Guard watchtower near RAF Gatow carefully monitored the comings and goings at the airfield. This one was similar in design to the one at Gross Glienicke Border Guard barracks. (Photo: Dallas Payne)

23 View from a Pembroke shortly after take-off from Gatow. The Border with the GDR (The Wire) formed part of Gatow's boundary and one of the watchtowers is clearly visible in this shot. (Photo: Dallas Payne)

24 Andover C(PR)1 XS596 succeeded the photo-Pembrokes but by then the operation was all but over. A short while later the aircraft left 60 Squadron to become the UK's 'Open Skies' platform and here is seen flying over southern England soon after taking on its new role. (Photo: via Kevin Wright)

25 Douglas C-47B Gabriel, 43-49454 F-UJGN of ELA 55. Prior to being assigned to Corridor flights, Armée de l'Air C-47s had taken part in the French North African colonial wars. (Photo: Peter Seemann)

26 Nord N2501 Noratlas No. 036 of EÉ54 Dunkerque at Berlin-Tegel in 1964, fitted with the Furet III (Ferret III) system. (Photo: Peter Seemann)

27 C-160G Transall Gabriel VI, F-216, F-ZJUP. Introduced in the closing days of the Cold War, the two converted Transalls continue to serve in the SIGINT role with the Armée de l'Air. This image shows the aircraft in a more contemporary external configuration. (Photo: Armée de l'Air)

28 De Havilland Canada DHC-1 Chipmunk T.10 WG486 of RAF Gatow Station Flight over the Brandenburg Gate in 1994. Of 1940s vintage, the venerable Chipmunk outlasted all the other aircraft types by successfully operating for forty years in the BCZ. (Photo: Crown Copyright via Mike Neil)

29 View from a BRIXMIS Chipmunk under fire from a Soviet soldier. Flying at low level over Soviet installations clearly carried a risk and on occasions aircraft returned with the odd extra hole. Fortunately no one was ever hurt in such incidents. (Photo: Crown Copyright via BRIXMIS Association)

30 De Havilland Canada DHC-2 U-6A/L-20 (Beaver) 58-2020 of US Berlin Aviation Detachment. The Beaver was an excellent observation platform possessing a good field of view and proved to be rugged and reliable. (Photo: Peter Seemann)

31 Pilatus UV-20A Chiricahua (Turbo Porter) 79-23253 of US Berlin Brigade Aviation Detachment. A pilot's favourite because of its excellent handling characteristics and ability to land in strong crosswinds on the Tempelhof taxiway as this one is demonstrating in 1982. (Photo: Ralf Manteufel)

32 Max-Holste MH-4521 Broussard No. 208 of AdlA at Tempelhof Open House in 1977. A long-serving utility and observation aircraft with the French military, it was a stable photographic platform. (Photo: Peter Seemann)

33 De Havilland Canada DHC-6-300 Twin Otter No. 603 of Adl'A at Tempelhof in 1988. Arriving in Berlin late in the day, the aircraft was well suited to its role. (Photo: Ralf Manteufel)

34 Cessna L-19E Bird Dog No. 24557 F-MCMO of DETALAT at Tempelhof Open House in 1993. Like the Chipmunk these aircraft had good handling characteristics at low speed but their narrow fuselage posed major challenges for photographers with long lenses. (Photo: Peter Seemann)

35 Sud Aviation SE3160 Alouette III of DETALAT. The Alouette III was another long-serving type with the French military, although it did not regularly operate from Berlin until 1987. The type remained there until the termination of French operations in 1994. (Photo: Hugo Mambour)

36 Mi-24 Hind attack helicopter at Mahlwinkel in the Centre Corridor in 1993. The Hind was a serious concern to NATO forces because of its potent weapon load and sustained field operations capability. (Photo: MMFL Association via Roland Pietrini)

37 Sukhoi Su-24 Fencer at Welzow, which was well outside even the expanded 1990 airspace boundaries, pictured in 1993–94. The Su-24 was considered a serious threat because of its long range and large weapons load. It was among the last Russian aircraft to be withdrawn from Germany in 1994. (Photo: MMFL Association via Roland Pietrini)

38　AW Gazelle AH 1 similar to those used by 7 Flight AAC from Gatow until the end of operations in Berlin in 1990. (Photo: Kevin Wright)

39　Bell UH-1H 67-17305 of the US Army's Berlin Aviation Detachment stored at Tempelhof. Always immaculate in their special VIP colour scheme, they used the call sign 'Freedom City'. (Photo: Ben Dunnell)

40   The Georg Wilhelm Haus in Bad Eilsen was the home of the RAF and Army PI units until 1954 when they moved to Rheindahlen. (Photo: Bad Eilsen reunion website)

41   The JHQ building at Rheindahlen was central to British military operations in Germany from 1954 until its closure at the end of 2013. (Photo: Crown Copyright)

42 The Schierstein Compound in Wiesbaden was the home of the 497th RTS/497th RTG from 1954 until 1991 and central to American photographic intelligence operations. (Photo: USAF)

43 The Type 'D' stereoscope provided a 2x magnification and could be folded to fit into a small soft spectacle-type carrying case. (Photo: Peter Jefferies)

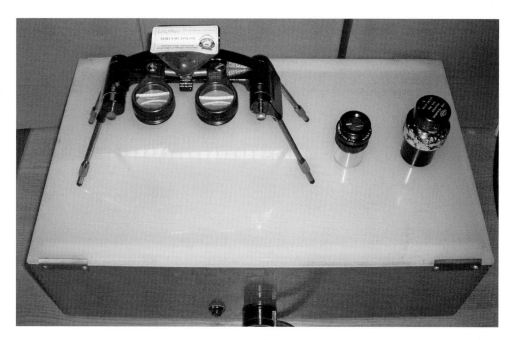

44 The simple interpretation tools used by the British until the late 1960s: the SV8 stereoscope with up to 4x magnification, the measuring magnifier and simple light box. (Photo: Peter Jefferies)

45 The Richards MIM-4 light table with Bausch & Lomb zoom 240 microscope head, motorised film drives and split light platen provided a quantum leap in interpretation capability. (Photo: Peter Jefferies)

46 A SS-1 Scud Battalion training on the Letzlinger Heide. Annotation Key:
1 – Scud Missile being loaded on to Scud transporter-erector-launcher on an MAZ-543;
2 – Scud transporter-erector-launcher on MAZ-543. (Photo: Crown Copyright via
Medmenham Collection)

47 A Divisional Free Flight Rocket Battalion (FFR Bn) deployed on a local training
area. FFR Battalions were notoriously difficult to find in barracks and only their associated
equipment was generally seen at their home locations. The BTR-60 PA command vehicle
No. 952 – at the bottom centre – was subsequently seen in a barracks area suspected to
belong to the FFR Battalion. (Photo: Crown Copyright via the Medmenham Collection)

48   Schlotheim in the South Corridor housed a BMP-2 equipped Motor Rifle
Regiment. Note the Soviet taste for fencing between units. Annotation key: 1 – Engineer
Company; 2 – Air Defence Battery with 2S6 Tunguska; 3 – Reconnaissance Company
with BMP-2; 4 – Tank Battalion with T-80; 5 – Motor Rifle Battalion with BMP-2;
6 – Mortar Batteries with 120mm mortar; 7 – Anti-Tank Battery with AT-5 Spandrel
on BRDM-2; 8 – Artillery Battalion with 2S1 122mm self-propelled gun and 1V series
command and reconnaissance vehicles; 9 – Fuel re-supply Company with KrAZ-255
fuel bowsers (tank truck); 10 – Maintenance Company; 11 – Two T-80 Main Battle Tank
(MBT); 12 – Aircraft/Helicopter refuelling unit (lodger unit). (Photo: Crown Copyright
via the Medmenham Collection)

49   Detailed image showing the breech of a 2S5 Giantsint-S 152mm self-propelled howitzer. The shot allowed analysts to determine its operation and layout. (Photo: Crown Copyright via Bob Hamilton)

50   Mi-8 Hip helicopter undergoing maintenance at Rangsdorf. The photograph shows details of the engine compartment layout. Shots like this, of newly arrived equipment, were of great assistance in understanding how a vehicle, helicopter or aircraft were constructed and worked. (Photo: Crown Copyright via Bob Hamilton)

51   A Flat Face B search radar. The shadow shows the shape of the radar sails, which helped the PI considerably. (Photo: MMFL Association via Roland Pietrini)

52   IPR underwater reconnaissance vehicle taken from a Chipmunk. An experienced PI could extract a wealth of technical intelligence from images such as this. (Photo: Crown Copyright via the Medmenham Collection)

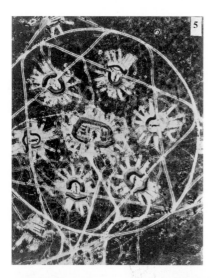

53 SA-2 Guideline SAM site in Cuba. This is a similar configuration to the one discovered at Glau in the late 1950s which became the centre for a considerable intelligence gathering effort to try and discover the SA-2s full capabilities. (Photo: USAF)

54 S-75 Dvina (SA-2 Guideline) missile on a launcher and with another missile on the re-supply trailer to the left. (Photo: Crown Copyright via the Medmenham Collection)

55 SNR-75 (Fan Song) SA-2 target acquisition and fire control radar mounted on top of a hardened facility to improve its range and operation. (Photo: Crown Copyright via the Medmenham Collection)

56 Spring 1981. BM-21 multi-barrel rocket launchers and other vehicles marked with the letter 'K' on the cabs. The application of these markings concerned senior NATO commanders who feared it might have been part of preparations for a 'fraternal intervention' in Poland. (Photo: MMFL Association via Roland Pietrini)

57 SA-9 Gaskin low-level SAM systems on BRDM-2 armoured cars in their home barracks outside their parking shed. (Photo: Crown Copyright via the Medmenham Collection)

58 'Let's call them Fred'. A PRP-3 on BMP-1 Chassis (Small Fred) and SNAR-10 Leopard battlefield radar on MT-LB (Big Fred). (Photo: Crown Copyright via the Bob Hamilton Collection and Hugo Mambour)

59   A BTR-60PB equipped Motor Rifle Battalion undergoing routine maintenance and inspection. The PI could extract a wealth of information such as: the shed occupied by the unit, the number of equipments, and side numbers indicating each vehicles position in the the unit organisation. Close-up images taken at the same time produced technical intelligence on the vehicles such as the content of the vehicle tool kit from which we could deduce the level of maintenance carried out at unit level.

60   A T-64 MBT power-pack change was a major operation and revealed a wealth of internal detail. (Photo: Crown Copyright via the Medmenham Collection)

61   SPN-30 Paint Box radar jamming system. This significant system was intended to interfere with the terrain following radar of NATO F-111, Tornado and even some components of the E-3 AWACS systems. It was the subject of a major international technical intelligence programme. (Photo: Crown Copyright via Bob Hamilton)

62 R-408 Twin Plate tropospheric scatter communications system. (Photo: Crown Copyright via Roy Marsden)

63 R-412 Twin Ear tropospheric scatter communications system in barracks. (Photo: Crown Copyright via Roy Marsden)

64 MiG-25RBV Foxbat or MiG-25RBT Foxbat Bort No. 74 at Werneuchen. The RAF PIs could deduce the layout of the reconnaissance equipment carried by these versions. (Photo: MMFL Association)

65   Yak-28 Firebar undergoing maintenance at Werneuchen with ARA-4 ground power unit on URAL-375 chassis. In 1966 a Firebar crashed into the Havelsee resulting in a major British intelligence effort to recover certain engine and electronic components. (Photo: MMFL Association)

66   Colbitz under the Centre Corridor hosts an army-level air defence equipment display. The intelligence community suspected that these were a deliberate 'show and tell' by the Soviets. Annotation Key: 1 – Air defence radars: Long Track; Spoonrest D; Thin Skin B; Flat Face B; 2 – Army-level SAM systems: SA-11 Gadfly and SA-4 Ganef and their associated radars; 3 – Regimental-level Air Defence systems: 2S6 Tunguska, BMP-2 MANPADS carriers and their associated radars; 4 – Divisional-level SAM system: SA-8 Gecko and associated radars; 5 – Air defence command and control vehicles; 6 – Mi-8 Hip helicopters, probably VIP transports. (Photo: Crown Copyright via the Medmenham Collection)

On return to Gatow, regardless of the flight's purpose, the procedure was the reverse of that for departure. The aircraft was taxied up to the hangar and the engine shut down. The Chipmunk was then pushed into the hangar, doors closed, with the crew disembarking and exiting via the back door. The front hangar doors were then reopened and the aircraft pushed out for refuelling, after which it was pushed back in again before the doors were finally closed. This procedure was described by Peter Kirkpatrick, a member of the Gatow ASF, as the 'proverbial pain'.

The crew then returned to the BRIXMIS HQ, in West Berlin, where the sortie was debriefed and recorded and the film processed and initially evaluated by BRIXMIS staff before being sent to the PI units at Rheindahlen for detailed analysis. One of the problems experienced during this debriefing phase was correctly recording the targets, film and frame numbers and the time-on-target. If crew notes were wrong, many hours of innocent amusement could be spent identifying individual targets, films and frames on the 20-plus rolls of film generated by the flight. In the 1970s this problem was solved using a senior NCO, who supported the SO2 Weapons Officer, always being an Intelligence Corps PI, with recent 6 Intelligence Company experience, who therefore had intimate knowledge of BCZ targets.

Techniques

A successful photographic sortie required a combination of strong crew co-operation, skill, determination and stamina to achieve the objective of bringing back high-quality photographs for exploitation. Excellent crew communication and co-operation were vital to success. Pilot and observer had to work together and understand what each was doing at all times during the flight. High-level navigational skills, a knowledge of local targets, order of battle, quick thinking and good airmanship all contributed to a successful flight. These qualities came to the fore if a sortie had to be replanned in-flight because of significant activity or important equipment sightings. Although the observer was equipped with a microphone, he could not talk to the pilot on the aircraft's intercommunication system because the assumption was that all electromagnetic emissions, even those within the cockpit, could be intercepted by the network of Soviet and East German static listening posts around Berlin and the Soviet air-related electronic countermeasures (ECM) regiment at Schönwalde, who were always looking for actual Western targets on which to practise. Consequently, hand signals and shouting were the normal communication methods.

Unlike the French and US aircraft, the Chipmunk had a low-set wing that limited the observer's view and often obscured the camera's view of the target when flying straight and level. Successful photography called for flying techniques that would cause an apoplectic fit to flying purists. To ensure that the observer had an unobstructed view of the target, the forward part of the canopy had to be opened, producing a considerable draught from the slipstream. Whilst this could be relatively pleasant during the warmer months, it was very uncomfortable in the colder ones, with the combination of sub-zero temperatures and slipstream producing a chill factor that whistled around the crew's exposed, and not so exposed, bits. To operate the camera the observer had to wear either thin gloves or no gloves at all. Long focal length lenses had to be kept within the confines of the cockpit so they were not buffeted by the slipstream and held sufficiently steady to achieve optimum results. To achieve this steadiness the observer often had to lean backwards across the cockpit with his head out of the other side, directly in the icy blast.

To acquire the best possible images pilots positioned their aircraft so that the target was kept in a fairly constant position relative to the aircraft's movement. A steady, sometimes steeply banked, turn, whilst maintaining altitude was used to ensure that the camera could be kept on target. These turns were mainly to the left because few people can naturally take photographs out of the right side of a cockpit and it gave the observer a better angle to look to the left. During these turns the observer fine-tuned the aiming, focusing and exposure. This turning technique often resulted in the aircraft fuel load becoming unbalanced. To restore it the Chipmunk would have to 'skid' the opposite way between targets. This technique and the low-altitude turbulence that was always encountered made for 'challenging flying!'[21]

The observer/photographer was always a very busy man. With only limited time to keep the target in the viewfinder he needed to act instinctively and cope with the skidding technique if he was to get good photographs. The low-altitude turbulence and restricted view through the viewfinder, often at 90 degrees to the direction of flight, was enough to turn the strongest stomach. Even the most hardened and experienced aircrew regularly suffered the symptoms of motion sickness. He also needed a good knowledge of aerial photographic and film uprating techniques. Besides all the normal flight paraphernalia such as target maps and recording media, he had two camera bodies fitted with different lenses as standard to reduce the need for in-flight lens changes, a time-consuming and awkward procedure. When a lens change was needed it often meant a film change too because the film speed needed to be compatible with the new lens. Film would be routinely uprated when using the 500mm and 1,000mm lenses, so that the higher shutter speed necessary to minimise camera shake was achievable and to ensure there was sufficient light to provide properly exposed images. In winter, photographic light time was short and light levels lower, so the film was uprated to 6400 ASA. As well as managing these problems between targets the observer also had to make a note of the target name, the time-on-target, the film number, frame numbers covering each target and notes of any significant items or incidents.

If the observer was particularly busy, the pilot would take over recording duties, leaving the observer free to concentrate on photography. Pilots were also trained as observers, becoming familiar with camera operation and the photographic techniques employed. This also meant that if no observer was available they could assume the role.

Flight Hazards

Flight hazards mainly came from three sources: avoiding other air traffic, the possibility of a forced landing in the GDR or East Berlin and the hostile intent (and sometimes behaviour) of Soviet and East German troops. Avoiding other VFR air traffic at the lower levels in the BCZ was not just a matter of watching out for Soviet and East German aircraft but also Allied ones. The AMLMs co-ordinated their air activities, but until the 1980s this was somewhat haphazard. The reality was that a sharp lookout had to be kept for other aircraft, especially if there was a lot of activity at a particular location, or a new piece of equipment had made an appearance that everyone wanted to photograph. Sometimes the Chipmunk arrived over a target on its allocated day and time only to find one of the other Allied aircraft already there – consternation all round.

Crews had to be alert for Russian and East German air activity, especially in the vicinity of the fast jet base at Werneuchen, on the north-eastern boundary of the BCZ, and the helicopter base at Oranienburg inside the Zone. Tangling with Werneuchen's MiG-25 Foxbats or Oranienburg's Mi-6 Hook or Mi-8 Hip helicopters would not have had a happy outcome. Russian and East German airborne reaction to the Chipmunk usually involved flying in close proximity and exchanging 'friendly' waves. On one occasion, however, the Chipmunk was subjected to aggressive flying by a pair of Mi-24 Hind helicopters that apparently tried to force it down.[22] Werneuchen airfield, because of its location, the aircraft based there and the many 'intelligence priority' types that frequently staged through, was a high-priority target for both Corridor and BCZ missions. But there were inconsistencies in Soviet attitudes and protests. At times the response to overflights would be robust and provoke protests. At others, as Roy Marsden has described, ground crews would sometimes wave to them as the Chipmunk appeared overhead. Others experienced a full air display routine directly above the airfield, from a Chipmunk pilot coming to the end of his tour in Berlin, with no protest at all. He asserts that the Soviets never admitted there was anything of importance in the BCZ because drawing attention to activities at the airfield would have been tantamount to admitting just how important it was.[23]

The biggest concern for Chipmunk crews was the possibility of a forced landing in the GDR or East Berlin, for whatever reason. In the event of engine failure it was unlikely that the aircraft would have been within gliding range of West Berlin, so it was pretty certain that a forced landing would be in either the GDR or East Berlin. Flying below 1,000ft gave the crew little time to respond to emergencies – about two minutes at 1,000ft – before the inevitable landing. David Cockburn said: 'If anything did go wrong with the aircraft when flying at 800ft there was little enough time to select a suitable landing area, let alone dispose of the evidence!' If the aircraft and crew had been found on the ground with the cameras, maps and notes it would have been totally incriminating and handed the Soviets clear proof of 'spying' unless a very, very convincing cover story was in place. So during the descent the crew were expected not just to find a suitable landing place, but to destroy any potentially incriminating evidence to provide the all-important 'deniability'.

The official disposal instructions were for the crew to put cameras, film and other potentially incriminating evidence such as marked target maps and records into a bag provided for the purpose and then drop it into the nearest lake, of which there are plenty around Berlin.[24] If this was not possible, the cameras were to be placed in the compartment behind the rear seat in the somewhat forlorn hope that any searchers would not discover them. Roy Marsden believed that the Soviets had diving teams on standby to search any lakes into which a bag might have been dropped. The crews' preferred solution was to land the aircraft in the nearest suitable place, drain some fuel from the tanks and then set fire to it with the kit onboard in the hopes that the evidence would be destroyed.[25] All this presumed that the crew were still sufficiently compos mentis after the 'landing' to do so. If they were unable to destroy the evidence before the authorities arrived, the crews carried a couple of pre-exposed films in the hope that they could convince the Soviets that, although they were carrying cameras, their purpose was 'innocent'. Disposal of exposed film presented its own problems. Before the 1980s the crew would simply open the film cassettes and pull the film out, exposing it to daylight. In the 1980s, as Bob Hamilton remembers, because of the amount of film carried, both crew members carried an old-fashioned beer can opener on their flying overalls. This could be used to flip off the ends of the film cassettes and expose the films to daylight. As Bob says, 'It was all a bit Heath Robinson but worked well in practice.'[26] However, with all these potential dangers it is testimony to the reliability of the Chipmunk's De Havilland Gypsy Major engine, and the skills of the RAF engineers at the RAF Gatow ASF, that there was never a loss of an aircraft due to engine or mechanical failure during the operation's forty-four years. But there were close calls. On 17 June 1957, Hans Neubroch accompanied by Major Pilsbury experienced a partial engine failure at 1,500ft, when the engine would not advance beyond 1,000rpm, which was insufficient to maintain level flight but enough to carry out a powered descent into a landing place of choice. A successful precautionary landing was made at Tempelhof.

In addition to airborne 'hazards', Chipmunk flights sometimes provoked hostile reactions from Soviet and East German ground troops too. Again it is difficult to determine if these acts were the result of official orders or over-zealous reaction by individual sentries, who always carried weapons loaded with live ammunition. In image 29 of the picture section, a Soviet soldier (circled) is pointing an AK-47 semi-automatic rifle and firing at the aircraft. Whether he was reacting this way because he didn't want to appear on camera, or the crew were not photographing his best side, remains undetermined. This incident placed British authorities in a quandary. On one hand, here was prima facie evidence to support a formal complaint to the Soviets of an overtly hostile act against an RAF aircraft going about its 'innocent' lawful occasions in airspace it was entitled to use. On the other hand, producing the photograph as evidence to support any complaint would have compromised the operation and given the Soviets unequivocal confirmation of Allied clandestine photographic reconnaissance. There were other occasions when the Chipmunk returned to Gatow with bullet holes in the airframe. Flares fired at the aircraft were also a common form of harassment.[27] Peter Jefferies often saw photographs of self-propelled and towed anti-aircraft guns, man-portable, mobile and static SAM systems tracking the aircraft as it passed by. This probably provided the operators with practice using a 'live' target. Roy Marsden has also described how, soon after take-off, in the local Potsdam area were several 'target' installations. That one unit in particular, the 34th Artillery Division, 'had the disturbing habit of training their guns on the aircraft as we flew round the installation'.[28] The Chipmunk crew had no way of knowing if the guns and missiles being pointed at them were loaded with live rounds, or what the operator's rules of engagement were – which must have been a very discomforting thought, if they had the time to dwell on it.

Protest and Compromise

The Soviets were never happy about the Allied flights as evidenced by the 'safety of flight not guaranteed' endorsement on the BASC flight cards. The flights only came about because of the Allies' assertion of their access rights to BCZ airspace from airfields in West Berlin. The Soviet representative in the BASC regularly protested about Chipmunk flights in particular, usually citing 'interference' with civilian air traffic at Berlin-Schönfeld (now Berlin-Brandenburg) international airport, regardless of where the Chipmunk actually was at the time of the alleged offence.[29] This was probably a means for the Soviets to protest about the flights, but without drawing the Allies' attention to the actual area of the alleged incursion, which they may have considered 'sensitive' for some reason at the time.

The intensity of air activity along the Corridors and inside the BCZ saw opportunities for ground and air-based efforts to sometimes overlap. These could be complementary, but equally, on occasions, they could undermine each other. One BRIXMIS officer has recounted the targeting of the high-priority objective at Werneuchen airfield. He described how the Soviets appeared to be aware when Allied overflights were likely to take place. When they suspected one was about to happen, they would often cover up, or move, items of sensitive equipment that they did not want the overflights to see. This could undermine the BRIXMIS 'Tourers' efforts, who had spent a long time creeping undetected to an observation point close to the airfield, which was within a PRA, to view those sensitive items rapidly being concealed from overhead flights.[30]

Despite the British suspecting that the Russians and East Germans knew what the Chipmunk was doing, knowledge of the operation and its products was strictly 'need to know' and security was taken very seriously. However, inadvertent compromise of the operation could happen, as recalled by Major General Peter Williams, a former BRIXMIS member. He was escorting some senior RAF visitors, including RAF Gatow's Station Commander, on an official visit to Potsdam. The party had the inevitable Stasi minders in tow. The party was standing on the Sansouci Palace terrace when the Chipmunk appeared overhead. The Station Commander's wife was heard to say: 'Look darling, it's a small plane – Goodness me! Isn't that your Chipmunk?' The Station Commander hissed at his wife out of the corner of his mouth: 'Listen to me. You can't see anything.'[31] Drawing attention to the flight in this way would certainly have interested the Stasi representatives, who would have passed the information up the chain of command.

Bob Hamilton was involved in one of those 'oops' moments. In mid 1990 Nikon developed a 500mm autofocus lens and Bob was selected to try it out. The lens was larger, heavier and more cumbersome than the 1,000mm lenses then in use. After getting airborne Bob prepared to do a few test shots before crossing into the GDR when they hit air turbulence. The lens rose about 6in and then rapidly came down to hit the canopy rail. The result was a very bent lens, costing some £2,000, that had to be written off.

A totally unofficial piece of intelligence-gathering carried out from the air over East Berlin brought considerable personal benefit to David Cockburn. A restaurant in East Berlin, frequented by BRIXMIS personnel, was a rather dilapidated establishment, not really the place to take a family, but the chef produced excellent meals in the poor facilities. Suddenly it closed but an Army officer was told by the chef that he intended to open his own restaurant in another part of the city. During the next few weeks they discovered that the chef had moved to a building near an S-Bahn (overground) station in one of the villages outside the city itself but within the city boundary. It was also on the Berlin Railway Ring that was regularly overflown by the Chipmunk in the hope of spotting 'kit' loaded on trains. Although the station was regularly overflown, it was not an important target but it now assumed greater significance.

On the next flight a building, near the station, was visibly being refurbished – an almost unknown occurrence for a private establishment in the GDR because of near-permanent material shortages. Over the next few months the building was kept under air observation and photographs were taken to confirm that the place looked like a restaurant. When signs of occupation appeared, a ground reconnaissance was called for. They found that the restaurant had the same name as the previous one and was open for business. The food was even better than before, the surroundings were very pleasant, and the staff friendly. This started a very enjoyable series of meals out, with food and service which would not have been out of place in a 5-star establishment in London. Sadly, the proprietor's success meant that he fell foul of the local SED Party elite. His restaurant was classified as a 2-star establishment, and so his prices were set to reflect this, but it was insufficient to make his business viable, so it eventually closed.[32]

Other British Light Aviation Activity

Before 1954 the RAF's Air Observation Post (AOP) Squadron and AOP Flights based in the BOZ provided light aircraft support to Berlin by deploying one or two Austers there as required. These aircraft were owned and maintained by the RAF but aircrew were usually from the Army (mostly Royal Artillery). They flew visual observation flights in response to such events as the 1951 East German workers' uprising. There is no evidence that any officially tasked photographic reconnaissance was undertaken, although there may have been enthusiastic amateur photographers in the crews who made personal photographic records.

In April and May 1956 there is some evidence of a number of flights by a Percival Prentice lasting about one to two hours, flying throughout the whole BCZ and carrying passengers, possibly BRIXMIS personnel and Berlin-based intelligence officers.[33] Whether these flights were photographic or visual reconnaissance is not recorded. The Cabinet approved Chipmunk photographic flights in 1956, although the Chipmunk had been at Gatow since 1954, so the Prentice flights may have been a precursor to this. However, the Prentice could carry up to four passengers, so they may have been familiarisation flights for observers.

In 1970 the Army Air Corps (AAC) formed '7 Aviation Flight' AAC (7 Avn Flt AAC), later renamed '7 Flight' AAC (7 Flt AAC), at RAF Gatow. The flight initially had four Westland Sioux AH-1s that were replaced by three Aerospatiale Gazelle AH-1s in 1975. The flight belonged to the British BIB and flew visual reconnaissance patrols along the inner city border (The Wall) and the border between the city and the GDR (The Wire), liaison flights and photographic reconnaissance missions. HQ BIB tasked the latter via 3 Intelligence and Security Company (3 Int & Sy Coy). Their main targets were the Grenzkommando Mitte installations adjacent to The Wall and The Wire. The results of these missions were mainly used by HQ BIB but were sometimes sent to HQ BAOR.

United States Light Aviation Activity in Berlin

In 1967 the USA authorised Project Lark Spur to photograph Soviet and East German installations in the BCZ using fixed-wing aircraft of the US Berlin Brigade Aviation Detachment.[34] The programme's original aim was to add to the large volume of photographs of Berlin produced by the US Corridor missions, but the Americans soon found that the Lark Spur photography did far more than just complement their other imagery collection programmes. It was particularly useful in supporting technical intelligence reports. The operation started in 1968 using a single Cessna O-1 Bird Dog (L-19) aircraft, which was replaced early in the programme by the more capable De Havilland Canada U-6/L-20 (DHC-2 Beaver) that arrived in Berlin during 1958 and stayed until 1979. It, in turn, was replaced by two Pilatus UV-20A Chiricahua (Turbo Porter) that were used until the Detachment's disbandment in 1991. Lark Spur flights were conducted in a similar fashion to the BRIXMIS Chipmunk missions with the observers drawn from the USMLM, at least from the 1970s . 'Lark Spur' photography was exchanged with the French and British under the Tri-Mission agreement.

The Berlin Brigade Aviation Detachment started in 1951 when three Hiller OH-23 Raven helicopters began operations at Tempelhof as part of US 6 Infantry Regiment. Their primary task was mounting air patrols over Western Sectors of the city. They also supported British and French forces who, at that time, had no Berlin-based aviation assets. Although they could have legally flown throughout the BCZ, they confined themselves to the Western Sectors of the city. By 1958 Bell OH-13 Sioux and Sikorski H-19 Chickasaw's had arrived, replacing the OH-23s which eventually left in 1962. In the same year a single U-6/L-20 (DHC-2 Beaver) arrived, staying until retirement in 1979 and subsequently it was donated to the Berlin Transportation Museum in 1982.

The unit was renamed the 'US Berlin Brigade Aviation Detachment' in 1962 and remained so until its disbandment in 1994 when Allied forces left Berlin. It continued to support US Berlin Brigade and United States Command Berlin (USCOB) activities with helicopter patrols along the inner city border ('The Wall') and GDR border ('The Wire'). Between 1962 and 1964 the rotary-winged component had a short-lived acquaintance with the H-34 (Choctaw) until they were replaced by the ubiquitous Bell UH-1 (Huey) that served in various versions. The detachment's fixed-wing element included a Cessna O-1 (L-19) Bird Dog until 1975 when it was replaced by a Cessna O-2 that itself left in 1979. The twin-engined Beechcraft U-8 Seminole of the 1960s was succeeded by a Beech U-21, and superseded by a Beech C-12 from 1986 to 1991. Two Pilatus UV-20 Chiricahua (Turbo-Porters) were also flown from 1980 until 1991 when Project Lark Spur ceased.

In the summer of 1962, at the time of the second Berlin crisis, there were numerous complaints by the Soviets about US helicopter flights. One protest from the Chief Soviet Controller read:

> Today July 19, 1962 an American helicopter No. 640 which took off from Tempelhof airport at 0824Z, irrespective of the fact that the region of its flight was limited to West Berlin, flew over democratic Berlin and from the open door of the helicopter pictures of different objects of the GDR were taken.[35]

The American response reasserted the Western 'freedom of movement' and the intent to continue exercising it, but ignored the photography issue. By the end of the month the exchanges became much more heated after the Soviet Controller twice demanded that a US helicopter flight leave the area over Berlin-Karlshorst on 30 July. The record says that the Soviet Controller stated to the US Controller, 'If the American helicopter does not leave the area over the Soviet objectives [sic] in Karlhorst, he will be shot down.' The Chief American Controller's reply, 'Was that statement a protest or a threat?' to which the Soviet response was 'I will tell you later'.[36]

The following day more information became available from USCOB who reported that the flight over Berlin-Karlshorst had been undertaken 'at an altitude of 100ft in order to obtain the required photographs'. The British representative at 'Live Oak' expressed his personal opinion to US General Wheeler 'that the manner in which the flight was conducted was highly provocative and unnecessarily rude'.[37] A few weeks later USCINCEUR issued new instructions covering Berlin that set 1,000ft as the minimum altitude for helicopter flights, with altitudes down to 500ft permitted when overflying East Berlin in poor visibility or to keep them clear of airfield traffic patterns in the BCZ.[38]

The Stars and Stripes of August 1968 reflected on life in the Aviation Detachment and stated that although flights had been conducted on a 'regular basis since the late 1940s, they gained greater significance when The Wall was erected in 1961'.

In 1968 the detachment was flying six UH-1Bs, one Cessna O-1 Bird Dog and one Beech U-8D Seminole 'command plane' from the USAF's Tempelhof AB. The unit comprised eight officers and fourteen enlisted men who flew around 1,200 flying hours a year. Unless weather conditions prevented it, the detachment flew at least once per day, and once or twice a week it flew a longer flight covering the city's western sector borders in detail. A patrol crew consisted of a pilot, co-pilot and crew chief. For reconnaissance flights an observer from Brigade G2 (Intelligence) would be picked up at Andrews Barracks. Sometimes specific objectives would be briefed 'but generally we just keep our eyes open, trying to observe any changes to the border fortifications'.

Besides the patrols, the detachment would undertake troop lifts to support exercises and give border orientation flights to visitors, including French and British officials who, at the time, didn't have Berlin-based helicopters. Another important task was to resupply the US Army Military Police who guarded the Steinstücken enclave. The helicopters had to land on a tiny plot completely surrounded by East German territory and this led to occasional exchanges of 'repartee' with the Vopos (East German Police). CWO Eugene Kollar recalls that 'the Commies are so close they practically breathe down our necks'. 'One day he called "Good morning" to them and a Vopo replied in perfect English: "It isn't a very good morning in Vietnam."'[39]

A newly arrived pilot's priority was to become mission qualified on the UH-1, which usually took six to nine months. As well as being expected to operate effectively in the busy and heavily restricted Berlin airspace using 'Freedom City' call signs, pilots had to learn a detailed brief on Berlin and its history for the benefit of VIP passengers during 'historical overflights' of the city.

Later the unit's three fixed-wing aircraft were a Beech C-12 for inter-European transport and two remarkable, Swiss-built, Pilatus UV-20 Turbo-Porters, known as 'Chiricahua' in US military service. They arrived in 1980 and were subject to special modification including replacement of the two windows on the right side sliding door by a single, large, optically flat rectangular window to facilitate photography, although the aircraft probably frequently flew with the door open. In addition the right side exhaust nozzle of the Pratt & Whitney PT6A turboprop was extended downwards to deflect the hot exhaust gases, that could otherwise have blurred pictures taken through, it clear of the windows.

New crews followed the unit's own qualification course and because there was no Chiricahua simulator, pilots had to go to the Pilatus factory in Switzerland for currency training, where much of the deeper servicing work was also carried out. The UV-20 was popular with the ground crews because of its simplicity and robustness. The type was very adept at Short Take Off and Landing (STOL) manoeuvres, needing less than 1,000ft to take off; its 'party piece' was to land at very low speeds on the taxiway between Tempelhof's two main runways if strong crosswinds affected them.[40]

USCOB ran the Lark Spur collection programme, providing both the aircraft and staff. However, in 1974 Colonel Peter Thorsen, recently assigned as Chief, USMLM, managed to convince his commanders that USMLM officers should participate as observers in Lark Spur. Researcher Hugo Mambour gained a detailed insight on some of the Lark Spur operations interviewing former USMLM participants Nicholas Troyan and Thomas Spencer.

Troyan was involved from the very start of USMLM member involvement with Lark Spur, one of the initial pair of officers assigned to those duties. He said he was 'thrilled at having the opportunity to be an observer for Lark Spur'. He explained the extent of tri-national co-operation in BCZ flights:

> In 1975–76 there was little coordination with aerial missions flown by the British and the French – this was probably a consequence of Lark Spur programme being managed by USCOB instead of the USMLM. If one of their aircraft was seen over an area or a target, it was not appropriate to invade their airspace for security reasons, nor was it wise to unnecessarily disturb the Soviets or East Germans. However, everyone consulted each other when a target had a particular interest, the co-operation among the military liaison missions continuing into the air.

Lark Spur coverage of the BCZ was scheduled for every third day, weather permitting. Troyan explained that he flew with Sergeant First Class (SFC) St John, from the Berlin Brigade who was regarded as a 'true expert' having flown missions for a long time. Captain Troyan described flights in the Beaver:

> I do recall that the briefing that I received from SFC St John on the programme was that the aircraft could fly a 40-mile (64km) circle around Berlin, and had to maintain a 1,000-foot above ground level (AGL) ceiling. Sitting in the co-pilot seat of the aircraft, I noticed that it was very difficult to observe, let alone achieve a clear photo, through the front triangular window of the aircraft. SFC St John sat in the rear, and had a larger window; however, it also limited his ability to take very clear shots. In my 'youthful exuberance,' I asked the pilot to remove the right door from the aircraft. After finding out that the 'Sovs' did not have, or did not use, height-finding radar against our programme, I had the pilot fly lower than the 1,000ft AGL required. This, plus the opening with the door removed, allowed both the person in the co-pilot seat and rear-seat occupant to get much clearer shots of activities on the ground. On one of our flights, as we approached the Dallgow-Döberitz barracks area, we saw what appeared to be the entire tank regiment that had apparently just returned from manoeuvres lined up in front of the vehicle wash ramps. SFC St John and I also noticed what appeared to be a new version of a BMP armoured personnel carrier. At that moment, I asked the pilot to let me take the 'control yoke.'
>
> 'I made a hard right bank, relinquished control back to the pilot, and began photographing the equipment around the wash ramp. At that time, I heard SFC St John tell me over the intercom that a lens he was changing on his camera had slipped from his hand during my hard banking of the craft, and he thought it had fallen on top of the 'Sovs'. He also said we should immediately head back to report this occurrence to HQ. I saw that most of the 'Sovs' around the wash ramps were pointing up at us, some with their AKs. However, this was not unusual, since any time we flew over their installations, the 'Sovs' and East Germans would point at us, some would wave, some shook their fists, and some pointed their weapons.

He added that he believed the Soviets protested to Henry Kissinger via the Soviet Ambassador about the 'bombing' as they called it, but because British and/or French aircraft also arrived overhead the same barracks at the same time it was difficult to definitively verify 'who had dropped what on the Soviet wash ramp.' Indeed this event passed into the folklore of the three allied missions told and retold many times.

When we returned to USMLM and I reported to Colonel Thorsen, his first reaction was: 'Troyan, you again, I hope you have your bags packed,' or words to that effect; however, SFC St John saved my hide by saying that it was he who dropped the lens. At this point then, Colonel Thorsen became very gracious to SFC St John, stating that, after all the time he had been running this programme, the odds that an unforeseen event would occur was only natural. He told me to accompany SFC St John to Berlin Brigade and pass on to Colonel Baker, the Berlin Brigade Deputy Chief of Staff for Intelligence, not be too hard on SFC St John. He also ordered me to come up with a Standard Operating Procedure that would ensure that all 'lens swapping would be done inside the flight bag, which would be secured to the aircraft seat'.

Another participant, Major Thomas Spencer, explained how he became involved in the programme:

In 1975, a Lark Spur observer position become available and I volunteered to extend my tour at USMLM for one year if I could be the USMLM Lark Spur programme officer. I had undergone pilot training earlier and I knew my two years of ground touring in East Germany had prepared me well for equipment identification, map reading, and the like. Two previous USMLM officers, who worked part-time on Lark Spur, had proven that the combination of proficient USMLM officers, with their equipment identification skills and local area familiarity enhanced that programme. USCOB owned the Lark Spur programme and its assets (planes and people) and realized that USMLM augmentation made for a more effective intelligence collection effort. This was a real win-win for the American intelligence aerial collection efforts within the BCZ.

When his request was approved he became the first full-time USMLM Lark Spur Officer:

A Berlin Brigade NCO, Staff Sgt St John, and I flew as aircraft crewmen out of Templehof Airfield. We both studied extant Specific Intelligence Collection Requirements that were submitted by various governmental agencies to guide us in our collection efforts, but also never missed an opportunity for targets of opportunity.

During our missions, we wore fire-retardant Nomex flight suits with no insignia to provide some superficial masking of our identities. We did carry our military identification cards in case of having to land in East Germany. In actuality, we were pretty certain that the Soviets and East Germans knew what those aboard the Lark Spur aircraft were doing. It sometimes felt ridiculous knowing that the only people who really didn't know the Lark Spur programme existed were our own American people. But those were some of the games played during the Cold War.

He continued:

> Our aircraft were always outside the hangars so we carried our camera equipment in
> our aircraft helmet bags from the hangars to the aircraft and usually wore our helmets
> walking to the aircraft. As a photography lover, it was a privilege to have photographic
> equipment that I personally could not afford. We used Nikon F camera bodies, with
> or without motor drives, 50mm, 135mm, 500mm, and 1,000mm lenses, plus unlim-
> ited amounts of Kodak Tri-X black and white and Ektachrome colour film. Our
> onsite USMLM photo-processing laboratory completed the job and we could get
> film developed within hours in a rush. USMLM's wide range of camera equipment,
> and especially our quick turnaround photographic laboratory, plus the experienced
> USMLM officers, who were quick at military equipment identification, may well
> have been the deciding factors for USCOB agreeing to our joint LARKSPUR oper-
> ations and reports but USCOB retained programme 'ownership' and got first credit
> for outstanding reports. However, overall results were much better, more responsive,
> and we produced a very large number of Intelligence Information Reports (IIR) that
> helped greatly in satisfying the American intelligence community's requirements.
>
> We removed the Beaver's upper trapezoidal windows from the rear doors for
> several reasons. First, there was a firm mandate to minimize dropping any equip-
> ment from the aircraft while doing our 'wing over' at 45-degree-plus angles as we
> circled over targets for the best shots. Typically, SFC St John and I sat in the back,
> each looking out one side for designated targets that had outstanding intelligence
> requirements from the myriad of intelligence agencies, plus always seeking targets
> of opportunity. Generally, the Soviets and East Germans paid little attention to us;
> however, if we did experience any signs of hostility, we took it as an indicator that
> we might be observing new equipment or something out of the ordinary. This usu-
> ally just doubled our interest. On such occasions, if we had an adventurous pilot,
> we would ask for a 'wing over.' Aerodynamics being what they are, this manoeuvre
> resulted in the aircraft spiralling down in altitude and we would 'accidently' slip
> below the 1,000ft AGL we were supposed to maintain.

Major Spencer explained the outcomes:

> This resulted in much closer photos that were hand-focused at 1000 AGL (no auto-
> matic focus cameras were available in the 1970s). One had to concentrate, because
> the 500mm and 1,000mm lens on the Nikon F motor-driven body could eat up the
> 36 frames of a Tri-X 35mm film in a very few seconds. By putting the wing over and
> circling a target, we were able to capture many pictures of the same subject, which
> could then be viewed by special optics that yielded three-dimensional views and
> provided intelligence analysts with more information. We even were able to look
> down into the interior of targets such as tanks, self-propelled artillery, and armoured
> personnel carriers. The aircraft transponder, which sent our position and altitude to
> Berlin air traffic controllers, sometimes 'accidently' failed to work on such occasions

and the pilots would receive a radio call notifying him that they had lost contact with us. It was always interesting that the transponder would magically come to life again when we reached 1,000ft AGL. The full-frame, better-quality pictures sometimes resulted in questions from Colonel Thorsen as to how we were able to obtain such great pictures at 1,000ft AGL. (I don't remember Sgt St John's superiors ever asking that question.) My response to our commander Colonel Thorsen was that it was just the effect of flying at 1,000ft AGL using a 1,000mm lens that makes it look like you are only one-foot away. He would only smile, shake his head, and walk away. He had been a military attaché in Warsaw, so knew very well that attachés and USMLM Air and Ground tour officers sometime took chances in order to succeed. And, sometimes it just was the better part of valour to not tell all.

There were several intelligence-gathering advantages to the Lark Spur programme. Primarily, our aerial photographs presented equipment in a totally different perspective and provided details for analysts that satellites at the time could not obtain. They supplemented any ground-level views and gave a fuller picture of capabilities. Secondly, we enjoyed relative safety as compared to being detained, run off roads, assaulted, and especially being shot at by the Soviets and East Germans. However, it was not unusual to have weapons pointed at us and, more frequently, flare guns fired at the aircraft. The pilots had complete freedom to fly the plane as necessary to avoid flares, other aircraft, and so on. This allowed Sgt St John and me, as aircraft crewmen observers and photographers, to concentrate on our targets. After flying missions in the 'ring' for several months, we were able to discern patterns of behaviour such as what days training took place and where, what days were wash days, maintenance days, and inspection days, and so forth. Understanding these patterns helped guide us in our collection efforts. Our observations also enabled us to provide subjective comments and personal analysis of activities, tactics, and training that a desk analyst could not do as well as someone who actually had eyes on the target.

Then Army Captain Tim Bloechl ran the programme from August 1984 to December 1986 as the Reconnaissance and Surveillance Officer for the Office of the Deputy Chief of Staff, Intelligence (ODCSI). He described flying in the UV-20A:

The aerial view of Soviet and East German facilities also provided a perspective of the difference between these forces. Soviet garrisons were often untidy and poorly maintained. Indeed, when one flew over the aircraft hangars at Oranienburg, you could look through the holes in the roof to count the helicopters housed inside. Trash was everywhere. On the other hand, the East German barracks were very well maintained. One could sense a higher degree of discipline and morale within the East German forces.

Periodically USMLM officers would go on missions with us to check areas they were thinking about checking out the next day on the ground. On another occasion, in December of 1985 if I recall correctly, while in the vicinity of Oranienburg Airfield, three Soviet helicopters tried to interfere with our flight and it appeared to the pilot and crew members this was an attempt to force the plane down. So the plane left the area for a time, but when the crew felt the coast was clear, went right back to the airfield to see what they might be hiding. Our higher HQs was not very happy that they did so!

Otherwise, we largely conducted each mission without incident. Our biggest challenge was usually weather. Low cloud ceilings and reduced visibility, particularly in the winter months, caused many mission cancellations. Also during the winter, it got awfully cold with the side door open on the plane!

Describing the altitudes at which the aircraft operated then he said:

> The flight altitude was routinely 1,000ft (But when deemed important to mission execution, we flew below 1,000ft to as low as 500ft for short periods) and 3,000ft over the airfields. The MiGs used to routinely buzz us to mess with us. We sat sideways in the plane and opening the door – left to right – to hang out and take pictures.[41]

An article from the US Army publication Soldiers in 1990 illustrates the rapidly changing situation in Berlin following The Wall's collapse. The detachment now had six UH-1Hs and had three main tasks: providing priority air transport for US, British and French military personnel as well as US and West German government officials; conducting 'special air missions as directed by the Deputy Chief of Staff for Intelligence'; and providing support to the US Berlin Brigade's three infantry battalions. The unit establishment was some twenty-one soldiers and sixteen civilians, several of the latter being German mechanics responsible for unit-level maintenance and technical inspections, together with the US Army enlisted crew chiefs. The ten pilots were rated to fly both helicopters and fixed-wing aircraft. The two UV-20As left in August 1991 as US activities in the city wound down.

French Light Aircraft and Helicopter Flights in the BCZ

French photographic flights over the BCZ started around 1960 using a single Cessna L-19E Bird Dog detached from the Platoon Aviation Légère de l'Armée de Terre de Commandant Chef de Forces Français en Allemange (Pl ALAT CC FFA). The aircraft was flown by ALAT pilots detached from Baden-Baden and Armée de l'Air (AdlA) pilots on the MMFL's strength. Army and Air Force observers, of all ranks, were drawn from the MMFL. A Berlin detachment of Pl ALAT CC FFA formed at Berlin-Tegel on 1 August 1968 following the arrival of a second L-19. The L-19s were small and their tandem seating arrangement was far from ideal for photographic operations because the narrow cabin gave the observer very little manoeuvring room to use the large 400mm lenses, but provided the MMFL with an airborne photographic reconnaissance capability. The L-19s continued in service until 1993, close to the end of French operations in the city.[41] The ALAT CC FFA title was used from 19 June 1969 until 1 September 1978 when it became the Liaison Squadron: 1 Army which itself disbanded on 31 May 1987.

In May 1987 two SE3160 Alouette III light helicopters were detached from 12 Groupe d'Hélicoptères Légères (12 GHL) to provide security for a Berlin state visit by French President François Mitterrand. After the visit they remained in the city and continued operations within the Western Sectors until 1990. The two ALAT detachments at Berlin-Tegel were combined on 1 July 1989 to become the Détachment Aviation Légère de l'Armée de Terre Berlin (DETALAT BERLIN), subordinated to the Commandant of the Forces Français en Berlin (FFB). The combined detachment had two L-19Es that left Berlin on 21 April 1993 and the two Alouette IIIs departed on 30 June 1994.

The ALAT L-19s were supplemented by Armée de l'Air (AdlA) Max-Holste MH-1521M Broussards based at Berlin-Tegel. These were flown by AdlA pilots on MMFL's strength, in a similar way to the British use of their Chipmunks, to maintain their pilots' qualifications as an overt justification for their presence. Observers were Army and Air Force officers, or NCOs, from the MMFL. The Broussard, being a larger aircraft, could carry up to six people in its cabin, which significantly improved the observation capabilities. The Broussard was replaced in 1988 by a De Havilland Canada DHC-6–300 Twin Otter which left in 1990 when the MMFL ceased operations.

French flights in the BCZ were conducted in a similar manner to those of the other Allies. However, the French pushed the boundaries by using 'technical' flights to return aircraft to France for maintenance as an excuse for additional intelligence collection. Peter Jefferies recalls a flight in late 1969 when the French flew down the Centre Corridor, during which they took photographs and circled Soviet installations, in a similar fashion to a BCZ mission. Flights down the Centre Corridor allowed observation of several significant targets that were in PRAs, such as the Letzlinger Heide major training area and Mahlwinkel helicopter base. The flight attracted a very robust Soviet response. The French were very lucky that the aircraft was not engaged because nearly all Soviet installations outside the BCZ had active air defence sites in close proximity to them. They were certainly not used to seeing strange light aircraft manoeuvring at low level.

Although there is no definitive evidence, Peter believes that subsequent French flights along the Centre Corridor were non-photographic because he never saw further photographs from these 'technical' flights. The French possibly decided that any photographs taken by these flights fell outside the Tri-Mission exchange agreement, so perhaps kept them to themselves. Following the Soviet protest to the 1969 flight, the French modified their procedures. Subsequent 'technical' flights required the aircraft to fly directly to West Germany without orbiting any Soviet installations en route, so these flights were probably confined to visual reconnaissance.

A 1975 British report gives an example of French procedure. On 12 June the French posted a VFR flight plan down the Centre Corridor at below 2,500ft. The Soviet Controller raised the standard objection to Allied flights below that level, whilst the British and French maintained that in order to stay VFR and avoid cloud they might have to fly below 2,500ft. The exchange ended with the Soviet Controller stating that 'in view of the fact that you are planning an unauthorised flight level that may bring about a dangerous situation in the air, I do not guarantee the safety of its flight'.[43]

He stamped the BASC flight card accordingly. Flying without radio or IFF contact, the aircraft flew along the Centre Corridor and landed at Braunschweig (Brunswick), and the crew informed the BASC French Controller that they had exited the Corridor.

The DETALAT BERLIN's main role was helicopter surveillance of The Wall and The Wire and the installations close to them from within the Western Sectors. The fixed-wing element often ventured beyond the city boundaries into the BCZ. After the MMFL stood down in September 1990, DETALAT BERLIN provided a local photographic reconnaissance capability to the FFB, tasked by the 2ème Bureau at HQ FFB. In 1991 the German authorities opened up the airspace between the north boundary of the North Corridor and the south boundary of the Southern Corridor to military aircraft. Unlike the British and Americans, the French took full advantage of this airspace liberalisation. They had a cavalier approach to this 'restriction' and allowed the Alouettes to roam at will both inside and outside the designated airspace on photographic sorties. Images 36 and 37 were taken by DETALAT in 1993 and 1994 of Mahlwinkel and at Welzow, which was well outside the designated area. A YouTube video of the Soviet farewell parade and Open Day at Sperenberg on 27 May 1994 shows it being overflown by a DETALAT Alouette III.[44]

Conclusions

The Allied light aircraft and helicopter photographic operations in the BCZ provided close-up photographs of equipment that contributed to the technical intelligence effort; images of vehicle groupings in barracks helped to establish parking patterns and shed occupancy and they were a prime source of turret/side numbers that helped establish unit organisations. They were an important adjunct to tri-national AMLM work close to the city, each significantly complementing the other's work. Combined with the Corridor imagery programmes they were a core element of the Western PHOTINT effort in Germany.

Notes

1 The National Archive: PRO DEFE 71/128. Allied Control Authority, Air Directorate, Flight Rules for Aircraft Flying in Air Corridors in Germany and Berlin Control Zone. Section 1, para 3c, 22 October 1946.
2 The National Archive: PRO AIR 2/18561 Memo HQ British Forces Germany to MoD London, 30 October 1962.
3 Email from Hans Neubroch to Peter Jefferies, 1 May 2014.
4 The operation had numerous code words, including Eldorado, Philaria, Schooner, Medius, Farnborough, Nylon and Oberon.
5 David Cockburn in K. Wright (2009), p. 68.
6 The National Archive: PRO PREM 11/3698 – minute from Chairman JIC (Sir Norman Brook) to PM, 30 May 1961, and PM's approval of flights, 1 June 1961.
7 The National Archive: PRO AIR 2/18561 (RAFG/TS.1247/Ops, 17 Jul 1962).
8 The National Archive: PRO PREM 11/3698 minute to PM, 20 February 1962.

9 The National Archive: PRO PREM 11/3698 minute to PM, 24 April 1962.

10 Telephone conversation between Peter Jefferies and Roy Marsden, 27 April 2006.

11 Email from Hans Neubroch to Peter Jefferies, 19 April 2014.

12 The National Archive PRO AIR 2/18561 RAFG/TS.1247/OPS, 17 July 1962.

13 Telephone conversation between Francis Bacon and Peter Jefferies, 8 May 2014.

14 The National Archive: PRO PREM 11/3698 Memo from Chairman JIC to Prime Minister, 18 December 1961.

15 Email from Bob Hamilton to Peter Jefferies, 23 March 2012.

16 R. Marsden (1998), 'Operation "Schooner/Nylon": RAF flying in the Berlin Control Zone', *Intelligence and National Security*, Vol. 1, No. 4, p. 181.

17 T. Geraghty (1997), *BRIXMIS: The Untold Exploits of Britain's Most Daring Cold War Spy Mission* (London: Harper Collins), p. 90.

18 Marsden (1998), p. 181.

19 R. Bates (2001), 'BRIXMIS: History and Roles', *RAF Historical Society Journal*, No. 23, p. 19.

20 Marsden (1998), p. 190.

21 David Cockburn in conversation with Peter Jefferies, and Wright (2009), p. 69.

22 Marsden (1998), p. 191.

23 Ibid., p. 189.

24 Ibid., p. 186.

25 Ibid.

26 Email from Bob Hamilton to Peter Jefferies, 23 March 2012.

27 David Cockburn in conversation with P. Jefferies, and Wright (2009), p. 69.

28 Marsden (1998), p. 187.

29 Ibid., p. 191.

30 A. Pennington (2010), 'BRIXMIS & The Corridor', *Medmenham Club Newsletter*, p. 23.

31 P. Williams (2006), *Brixmis in the 1980s: The Cold War's 'Great Game' – Memories of Liaising with the Soviet Army in East Germany*, Parallel History Project on Cooperative Security (PHP), p. 23.

32 D. Cockburn, personal memories of BRIXMIS (unpublished), 9 September 2012.

33 The National Archive: AIR 28/2016, *RAF Gatow ORB*, August 1956.

34 Memo for Director of Central Intelligence from Deputy Director Intelligence, *JRC Monthly Reconnaissance Schedule for January 1968*, 2 January 1968.

35 The National Archive: PRO FO371/163670, Telegram 639, Gen. Dunbar to Foreign Office, 19 July 1962.

36 The National Archive: PRO FO371/163670, Telegram 657, Gen. Dunbar to Foreign Office, 30 July 1962.

37 The National Archive: PRO FO371/163670, LOUK 75, LIVE OAK to USCOB Berlin, 31 July 1962.

38 The National Archive: PRO FO371/163670, LOUK 80, LIVE OAK to USCOB Berlin, 15 August 1962.

39 P. Kuhrt (1968), 'Looking Down on Berlin's Wall', *Stars and Stripes*, 11 August.

40 S. Harding (1990), 'Freedom City Flyers', *Soldiers*, Vol. 45, No. 22, pp. 42–4.

41 H. Mambour: http://www.16va.be/vols_mmfl_part1_eng2.html.

42 Thanks to Hugo Mambour: http://www.6va.be/operation_larkspur_part1_eng.html and http://www.16va.be/operation_larkspur_part2_eng.html (Accessed 14 September 2016).

43 The National Archive: PRO DEFE 71/8, British Element BASC to Deputy Political Adviser to BMG Berlin, 13 June 1975.

44 http://www.youtube.com/watch?v=MhaThUN-WZc from 36 seconds to 52 seconds.

Exploiting the Imagery: Units, Methodologies and Reports

The British and Allied photographic operations in the Air Corridors and BCZ presented the Allied intelligence community with an incredible opportunity. They provided almost daily cover of GSFG and NVA troops in this most forward of areas that were often the most fully manned and best prepared of the Red Army. They frequently received the latest equipment and would have been the vanguard of any Soviet attack on NATO. They were kept at high states of preparedness with armoured vehicles at battle readiness, fully fuelled and with ammunition preloaded. Similarly, logistic vehicles were kept loaded with fuel and ammunition ready to deploy directly into the field without having to pass through static logistic facilities for loading.

This high state of readiness meant that the Allied intelligence community needed early warning of any changes to a unit's posture, organisation, equipment and location. Such changes could have been an indicator of an increased state of alert and, perhaps, hostile intentions. The coverage provided by the Corridor and BCZ photographic flights was a major element in determining Soviet and East German military intentions and tracking force developments. To extract the maximum intelligence from the flights' products, acquired at considerable risk to the aircraft's crews, required well-trained, skilled personnel backed by an effective organisation to manage the huge quantities of imagery and data they generated.

British and US Photographic Intelligence and Interpretation Units

The British and Americans possessed a worldwide network of processing and photographic intelligence units, covering tactical and theatre-specific requirements. Additional home-based units also looked at the output from all the overseas units, including Germany. In Germany, the British and Americans each had a major presence devoted to film processing and interpretation.

British Photographic and Photographic Interpretation Units in Germany

The Army's theatre-level PI unit in Germany started as the 21st Army Group Photographic Interpretation Unit (21 AGPIU), formed in 1943, to support Montgomery's HQ 21st Army Group (HQ 21AG) for the 1944 invasion of Europe. At the end of the Second World War in May 1945, it was based in the spa town of Bad Oeynhausen near Hannover. One PI officer from 21 AGPIU was deployed as a liaison officer to the Headquarters British Air Forces of Occupation (HQ BAFO) in the nearby spa town of Bad Eilsen. On 25 August 1945 HQ 21AG became Headquarters British Army of the Rhine (HQ BAOR), the British Army Headquarters in Germany until the end of the Cold War. As a result 21 AGPIU was renamed Army Photographic Interpretation Unit (British Army of the Rhine) (APIU (BAOR)), which title it retained until 1960. It moved from Bad Oeynhausen in late 1946/early 1947 to Bad Eilsen to co-locate with the RAF PIs at HQ BAFO as part of the short-lived Joint Air Photographic Interpretation Centre (Germany) (JAPIC (G)). Although designated as a joint service unit, both APIU (BAOR) and the RAF's Photographic Interpretation Detachment (PID) retained a high degree of individual autonomy.

At the end of the Second World War the majority of RAF PIs were attached to various tactical reconnaissance squadrons at RAF bases in Germany and the Low Countries. In July 1945 HQ 2TAF was redesignated HQ BAFO and together with the retitled PID BAFO was housed in the commandeered Bade Hotel and other buildings in Bad Eilsen. In 1947 PID BAFO was subsumed into the JAPIC (G). The rationale behind JAPIC (G) was to bring the Army and RAF theatre-level PI units into a single joint command structure, in a similar manner to the other British theatre-level PI units around the world. JAPIC (G) also had an outstation at RAF Bückeburg where 3 Photographic Reproduction Section (3 PRS) was responsible for camera maintenance and print production alongside the Bückeberg-based element of 4 Mobile Field Photographic Unit (4 MFPU). Throughout the Cold War there were regular proposals to either resurrect JAPIC (G) or form a Joint Air Reconnaissance Intelligence Centre (Germany) (JARIC (G)), in common with the JARICs in other UK theatres, but the balance of opinion was that the co-located single-service units with shared infrastructure worked well – a case of 'if it ain't broke, don't fix it'.

During the 1945 to 1954 period the various Mobile Field Photographic Sections (MFPS) and Mobile Field Photographic Units (MFPU) attached to RAF tactical reconnaissance squadrons were responsible for the bulk processing of film and production of photographic prints. The mobile element of 4 MFPS/MFPU at Bückeburg supported II (AC) Squadron and the Corridor flights carried out by the co-located Command Communications Squadron. The static section was co-located with HQ BAFO to provide second and third phase photographic support to the HQ and the PI units.

In 1954, following German pressure to vacate the two spa towns, the two headquarters together with their associated photographic and PI units, moved to the purpose-built Joint Headquarters (JHQ) complex at Rheindahlen, just outside Mönchengladbach, close to the Dutch–German border. The site housed not only HQ BAOR and HQ 2TAF but also the two NATO commands of Northern Army Group (NORTHAG) and 2nd Allied Tactical Air Force (2ATAF).

There was a seminal change to Army PI in 1956 when the Intelligence Corps assumed the responsibility for the provision of Army PIs. This brought some organisational and command changes, with the creation of the Theatre Intelligence Unit (TINTU) responsible for operational intelligence and security matters, which was administered by Headquarters Intelligence Corps (British Army of the Rhine) (HQ INT CORPS (BAOR)). Under this regrouping APIU (BAOR) changed to Photographic Interpretation Company (Theatre Intelligence Unit) (PI Coy (TINTU)) in 1960 and by 1962 PI Coy (TINTU) had been renamed Photographic Interpretation Company (British Army of the Rhine) (PI Coy (BAOR)). Following the adoption of the Intelligence Group concept in 1965 the group's subordinate companies were numbered and PI Coy (BAOR) became 6 (Photographic Interpretation) Company (6 (PI) Coy).

During the 1950s and 1960s the RAF's PID was a large organisation with some fifteen to twenty PIs and ten support staff of all ranks and both sexes. In the mid 1960s the unit was reduced to seven PIs and a similar number of support staff, coinciding with the arrival of viable reconnaissance satellite imagery that gave the RAF the wider view it needed to assess the totality of the Soviet air threat from mainland Russia and other Warsaw Pact states. This saw Germany's importance in assessing this wider threat reduced, so the scarce resources were redeployed to exploit this new material. In January 1959 HQ 2TAF became Headquarters Royal Air Force Germany (2nd Tactical Air Force) (HQ RAFG (2TAF)) and so PID 2TAF became PID RAFG, a title it retained until the end of the Corridor operations in 1990.

There were major changes to the reporting emphasis of PI units too, moving from simply recording all equipment seen at an installation to the detailed analysis of it. This sometimes utilised material from other intelligence sources as well to produce assessed intelligence, (rather than just raw information), with the resulting product called Photographic Intelligence. This prompted yet another name change for the Army PI unit with 6 (PI) Coy becoming 6 Intelligence Company (Photographic Intelligence) (6 Int Coy (PI)) in 1970. The unit's name changed to 6 Intelligence Company (6 Int Coy) in 1974 to conform with other companies in the group and continued in being until 1 Military Intelligence Battalion (1 MI Bn) formed in 1992.

Until the early 1970s the Army PI unit was organised into a PI section and a Support Section. Tasks were passed to either individual PIs, or ad hoc sections, formed to fulfil a specific task. From the late 1960s until 1990, the predominant role was analytical reporting and to meet this requirement the unit consisted of five subsections covering Current and Immediate Reporting (First and Second Phase); Longer-Term Detailed Analysis and Special Studies; Technical Intelligence; Graphics Support; and Clerical Support. In the 1980s a Computer Development Section was added to design and introduce the Double Vision (DV) Information Technology (IT) system into the unit.

4 MFPU became the Photographic Reproduction Unit RAFG (PRU RAFG) but this didn't change the unit's responsibilities, although it more accurately reflected the unit's static status.

The Units' Roles

Throughout the Cold War the roles of the eventual PRU RAFG did not radically change. It was responsible for the bulk processing and printing of film produced by the Corridor and BCZ missions and other aerial reconnaissance activities over West Germany, ground photography and report printing.

In the immediate post-war period the responsibility of both PI units was to co-ordinate the photographing of the whole BOZ as part of the wider Allied programme to cover all the Western occupation zones. This enabled the existing obsolete mapping to be updated and helped to assess the resources required for German economic reconstruction. Photographic reconnaissance of the Soviet Occupied Zone (SOZ) started on a sporadic basis in 1945 with British material being exploited at Bad Eilsen. Other tasks included providing air photographic support to Army field exercises and other peace-time photographic tasks. Originally an Army responsibility, this was later transferred to PID, which maintained the library of current air photography of West Germany.

As the quantity of aerial photography from the Corridors and BCZ grew and the extent of the Soviet threat became apparent, the primary role of both units swung towards the exploitation of material from these missions and the dissemination of the resultant intelligence to the Allied intelligence community. Both the British PI units were peacetime-only and would have ceased to exist in the event of hostilities. During the Transition to War (TTW) period they would continue to exploit mate-rial from the Corridor and BCZ operations until flights halted. The units' personnel would then be deployed to either staff appointments in HQ NORTHAG, HQ 2ATAF and HQ 1(BR) Corps, or to the RAF's Germany-based tactical reconnais-sance squadrons and Royal Artillery Drone Troops. The UK-based Territorial Army (TA) and Royal Air Force Volunteer Reserve (RAFVR) personnel would also have provided reinforcements to these units to bring them up to their wartime strengths.

Besides the Regular PIs based in Germany, two other groups exploited Corridor and BCZ material. They were the TA personnel of 21 Intelligence Company (Volunteers) (21 Int Coy (V)) TA and the RAFVR personnel belonging to 7010 Flight RAFVR (7010 Flt RAFVR). Each section consisted of about twelve of the more experienced PIs who used their training weekends with JARIC at RAF Brampton in Cambridgeshire to exploit selected imagery. During their fourteen-day annual con-tinuation training period ('annual camps'), in Germany they did similar work. The Army section was known as 'The JARIC Team' and was established in the mid 1970s with the RAFVR's 'PID RAFG Section' formed in the mid 1980s.

Because of the limited time available to them, the reserve sections were given tasks lower down the exploitation priorities list that were less time constrained than others.

It is fashionable now to talk of 'one Army' and 'one Air Force' integrating Reserve with Regular Forces. The British intelligence community was clearly ahead of the game. The contribution made by those Reserve Forces personnel during live Cold War operations must be acknowledged. In fact, the valuable reports they produced might never have been written because the Regular PIs faced more pressing priorities.

United States Photographic and Photographic Interpretation Units in Germany

Until 1951 the US Germany-based photographic and PI units centred on Fürth-based 10 RG. They exploited material produced by the 45 RS split between Fürth and Fürstenfeldbruck and that from the 10 PCS at Fürth too. Both units flew missions over the SOZ in the Berlin Air Corridors and the BCZ.

As the Soviet threat increased, the emphasis of USAFE activities moved towards war preparation. The 497th Reconnaissance Technical Squadron (497 RTS) formed at Wiesbaden AB in May 1951 with a complement of twenty-four officers and 194 enlisted personnel. Its role was to provide processing, production, detailed photographic interpretation and the compilation and reproduction of aeronautical charts and related products for USAFE. Between July 1951 and January 1952 the 497 RTS was based at Shaw AFB in South Carolina, but returned to Wiesbaden to occupy the Schierstein Kaserne, later Schierstein Compound, to provide a central photographic processing and interpretation capability. In October 1967 it became the 497th Reconnaissance Technical Group (497 RTG) as its wider responsibilities increased. It remained at Wiesbaden until 1991 when it moved to RAF Molesworth in Cambridgeshire, UK, to become part of the Joint Analysis Centre (JAC).

The unit was initially manned by USAF personnel, but it gradually became joint service in all but name, with men and women of all four US services (Army, Navy, Marine Corps and Air Force) working as an integrated team. Over time its area of interest expanded beyond Germany to cover an area from the Baltic to the Black Sea and later the Mediterranean as USAFE responsibilities grew. One of its main tasks was providing immediate exploitation reports from US-origin photography taken in the Corridors and BCZ. These and other operations generated a prodigious quantity of imagery. Therefore the 497 RTS/RTG undertook relatively little analytical reporting and concentrated on providing raw data to support deeper analysis by other agencies, often outside Germany. Crises outside Europe in the Middle East and Africa made many calls on the unit's capabilities. This included supporting the British government during the Kuwait Crisis of 1961 when Iraq threatened to occupy Kuwait. By 1967 the unit's complement had increased to 73 officers, 296 enlisted personnel and 23 civilians.

In the 1980s and 1990s the unit provided imagery intelligence to support many other operations and crises, including analysis of the 1986 Chernobyl nuclear power plant accident, the bombing of Libya by UK-based USAF aircraft (Eldorado Canyon) in 1986, operations connected with the run up to and execution of the 1990–91 Gulf War (Desert Shield and Desert Storm), and evacuations of US and Allied nationals from Liberia, Zaire and Turkey.

In the mid-to-late 1950s the US Army had a small PI section co-located with the 7499 SG at Wiesbaden AB called Detachment 'B' (Provisional) of the 513th Military Intelligence Company (513 MI Coy) based at Oberursel. This small detachment of nine people (two officers, one NCO and about six enlisted personnel) exploited imagery taken in the Central and Southern Corridors under Project Red Owl, and occasionally Hot Pepper, for five and a half days each week. They reported on the types and numbers of equipment at the various locations. Their reports were sent

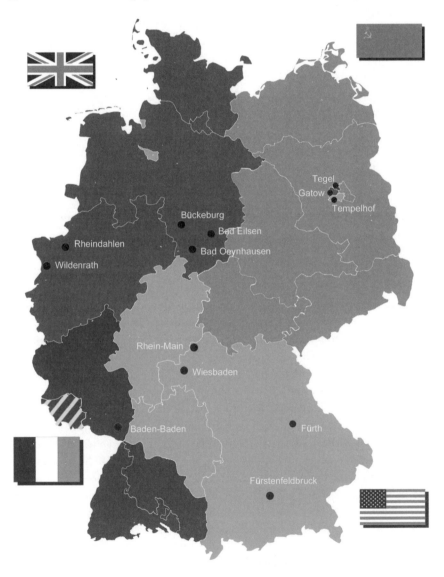

This map shows the historical operating locations of British, French and US HQs and PI units in Germany. By the 1960s US operations were largely centred on Rhein-Main and Wiesbaden and British ones on Wildenrath and Rheindahlen. (Wikimedia Commons)

to the Ground Liaison Office (GLO) at HQ USAFE and thence by courier to HQ USAREUR at Heidelberg.

The other US Army PI unit supported Headquarters United States Army Europe (HQ USAREUR) based at Coleman Barracks, Heidelberg. Like its British counterparts, the US Army PI effort in Germany was dispersed amongst various formations. In 1965 these personnel were combined to form the 2nd Military Intelligence Battalion (Air Reconnaissance Support) (2 MIBARS) that dealt with all aerial reconnaissance matters within USAREUR. 2 MIBARS was subordinated to the Office of the Deputy Chief of Staff Intelligence (ODCSI) at HQ USAREUR. It produced analytical reports by exploiting photography of the Warsaw Pact forces facing the US Army's V and VII Corps.

Extracting the Intelligence

To extract the maximum intelligence from imagery obtained required skilled people – photographers and PIs who are frequently the unsung heroes of these operations.

Photographic Training and Employment

RAF photographers processing film from photographic missions were mainly non-commissioned personnel, with commissioned photographic engineering officers providing technical and management expertise. They were trained at the RAF School of Photography in all aspects of wet film photography from using hand-held cameras, techniques associated with bulk film and print processing to aircraft camera installation and maintenance. Not for them the luxury of digital manipulation that is the stock in trade for the modern Image Analysts, but instead long hours using chemicals in dark rooms to produce the best-quality imagery for the PIs. The RAF photographer was a multi-skilled, flexible individual, who could be employed on almost any photographic task. For example, on a tour an RAF photographer could be involved in public relations, covering VIP visits one moment and then be part of the team involved in rapid film processing supporting tactical reconnaissance missions.

US photographers went through similar training but they were not as flexible as the British. John Webber, a former RAF warrant officer photographer, recalls that US personnel were very much part of a 'one man, one job' philosophy. This meant that an equipment operator was not easily redeployable to use another piece of equipment without additional training. Although this may seem inflexible to British eyes, the US personnel were often more experienced on individual pieces of equipment and so more aware of its particular capabilities and idiosyncrasies.

Photographic Interpreter Selection, Training and Employment

Throughout the Cold War there was never a time when PIs were not fully employed. Until the mid 1950s the Army and RAF trained only commissioned officers as PIs, but as the amount of material produced by the various worldwide operations grew, there

were insufficient commissioned PIs to meet the demand. As general population educa-
tion levels improved, the decision was finally taken to train non-commissioned ranks
as PIs. The effect of this change was somewhat blunted initially because only senior
non-commissioned officers (SNCOs) were accepted for training. By the early twenty-
first century the growth of imagery-producing systems with multi-spectral outputs,
some deployed in direct support of combat troops, led to junior non-commissioned
officers (JNCO) being trained as Image Analysts (IAs) as PIs were retitled.

Before 1956 Army PIs were an eclectic mix of commissioned officers from all
parts of the Army (e.g. infantry, armour and artillery, etc.) including the Intelligence
Corps (INT CORPS). During the Second World War there had been some NCO
PIs but this practice was soon discontinued. In 1956 the Intelligence Corps was made
responsible for the recruiting, training and provision of all male Army PIs and at
the same time started training selected SNCOs for PI duties. Following this change,
non-Intelligence Corps personnel in PI posts were offered the opportunity either
to transfer into the Intelligence Corps, or to remain in post until they retired or
were replaced by Intelligence Corps personnel. Female Army PIs were commissioned
officers of the Women's Royal Army Corps (WRAC) selected for PI training using
RAF and Intelligence Corps procedures. In the late 1970s a WRAC (but badged as
Intelligence Corps) sergeant qualified as a PI, becoming the first Army female SNCO
PI – the first of many. In 1992 women were integrated into the mainstream army
and the WRAC disbanded, with its former members joining the regiment/corps to
which they were attached. Thus female PIs became part of the Intelligence Corps.

In contrast to the Army where PI was seen as one of many intelligence-based
skills, the RAF viewed PI as a full-time career with its own exclusive Trade Group
– Trade Group 14. On commissioning, RAF officers of both sexes were sent to the
Joint School of Photographic Interpretation (JSPI) to be trained before joining a
PI unit. Non-commissioned RAF personnel started out as Plotters Air Photography
(PAP) whose job was to plot on traces the results of photographic sorties so that the
photographs could easily be retrieved for further exploitation. On reaching the rank
of senior corporal they could be selected for PI training. After completion of their
PI training, they would be posted to an appropriate PI unit. The Support Personnel
for PI units came from their respective services to provide drawing office, graphics
production and administrative staff.

After selection for PI training, a student of any rank joined the three-month training course at the JSPI, which was located at a number of places during its history,
including RAF Nuneham Park in Oxfordshire, RAF Bassingbourn and RAF Wyton
in Cambridgeshire. The JSPI is now the Imagery Intelligence Wing (IMINT Wing) of
the Defence Intelligence and Security Centre (DISC) at Chicksands in Bedfordshire.

JSPI taught a syllabus covering all aspects of PI from the basic skills of stereoscopy,
locating targets on maps and photography, scaling, measuring and identification of
objects through to analysing and identifying the key features of military and civilian
targets and organisations. British instructors were drawn from all three services, often
selected for their expertise in a particular area on which they taught during the course.

Successful completion of the thirteen-week course meant the new PI was ready for operational deployment. But like passing a driving test, it denoted that the PI had achieved a basic level of competence. Further on-the-job training and experience were needed to produce the well-rounded and experienced PI.

Unlike the British, where the training of PIs was a joint service matter, the USA trained its PIs at single-service establishments such as the US Army School at Fort Holabird, Maryland, although the syllabus was broadly similar. USAF PIs went through a twenty-six-week course that not only covered photographic interpretation but other intelligence-related subjects as well. Mike Mockford, who served as a UK exchange officer instructor at the USAF PI School at Denver, Colorado, described the course as a 'PI factory' where instruction was mostly by rote and more rigidly controlled and structured than its UK counterpart. Students were segregated into classes for officers, SNCOs and airmen that were each about twenty strong, although the subjects taught were the same whichever class the students were in. Instructors taught the subject of the day, regardless of their particular expertise or specialisation. Given US worldwide PI commitments and the large numbers of personnel required to undertake them, this production line approach was the only way to service them. Like their British counterparts, completion of the Denver course was only the start of the long road to becoming a fully effective PI.

At the height of the Cold War in the 1960s and 1970s the British PI cadre numbered about 600 personnel scattered over a number of worldwide locations. As Britain withdrew from its former colonies and commitments east of Suez, the number of PIs and operating locations decreased. One advantage of this small cadre, and the relatively small number of available postings, was that British PIs often returned to serve in the same unit on more than one occasion. This allowed them to build up considerable experience of a particular theatre and operations. For example, Peter Jefferies spent nine of his fourteen-year Regular Army PI career on three tours exploiting Corridor and BCZ imagery between the late 1960s and the early 1980s. This contrasts with the US PIs who would usually serve only a single tour with the 497 RTS/RTG at Wiesbaden. They were very unlikely ever to return there during the rest of their PI career, thus losing the value of prior experience that a subsequent tour could generate.

On arrival at their unit in Germany a newly qualified British PI started a period of theatre orientation and system familiarisation training that lasted about eight weeks but could be longer. For PIs on a repeat tour this period was shorter because of their existing knowledge and experience. Training included recognising individual target features and their immediate environs, equipment knowledge and unit organisations. This meant that an Army PI needed to be able to recognise some 2,500 individual pieces of Soviet and East German equipment and their many variants, unit organisations both in barracks and when deployed in the field, and any changes to equipment and organisation. Des Pemberton, a former Warrant Officer PI described this process as similar to a London taxi drivers acquisition of 'the knowledge' and it became so well ingrained that it allowed Des to recognise a former target in the

Dallgow-Döberitz complex when it featured in the TV series *Homeland* some thirty years after he had last seen it. As time progressed the new PI was gradually allowed to exploit 'live' photography, albeit under their mentor's supervision. When new PIs had demonstrated their mastery of in-theatre systems and procedures, they would be declared competent to work unsupervised.

Exploitation Equipment

All British PIs were issued with a standard PI kit in an attaché case containing all the equipment needed by them to ply their trade. This was developed by the Army primarily for its PIs operating in the field and although later adopted by the other services it was always known as 'The Army PI Kit'. Its contents included a stereoscope, measuring equipment (rulers, scales and a magnifying measurer), mathematical tables (logarithmic and trigonometric), drawing instruments and the very useful PI slide rule that on one side was a normal mathematical slide rule and on the other had scales that allowed a PI to determine the actual ground size of an object by setting the object's image size on a moveable scale against a fixed one that recorded the image's scale. One of the more bizarre items in the kit was a battery-powered headband lamp to provide a light when deployed in the field, which had little practical use.

Electronic calculators eventually replaced the mathematical tables. However, PIs being cautious animals often retained the tables as a fall-back in case of power failures. Individuals tailored their own PI kit to meet the needs of their specific wartime role. It could be reduced to the basics of stereoscope, measuring magnifier and slide rule that would be carried in personal web equipment, so the attaché case could be dispensed with. Individual PI kits often included many 'home-made' items including stereo pairs, equipment recognition material, organisation diagrams and tables and templates for marking maps, locating targets, rough and ready scaling, measuring and flight planning.

The basic tool was the hand-held stereoscope that could be used to view either paper prints illuminated by a desk top lamp or small-format tactical images (70mm × 70mm) using a light box. Stereoscopes ranged from the simple Second World War-era 2x magnification Type 'D', carried in a soft spectacle-type case, to the later 'SV8' and 'Vinten' types that gave up to 4x magnification and some with a limited zoom capability. The other basic tool was the Magnifying Measurer which came in many versions from multiple manufacturers. It consisted of a clear plastic cylinder on whose base was an etched scale that allowed measurements to be taken in millimetres and increments of 0.1mm. On top of the cylinder was a magnifying lens so that the scale could be seen clearly. This instrument allowed accurate measurements to be taken of objects on an image so that their actual ground size could be determined using the PI slide rule.

Desktop light sources came in a number of forms. One included a tungsten bulb lamp with an anglepoise-type mounting, which allowed photographs to be viewed in the best light. These lamps produced considerable heat and prolonged use caused fatigue and headaches. Later versions used fluorescent tubes that gave a more natural light source and remained cooler over prolonged operating periods.

Negative and positive film images were viewed on light boxes in which fluorescent tubes projected light through a translucent plate onto which the film was placed. Some light boxes had hand-wound spools at each end, so long rolls of film could be wound across them.

Until about 1971 exploitation of imagery from all sources was carried out using simple stereoscopes and light boxes. This was adequate for RAF and US Corridor mission images. Although the US missions were flown at higher altitudes than the RAF's, they used longer focal-length lenses, producing photographs at scales that were close to, or larger than, the RAF's. The US 9in × 18in (229mm × 457mm) paper-print format was exploitable at desk level, but was somewhat unwieldy in a desk environment. In 1969 the USA changed from framing to panoramic cameras with smaller focal length lenses that produced continuous rolls of film. These were routinely longer than 2,000ft (610m) with images at smaller scales than before. The only way to view this film efficiently was using a special light table that allowed the film to be wound quickly across it and examined through viewing optics with varying levels of magnification that could be moved over the image without having to reposition it.

The USA already possessed the machinery to cope with the change of film format, but the limitations caused by the continued British use of simple equipment were cruelly exposed. To view panoramic imagery stereoscopically, the best way to achieve optimum exploitation, the film had to be hand-wound over a light box. When a target was identified, the strip of film covering it was cut out of the roll and then further cut into individual frames so that they could be placed side by side for viewing. After exploitation the individual frames were rejoined into a strip using adhesive tape and then the complete strip taped back into the main roll of film. This film then had to be hand-wound back onto its original spool. The process was time consuming and inefficient and precluded the maximum extraction of information because of the low magnifications available with the hand-held stereoscopes. One contemporary PI commented: 'The only advantage of this exploitation method is that it keeps my shares in the adhesive tape manufacturer high.'

If the British were to keep pace with these new developments and the increased amount of material being produced, they needed modern exploitation equipment. In the early 1970s, 6 (PI) Coy took delivery of its first US-origin light table, which provided a quantum leap in both technology and exploitation capability. It met all the essential requirements and had additional features such as motorised file transport drives. The benefits were immediate. Photography could then be more quickly and efficiently exploited. The resulting intelligence product was more current as the backlog of photography awaiting exploitation decreased significantly. Productivity increased because the PIs could spend more time exploiting the images. But there were disadvantages: the tables were very large and required a considerable amount of floor space. They were over-complex for the German theatre and very expensive – around £50,000 per unit at 1970 prices. Finally they needed their own electrical supply because when they used the normal domestic supply they regularly blew fuses, plunging large parts of the JHQ building into darkness.

What was needed was a simpler, cheaper solution more suited to the German thea-tre and it came in the form of the Richards MIM-4 light table. It had most of the earlier light tables features, was more compact and was cheaper to buy and operate. By the mid 1970s each PI in the Immediate Reporting Section had their own light table whose settings – such as optics and table height – were tailored to meet their individual requirements. PIs became quite territorial about 'their' light table.

Whilst the problem of exploiting long film rolls was now solved, examining AMLM 35mm photography continued using light boxes and single lens magnifiers with limited magnification. These were becoming unreliable and the non-variable light source meant they could not be used for long periods. The PIs rapidly discovered that the MIM-4s with their optics, monocular zoom capability and variable-level light sources were far superior for exploiting this photography. This greatly increased the demands placed on them, leading to a major growth in the backlog of US-supplied corridor photography awaiting exploitation and an unacceptable delay.

To overcome this problem 'head-up' viewers, which projected the image onto an angled screen in a hood, replaced the light boxes and magnifiers. The viewers had variable magnification that was much better suited to exploiting the 35mm film format, allowing the PI to sit upright and examine the film using both eyes. They were very effective, well liked and capable of handling the majority of 35mm film exploitation requirements. If better resolution and higher magnification was needed, the PIs reverted to using an available MIM-4. BRIXMIS purchased the 'head-up' viewers (using hard currency DM or $) direct from the manufacturer, Carl Zeiss of Jena in the GDR! After purchase the viewers were taken to Berlin in a BRIXMIS vehicle and on to Rheindahlen by Army transport. The irony was not lost on the PIs and Intelligence Staff that the East Germans had supplied equipment to the British to exploit photography that produced intelligence on their own and Soviet armed forces.

Support Materials

The most basic requirement for any target is simply to know where it is geographi-cally. The Army PI unit used 1:25,000 mapping contained in four large books, covering the three Corridors and the BCZ, for this purpose. They preferred 1:25,000 maps as they were more detailed than the NATO standard 1:50,000 scale maps. Known targets were hand-drawn onto the individual map sheets as were any new installations and constructions to ensure the mapping was kept up to date; 1:50,000 maps were gradually adopted because of the decreasing availability, and obsolescence of the 1:25,000 maps, but they remained in use until the end of the operations. The RAF's PID used five books of 1:50,000 mapping, covering the three Corridors, the BCZ and the German Baltic coast, with the RAF's targets marked on them.

The US-origin Bombing Encyclopedia, later restyled as the Basic Encyclopedia (BE), recorded all targets worldwide. Each was allocated a unique number, based on its position in a World Area Chart (WAC) area whose boundaries were determined by latitude and longitude co-ordinates. The BE contained a wealth of information, primarily for Air Force planners, to plan attacks on targets and select the optimum weapons systems necessary to neutralise or destroy them. The PIs in Germany mainly used this very accurate location information for their work. The BE's use and dissemination was initially restricted to the 'Five Eyes' community of Australia, Britain, Canada, New Zealand and the USA, which sometimes created difficulties in sharing this material outside that group.

After several proposals, HQ USAREUR devised a system that was widely adopted. This used the name of the target's nearest town or village, initially followed by a four-figure number that was replaced in the early 1960s by a three-figure one. The first of the three numbers denoted the ownership or function and the installation, and the last two were the installation's individual number. For example Schönwalde 281 was a target in or close to Schönwalde belonging to the Soviet ground forces, indicated by the lead number 2, with an individual number of 81.

Determining the location of photography that had been taken by aircraft was achieved by one of three methods. First the flight's documentation detailed the cameras and frames used to cover a particular area. For long camera runs covering a number of targets, this was not the most accurate form of record. Second, the photographic coverage card recording all the coverage of a specific target was held in an individual target folder. Finally, the sortie trace plotted all the frames on a transparency that could be laid over a small-scale map to ascertain the areas covered. Indexing of photography is adequate for identifying individual sorties and targets, but successful PIs needed wide-ranging support materials that allowed them not only to refer to historical photographic images but also to compare the historical situation with the current one.

The main exploitation support tool was the Target Folder and one was created for each installation covered by the reconnaissance programmes, including those at the very edge of their capabilities. Each contained a map extract with the target's area marked on it and a single photograph, or photographic mosaic, showing the target's boundaries and any subdivisions. Cards for recording photographic coverage, equipment sightings and parking patterns completed the package. These were all contained in single or multiple A4-size manila wallets, depending on the target's complexity. Large target complexes had a master target folder containing a map covering the whole area and a photographic mosaic detailing all the installations in the complex. To illustrate the number of target folders involved, the combined Army and RAF target folders occupied ten four-drawer A4-size filing cabinets.

Other major reference tools were the various service recognition manuals that provided photographs and drawings of equipment used by the Soviet and East German forces. The ground force equipment manuals were organised into equipment roles, such as armour, artillery, engineer, communications and electronics. Similarly the Air Force manuals grouped aircraft and helicopters by function too (fighter, attack, bomber and transport). These official manuals were supplemented by 'home-made' recognition materials including the use of stereoscopic pairs of photography.

The British PI units also had a Photographic Data Index (PDI), which contained ground and air imagery of installations and equipment that had mainly been collected by the AMLMs but included imagery from other sources. The PDI was held in a number of four-drawer card index cabinets.

Photographic Products

The Allied Corridor and BCZ programmes produced a number of image formats. The British initially used 8½in × 7½in (216mm × 190mm) followed by 9in × 9in (229mm × 229mm) framing formats and finally the panoramic 5in × 24in (127mm × 610mm) format in the programme's latter years. The USA used 9in × 9in (229mm × 229mm) and 9in × 18in (229mm × 457mm) framing formats until 1969, when the 5in (127mm) panoramic format replaced them. The 5in produced frames up to 24in (610mm) or 48in (1220mm) long. Between 1953 and 1962 Project Pie Face produced the unique 18in × 36in (457mm × 915mm) format images, known by some PIs as 'Texas Postcards'. The French used 114mm × 114mm (4.5in × 4.5in) and 55mm × 250mm (2.1in × 9.8in) formats. Individual paper prints were widely used by the Allies until 1969 when the USA introduced continuous roll positive imagery. The British continued using paper prints until 1988 when the introduction of their own panoramic camera installation saw them switch to positive roll film.

Western light aircraft flights in the BCZ all used 35mm monochrome and colour roll film of up to thirty-six frames. French photographs were received in 5in × 7in (127mm × 178mm) format paper prints.

Exploitation Priorities and Responsibilities

RAF Corridor missions were the top priority for British exploitation. The intelligence extracted was rapidly disseminated to the Allies to alert them to any significant items or developments. The next priority was BRIXMIS Chipmunk imagery. Although HQ BRIXMIS in Berlin undertook an initial examination of the material, it was not scrutinised by trained PIs until it got to the PI units at Rheindahlen. US Corridor imagery was the next priority, followed by US and French BCZ imagery. The non-British imagery was exploited as and when it was received, but where possible in chronological order. Exploitation of any other imagery was exploited on a case-by-case basis, depending on the task's priority.

When an RAF Corridor flight returned to Wildenrath, the film and crew were taken to Rheindahlen for debriefing by the RAF and Army PI units' operations officers and relevant members of the Air Staff, especially if there had been a significant incident. During the debriefing, copies of the mission documentation recording the routes and targets imaged were passed to the Heads of the Army and RAF units' Current Exploitation Sections.

In the Current Exploitation Sections there was always an air of tension and anticipation when the documentation arrived. This was the first time that the PIs became aware of the mission's routes and targets. The section heads allocated individual targets to a specific PI for the immediate exploitation phase. From this a signal, detailing the mission highlights, was prepared for the Allied intelligence community. This period was rather like war – 90 per cent waiting for 10 per cent frenetic action. During the wait for the prints' arrival, there was still much to be done. The target folders relating to the assigned targets were retrieved and the latest information studied. It also helped PIs to know why the target had been selected for coverage. Was there a specific intelligence requirement or was it just routine? Or was it an opportunity target where the aircrew had seen significant activity like a major river crossing or tactical exercise and taken photographs, even though the target had not been formally tasked? Stereoscope lenses were polished, forms prepared. With better preparation came better exploitation – a case of the six 'Ps'.[1]

The PRU processed the film and made two print copies from it, one for each PI unit. After the prints had been subjected to immediate and later deeper exploitation, one copy was retained in the PID film library for twelve months and the second copy was sent by courier to the 497 RTS/RTG as part of the weekly imagery exchange.

Once the PIs received their prints it was a case of 'eyes down, look in'. Would there be any new equipment? Would there be a high level of activity somewhere? Competition between PIs was fierce in the hopes of pulling off a 'scoop'. Each target was reported on a pre-prepared proforma that already had the mission and target details completed, followed by a blank space to record any highlights. The Section Head collated the completed proformae for inclusion into the First Phase signal, later known as a RECCEXREP to conform to NATO terminology. This signal reported any unusual or high levels of activity including field exercises, river crossings, new equipment sightings and details of any new construction. It also recorded all the targets covered by the mission. The signal was distributed throughout the British, Canadian and US intelligence communities. There was a First Phase signal/RECCEXREP for each individual element of the mission: inbound leg, 'Chukka' (BCZ) and outbound leg. Unlike tactical reconnaissance signals of the same name, the First Phase signal/RECCEXREP was not the subject of any rigid time constraints but was transmitted on its completion. It was a matter of professional pride to have these signals transmitted within two hours of receiving the prints. The pace now slowed as the photographic images were subjected to detailed examination that resulted in the consolidated Second Phase report, later known as an Initial Photographic Interpretation Report (IPIR), in NATO terminology.

These IPIRs reported on all the installations covered, even if there was no apparent military activity. The report included detailed equipment counts by unit area, record any parking patterns, listed shed and bay associations and recorded any unusual or noteworthy activity. It was also disseminated throughout the British, Canadian and US intelligence communities. It provided input to the PI units' databases, forming the basis for any further analysis. After 1970, PID ceased producing IPIRs by consolidating their month's exploitation results into a Monthly Summary Report, containing details of all the equipment readouts carried out by them on their targets, together with illustrative imagery. If there was activity, PID would generate a specific individual report to cover this. The UK-produced IPIR was different from the US IPIR, which was subject to more rigid time constraints.

Production of the IPIR provided some lighter moments. All PIs had their own shorthand that they used to prepare the draft report. Usually the PIs used NAMA to indicate no apparent military activity and NAMA was transcribed in full in the final report by the unit's typist. One PI reported a target's status as SFAH and the new typist, not aware of PIs' foibles, dutifully typed SFAH into the final report. An Intelligence Staff officer enquired, 'what does SFAH mean?' A highly embarrassed operations officer explained that it meant that there was a very low level of activity.

The Chipmunk photography was initially examined at HQ BRIXMIS in Berlin, which produced its version of a First Phase signal recording items of significance. This was sent to HQ BAOR, MoD UK and the other AMLMs. BRIXMIS also generated its own reports, mainly Technical Intelligence Reports, for distribution to the British, Canadian, French and US intelligence communities. After this first look, the photography was sent by courier to PID where it was then made available for detailed exploitation by the PIs; Second Phase exploitation of BRIXMIS imagery was carried out by both PI units to add information to their databases for later analysis and the photography was sometimes used to illustrate Special Studies and Technical Intelligence Reports.

US Corridor imagery was initially examined and exploited by the 497 RTS/RTG, which produced an IPIR signal containing mission highlights and detailed equipment readouts of the targets covered by the mission. This IPIR conformed to US operating procedures and was disseminated at four-hourly intervals, regardless of whether the mission's exploitation was complete. Consequently an individual mission's IPIR could arrive at the British PI units in several parts. The sheer volume and coverage of photography received from the Americans precluded the small British Army PI unit from exploiting it all in detail. The Army operations officer selected targets for detailed exploitation based on the US IPIR's results. This system was still flexible enough to allow an individual PI to generate a report on their own initiative if they saw something significant. All installations covered by the US missions were recorded on the installation coverage cards to support any future requirements. The Army used US Corridor imagery primarily for database population, but it was also used to support and illustrate special reports. The RAF had fewer targets, so PID was able to fully exploit all relevant US Corridor photography. The smaller scale US photography made it eminently suitable for producing target prints because it could cover a target with a single frame or a small number of frames.

USCOB and USMLM imagery acquired under Project Lark Spur and imagery from the Forces Français en Berlin (FFB) and MMFL came to the PI units via BRIXMIS and could be up to four weeks old. This often limited its usefulness. The imagery was exploited in its order of arrival and was mainly used for database population and to support other reports.

To make the optimum use of the limited PI resources and avoid duplication of effort, target types were divided between the two units. The Army's responsibilities included the organisation and equipment of ground force units; surface-to-surface missile (SSM) units and their associated supply chains; air defence units including man-portable and mobile SAM and anti-aircraft artillery (AAA) units; ground force training areas (including ranges, river-crossing training areas and tactical manoeuvre locations); and static logistic installations such as major repair facilities, military stores, fuel and ammunition depots and new construction sites until their purpose and ownership had been determined.

The RAF's responsibilities included Air Order of Battle (AOB) for fixed-wing aircraft and helicopters; air-related infrastructure such as airfields, air-related headquarters and command and control facilities including radar and communications sites; air-related storage and maintenance facilities; and static and semi-mobile SAM and AAA sites to assess how they would affect the planned routes of NATO offensive air operations. It also examined mobile and man-portable SAM systems and mobile AAA systems to assess their capabilities and the threat they posed to British and NATO aircraft and helicopters. The RAF also examined new construction work until its ownership and purpose was established. The two areas of deliberate duplication were some air defence systems and new construction. The Army's interest was in where the air defence systems fitted into the Ground Force Order of Battle whilst the RAF was mainly concerned about the systems' technical capabilities and the threats they posed to NATO's aircraft and helicopters. Both sides took an interest in any new construction outside existing installations until its ownership had been determined, when responsibility was handed over to the relevant service.

Reporting Responsibilities

Before 1968 the British Army PI unit's main reporting responsibility was to provide evidence of any heightened air and ground force posture that could be a precursor to hostilities – Indicators and Warning (I&W). Other reporting priorities were ground force exercises and river crossing training. This was communicated through First and Second Phase reports that consisted of a 'washing list' of the equipment present in the target area, regardless of what units were based there. This confirmed the presence of certain equipment at a target but was somewhat imprecise in determining the occupying units. It did not add to knowledge of the unit's Table of Organisation and Equipment (TO & E) and certainly did not help detect any organisational changes. However, this system was capable of meeting the requirements of the time to provide as much warning as possible of any change in posture that may have preceded an imminent attack. Sightings of new equipment and re-equipment programmes generated many Technical Intelligence Reports that often represented the first time that the equipment had been seen by Western intelligence.

In the mid 1960s reconnaissance satellites became more reliable and provided wider coverage of the Soviet Union and Warsaw Pact territories without the risks attached to manned overflights. This coverage provided more opportunities to detect possible hostile intentions and reduced the importance of I&W information based solely on observations in Germany. Accordingly the reporting emphasis in Germany shifted towards in-depth analysis of units in the target areas. By dividing targets into functional areas and then recording the equipment present in them, the type of unit could be assessed more effectively. These findings could then be compared with the published Order of Battle (ORBAT) to ensure that the ORBAT information was as accurate as possible. This shift to unit analysis required the development of a new set of methodologies and reporting procedures which became the standard procedures for post-1968 target exploitation until the cessation of operations in 1990.

Technical Intelligence was an important exploitation priority. Although satellite imagery often discovered new equipment at the Soviet Union's Research and Development (R&D) establishments, it was often only when it entered service in Germany that the Allied intelligence community would acquire close-up images necessary for in-depth analysis. The lower security classification of photographs from Germany, compared to satellite imagery, which had a very limited distribution, eased the dissemination of technical intelligence to a wider audience in the intelligence community.

Detailed unit analysis required regular, repetitive target coverage so that changes could be quickly detected. It also demanded patience from the PIs, an eye for detail and the ability to detect changes.

An Area Print of the target would be produced. A single-occupancy target required the target's external boundaries to be determined, followed by the identification of the functional areas such as accommodation, administrative, vehicle and equipment storage, logistics and training facilities. A letter or number denoted these areas.

Multi-occupancy targets presented their own set of problems in identifying and establishing individual unit areas. After defining the external boundaries the PIs had to find the areas housing individual units. Soviet paranoia was a great help in this. Unlike NATO, where personnel from individual units mixed freely both at work and at leisure, and passed through another unit's area during their day-to-day duties, this concept was anathema to the Soviet mind set. In the Soviet Army personnel did not have free association either at work or at leisure. Although the units' domestic areas were not fenced off, a strict policy of personnel segregation was applied with each Soviet and East German unit having its own individual cookhouse and club that were for their exclusive use. Enforcing this segregation was simple – erect fences. Unit equipment areas were fenced off to mark the boundary between one unit and its next door neighbour. Within unit areas there were sometimes internal fences to segregate sub-units or denote 'sensitive areas'. Changes to fence lines indicated either an expansion of the occupying unit's area or a change of occupant. By following the fences and observing the equipment seen in the fenced areas, the PIs could soon deduce who lived where. Another aid to defining individual unit areas was the sand table-like models created in the unit's domestic accommodation area that showed unit personnel which part of the barracks housed their unit.

Within each unit's area were vehicle and equipment storage sheds. Analysing the unit's vehicle holdings and parking patterns helped to deduce the unit organisation. To do this each shed housing vehicles or equipment was individually numbered and the number of vehicle/equipment storage bays established. The convention for numbering bays was from left to right when facing the shed. So 'Shed 3 v 40' meant that it was shed number 3 in the area and it had forty storage bays. Bays came in several variations, such as double-depth, where two vehicles could be accommodated one behind another, and multiple-width bays that accommodated a number of vehicles abreast across the width. A record of sightings associated with a particular shed and bay was made on the Shed and Bay Card so that the parking patterns and vehicle associations could confirm the units or sub-unit occupying the shed. Any changes in parking patterns often indicated a unit reorganisation or a change of occupant.

The Table of Organisation and Equipment (TO & E) Card recorded overall equipment sightings in an area. These were compared against the unit's published TO & E and any anomalies reported. TO & E Card information formed the basis of any further in-depth analyses.

Recording and analysing the turret and side numbers painted on armoured vehicles was a very useful aid that often gave the first indication of an organisational change. The system was designed and developed by two Intelligence Corps warrant officer PIs around 1970 as part of a study covering two Soviet divisions. Although BRIXMIS had been recording these numbers for some time, this was the first occasion that they were subjected to in-depth analysis. This resulted in the accurate determination of an individual vehicle's unit, sub-unit and its position within that sub-unit. The study's boundaries were widened to cover all units within the BCZ. The Allies' light aircraft missions were the main source of turret and side numbers, although in the right circumstances they could sometimes be seen on Corridor photography. The turret number study had many successes, alerting the intelligence staffs to organisational changes before other sources confirmed them.

A Photo Coverage Card recorded all the photographic cover of an installation, regardless of whether it had been exploited. PIs reviewed this previous coverage to identify photography suitable for area prints illustrating reports.

Until the early 1980s sightings in all exploited areas were fully recorded. This involved the expenditure of considerable time and effort because recording was a manual process. The operations officer at that time changed the system to reporting by exception to improve output. This meant that a report was only raised if an equipment sighting did not conform to the published TO & E. Complete listings were periodically done to maintain database integrity and ensure that routine surveillance was not lost. This change sped up the reporting process and reduced the backlog of photography awaiting exploitation. The downside was that records were not as comprehensive as they had previously been, so there was a greater risk of something significant being missed. It also meant that if the target became the subject of detailed study, all the unreported photography of that target had to be reviewed.

Preparing material from the database for a detailed study was a laborious manual process that involved transcribing individual entries into chronological order so that the data was studied sequentially. One Warrant Officer PI remarked that: 'this is a good way of dealing with a junior soldier who has got up my nose. A few days of transcription should get the message home that I may be cross with them' – although cross was not the term used in the original remark.

Shed and Bay Card

Installation	Area	B	Shed No.	Unit
Schönwalde 281			15	1 SP Gun Bn/283 GAR

Mission	Date	Bay No. Frames	Area	B	Shed No.	Unit
RAFG 1234	15 May 77	F31 0025–0036 / F32 0026–0035 / F33 0025–0029	In Front of Shed BBV	2S3 2S3 2S3 2S3 2S3 1V13 1V14-2A 1V13 1V14-2A 7 x ZIL-131 2 x ZIL-131		2S3 2S3 / 2S3 2S3 / 2S3 2S3 / 2S3 2S3 — ZIL-131
LARKSPUR 77-029	19 Apr 77	Film 155 Fr 001–015	2S3 (022) 2S3 (021)	SP Gun 2S3	SP Gun 2S3 (025)	1V14-2A 1V13 — PRP-3 UAZ-452 PIM ZIL-131 — ZIL-131
BRX 77/034	22 May 77	Film 123 Fr 001–016	2S3 (024) 2S3 (023) 2S3 (022) 2S3 (021)	2S3 (025 2S3 (026	1V14 (020) 1V Ser (029) PRP-3 UAZ-452 PIM	UAZ-452 PIM
MMFL 277	14 Apr 77	Film 007 Fr 005–036	ZIL-131 ZIL-131 ZIL-131 ZIL-131			
RAFG 1237	22 May 77	F31 0001–0012 / F32 0002–0013 / F33 0002–0011	2S3 2S3 2S3 2S3 1V13 ZIL-131 ZIL-131 2S3 2S3 2S3 2S3 1V14-2A UAZ-452 PIM		PRP-3	ZIL-131 ZIL-131

Example of a Shed and Bay Card. This was used to record the associations of equipment with a particular storage shed and their parking patterns within bays, including turret/side numbers. (Document via Peter Jefferies)

TO & E Card

Installation / Mission	Area / Date	Frames	2S3 152mm SP Gun (B)	BM-21 122mm MBRL (Unit)	1V11 Series ACRV	1V12 ACRV	1V13 ACRV	1V14 ACRV	PRP-3 OPV	MT-LB M-1975 (Big Fred)	UAZ-452 PTM Veh
Schöenwalde 281			283 Guards Artillery Regiment / 20 Guards Motor Rifle Division (283GAR/20GMRD)								
Published TO & E as at 1 Jan 77			48	18	16	4	6	6	4	1	4
RAFG 1234	15 May 77	F31 0025-0036 / F32 0026-0035 / F33 0025-0029	20*	9			2	3			
LARKSPUR 77-029	19 Apr 77	Film 155 Fr 001 – 036	22	12		2	5	5			
BRX 77/034	22 May 77	Film 123 Fr 001 – 016	8	-	-	-	1	1	1	-	1
MMFL 277	14 Apr 77	Film 007 Fr 005 – 036	5	2	-	-	-	-	-	-	-
RAFG 1237	22 May 77	F31 0001-0012 / F32 0002-0013 / F33 0002-0011	66	17	-	5	6	6	3	1	4

Example of a TO & E Card. This card recorded all equipment sited in a unit area so that they could be compared with the published Table of Organisation & Equipment. (Document via Peter Jefferies)

Turret Number Analysis

Unit	Schönwalde 281 – 1 Bty/1 SP Gun Bn/283 GAR	Turret/Side Nos									
Msn	Date	020	021	022	023	024	025	026	027	028	029
BRX 99/77	22 May 77	1V14-2A	2S3	2S3	2S3	2S3	2S3	2S3	1V13		1V Ser
LKSP 029	19 Apr 77	1V14-2A	2S3	2S3			2S3		1V13		

Example of Turret Number analysis. A change in a unit's turret/side number system was often the first indicator of an organisational change. (Document via Peter Jefferies)

The study of the numbering sequence and the allocation of numbers to individual equipments allowed a picture of the unit's organisation to be built up. In this case it shows that that 020 was the Battery Command Vehicle, 021 to 026 were self-propelled howitzers and 027 was the Battery Fire Direction Centre Vehicle. The appearance of a 1V series with number 029 may indicate a re-organisation or allocation of turret/side numbers. A wider study of the unit's numbers revealed the following allocation within the regiment:

001-004	1st Battalion Headquarters	005-009	2nd Battalion Headquarters
010-019	1st Battery of 1st Battalion	040-049	1st Battery of 2nd Battalion
020-029	2nd Battery of 1st Battalion	050-059	2nd Battery of 2nd Battalion
030-039	3rd Battery of 1st Battalion	060-069	3rd Battery of 2nd Battalion

Photo Coverage Card

Location	Schönwalde	Installation	Flugplatz Kaserne 281
Mission	**Date**	**Frames**	**Remarks**
BRX 77/034	21 May 77	Film 123 Fr 01–36	
77 CY 123	21 Apr 77	Pan 0100–0104	
LARKSPUR 77–029	19 Apr 77	Film 155 Fr 001–036	
MMFL 277	14 Apr 77	Film 007 Fr 005–036	
RAFG 1234	15 May 77	F31 0025–0036 F32 0026–0035 F33 0025–0029	
RAFG 1237	22 May 77	F31 0001 – 0012 F32 0002 – 0013 F33 0002 – 0011	
77 CY 125	22 Apr 77	Pan 0010–0015	NAMA
77 CY 126	23 Apr 77	Obl 0056–0099	

Example of a Photo Coverage Card. This recorded all photographic coverage of an installation. (Document via Peter Jefferies)

Unlike their US counterparts who had been using IT since the early 1970s, the British PI units didn't adopt IT until the early 1980s when Project Double Vision (DV) was commissioned. DV speeded up exploitation and reduced the amount of card-held data, such as Installation Coverage, TO & E and Shed and Bay records. Data could be sorted chronologically which meant that analysts could look at the developing situation without resorting to manual transcription. To ensure that spurious or inaccurate data did not enter the records and to keep the raw data as pure as possible, any data underwent a rigorous quality control process before being committed to the main database. DV was a 6 Int Coy and PID internal system with no external connections. Reports for external distribution were prepared and edited on DV but the final product was distributed in hard copy because DV was not capable of managing electronic distribution. Despite its limitations and obvious inadequacy today, it gave the British a leap in capability and efficient data handling at the time. A modern networked system would really have speeded up dissemination beyond the wildest dreams of those late twentieth-century PIs.

Conclusions

Throughout the Cold War, Corridor and BCZ flights provided regular surveillance of the Soviets' area. There were frequent changes to the equipment and methods used to extract intelligence from operations' photography. A major challenge was always the capability to effectively, process, organise and interpret the information provided from the vast quantities of photography.

Before the advent of reliable reconnaissance satellite imagery the Corridor and BCZ programmes were the only constant and regular surveillance available to the Allied intelligence community that could give them any indications of preparations for hostilities in this most forward area of deployed Soviet troops. To meet this requirement, simple listings of the equipment within an installation were usually sufficient. The downgrading of the I&W requirement in the mid 1960s significantly changed the way information was managed. It led to the development of more sophisticated analytical methodologies that were eventually adopted throughout the British PI community. These encompassed the use of other intelligence sources to provide a final product that was much more thoroughly analysed and assessed than previously. These changes were themselves the precursor to the twenty-first century's multi-skill, all-source intelligence cells.

Technical intelligence was always a significant product throughout the Cold War because Germany was the theatre where new equipment was often seen first. Satellite imagery may have often given more warning of the impending introduction of new equipment and systems, but it was in Germany that the analysts could get 'up close and personal' to collect and analyse detailed close-up images.

Notes

1   Prior Preparation and Planning Prevents Poor Performance.

WAS IT WORTH ALL THE EFFORT AND WHAT DID IT ACHIEVE?

For forty-five years, the Allied Corridor and BCZ flights produced almost daily coverage of a substantial portion of GSFG, the NVA and the air, maritime and border forces stationed in the GDR at relatively low political and military risk. For the first fifteen years, before the arrival of viable reconnaissance satellites, they were the only regular photographic surveillance capability available to the Western intelligence community. Although the early reconnaissance satellites provided wider area coverage of target countries, they had two disadvantages: first, optical cameras cannot penetrate the cloud cover that abounds over Eastern Europe for much of the year; second, their orbits are predictable, which lets forces in the targeted areas take measures to hide activity and disguise any new equipment, whilst the satellite is in range. The Corridor and BCZ flights could fly beneath the cloud cover and their flight timing and routes were less predictable than satellite orbits, which made concealment measures more difficult.

Continuous Development of GSFG, NVA and Other GDR Forces

Throughout the Cold War, Soviet and East German ground and air forces went through unit and formation reorganisations that increased their size and capabilities. Alongside the reorganisations, extensive re-equipment programmes progressively advanced their technical capabilities too, from the relatively simple Second World War-era equipment to the much more sophisticated levels of the 1980s.

During this period, Corridor and BCZ flights captured on film major unit changes and reorganisations including:

- Identifying Divisional and Army-level Independent Tank Units. In the 1980s, the Army-level units were disbanded and their assets redistributed into Tank Divisions and Motor Rifle Divisions.
- Regimental artillery batteries that were increased to battalion strength.
- The introduction of an SS-23 Spider Brigade at front level.
- The establishment, in each of the five GSFG armies, of Air Assault Units equipped with BMD-1 armoured personnel carriers (APC), 2S9 air-portable self-propelled guns, Mi-17 HIP transport helicopters and Mi-24 HIND attack helicopters.

Individual re-equipment programmes are too numerous to mention but those involving ground forces included:

- Qualitative improvements to all types of armoured vehicle including main battle tanks (MBT), armoured personnel carriers (APC) and armoured infantry combat vehicles (AICV).
- The introduction of new towed and self-propelled artillery pieces at all unit and formation levels and the associated 1V series automated target acquisition and fire control systems.
- A new generation of multi-barrel rocket launcher (MBRL) systems at all levels which replaced the wartime simple rocket launchers.
- The introduction of SS-21 Scarab medium-range guided missile systems, replacing the unguided Free Rocket over Ground (FROG) systems in the Divisional FFR Battalion.
- The replacement of towed AAA systems by self-propelled radar-controlled anti-aircraft guns, combined AAA and SAM systems, and SAM systems including MANPADS.
- The introduction of sophisticated battlefield radar equipped reconnaissance vehicles and an ECM capability into Divisional Reconnaissance battalions.
- The PMP floating ribbon bridge, new ferries, amphibious load carriers, and tracked IPR river reconnaissance vehicle enhanced river-crossing unit capabilities at all levels.
- A complete review of the existing logistics train and its improvement through the introduction of modern, larger load-carrying capacity vehicles based on the URAL-377, URAL-4320, KrAZ-255, KrAZ-260 and KamAZ-5410 series chassis.

Air and air defence forces also went through a series of re-equipment and upgrade programmes, including:

- The transition from wartime piston-engined aircraft to jet aircraft, including fighters, tactical bombers and reconnaissance aircraft, which improved with each generation fielded.
- The development of helicopters from simple transports to attack, versatile troop and heavy lift machines in many variants, including command and control and ECM variants.

- Improving the defence of key points and airfields by introduction of semi-mobile SAM systems like the SA-2 Guideline, SA-3 Goa and SA-5 Gammon missiles. The first system deployed in the GDR was the SA-2 Guideline site at Glau in the late 1950s.
- The introduction of sophisticated, integrated command and control systems, combining all the elements into the one entity needed to control and co-ordinate aircraft and SAM system activities in a complex air picture.

The regularity of Corridor and BCZ flights meant that they were able to detect and monitor these organisational changes and re-equipment programmes as they took place. This made a significant contribution, together with other sources, to military capability assessments by in-theatre and national intelligence staffs. This information also contributed to the MoD Defence Industry Desk's assessments of Warsaw Pact equipment production rates, by monitoring the speed and progress of its introduction into service.

Before the mid 1960s, when satellites opened up Soviet research and development establishments to surveillance, the Corridor and BCZ programmes were virtually the sole source of new equipment photography. Satellite surveillance reduced the importance of the Corridor and BCZ programmes' contribution to the overall technical intelligence programme because it allowed technical assessments to be made before the new equipment appeared in the GDR. Despite this surveillance net stretching back to the heart of the Soviet Union, there was still some new equipment that slipped through the surveillance net and consequently the first sightings were in the GDR, captured by Corridor and BCZ flights.

Routine Reporting

Chapter 7 covered the production of the First Phase (RECCEXREP) and Second Phase (IPIR) reports that the British used to communicate the immediate results, detailed reporting and database population from their missions, whereas the Americans used their IPIR for immediate reporting and database population. The content of these reports formed the basis for subsequent analysis and report production. Both nations' units also produced special reports to meet specific tasks or intelligence requirements.

Briefing Notes (BN)
BNs were a quick response, time sensitive – usually within twenty-four to forty-eight hours – to meet a specific task, or draw attention to a significant sighting or event. They consisted of a single page of written analysis supported by either a photographic print or transparency. The Scud battalion training deployment on the Letzlinger Heide training area (see image 46) and the deployed Divisional FFR battalion (see image 47) is typical of the activity that would have prompted a BN's production.

Special Photographic Interpretation Reports (SPIR)

SPIRs were an in-depth analysis tool that used all available photography and any other collateral intelligence to produce a rounded, assessed intelligence product. SPIRs were initiated either in response to a formal Intelligence Staff tasking, or by an individual PI after the operations officer's authorisation. They were not usually time constrained. The analysis of the BMP-2 equipped Motor Rifle Regiment (MRR) at Schlotheim in the Southern Corridor is illustrated in image 48. Producing this level of detail involved many hours of study and analysis.

The Divisional Studies: The '1910' Reports 1968–73[1]

In 1968, G(Int) – the Intelligence Staff Branch at HQ BAOR – directed 6 (PI) Coy to carry out an in-depth study of two typical Soviet divisions. The initial report in 1969 became a seminal work proving the soundness of the analytical techniques used. Subsequent reports further refined them in the light of the experience gained. The initial report's main aims were:

- To analyse a barracks infrastructure, identify individual unit areas and calculate if there was sufficient accommodation to house the personnel, vehicles and equipment of the unit believed to be occupying that area.
- To confirm the divisional units and sub-units occupying individual unit areas.
- To confirm, or modify, the HQ BAOR Intelligence Staff's publication on Divisional organisation of Soviet/GDR forces.
- To record the units' and sub-units' vehicle and equipment holdings, compare them with the HQ BAOR Divisional Tables of Organisation and Equipment, and report any anomalies.
- To report the presence of any units not held on the HQ BAOR divisional organisation.

The two divisions selected as subjects for this mammoth study were the 19 Motor Rifle Division (19 MRD), subordinate to the 20 Guards Army (20 GA) housed in the Dallgow-Döberitz complex just to the west of Berlin, and the 10 Guards Tank Division (10 GTD), subordinate to the 3 Shock Army (3 SA) housed in Krampnitz and Potsdam. The choice of these two divisions was driven by the fact that their barracks lay under the BCZ so they could be subject to maximum coverage from Corridor, BCZ light aircraft and, in some cases, AMLM ground tour photography.

The report's production involved a large proportion of 6 (PI) Coy's resources, including the current activities section, reporting on all coverage of the target areas, regardless of activity levels, and the special studies section, which concentrated on data analysis by studying equipment parking patterns, associating vehicles with specific sheds and bays, studying the turret number sequences and then comparing the findings with the published TO & E.

The reports used the unit designators from the HQ BAOR ORBAT. These could not be derived from photography, which could only confirm or deny the type of unit occupying the area. The unit's designation had to come from other intelligence sources. In August 1968, 19 MRD moved to Czechoslovakia as part of the 1968 invasion but they did not return to GSFG because, unknown to Western intelligence, they were transferred to mainland Russia, as the Soviet authorities considered them 'tainted' by their time in Czechoslovakia. It was some time before Western intelligence discovered that their replacement was the 35 Motor Rifle Division (35 MRD). In the interregnum what was actually 35 MRD was being reported as 19 MRD.

The first '1910' report, published in 1969, was a massive tome recording in detail the construction and capacity of the barracks accommodation and other infrastructure, the location of individual divisional units in the barracks complexes and their equipment holdings, including any anomalies with the published TO & E. Subsequent reports in 1970 to 1973 were smaller works that recorded the changes from the previous year's report.

The reports were invaluable to the international intelligence community and became the 'gold standard' for analytical reporting. The highlights included:

- Confirmation that T-54/T-55 tanks equipped MRDs and T-62 equipped TDs.
- The discovery and confirmation of the existence of an Independent Tank Battalion in 19 MRD equipped with 51 T-54/T-55 tanks.
- Confirming the existence and locations of the Divisional Free Flight Rocket Battalions (FFR Bns). The signature items of equipment were often seen on local training areas but rarely in barracks (image 47). The BTR-60 A command vehicle, side number 952 seen with the battalion on the training area, was later seen in the barracks area associated with the FFR Bn which confirmed its occupancy.
- Confirmation of the reinstatement of the Divisional Anti-Tank Battalion, equipped with 100mm T-12 anti-tank guns, to the 19 MRD ORBAT when it joined a divisional-level exercise in 1971. The unit had previously been declared surplus to the Divisional ORBAT in 1970.
- The arrival of BMP-1 Armoured Infantry Fighting Vehicles (AIFV) in GSFG in 1971.
- The replacement of earlier equipment by modern, later generation, equipment in all arms and services.

A comparison study covering parts of two other divisions, one of each type, located outside the BCZ was done to assess the validity of the findings of the '1910 studies' and to ensure that the Soviets were not employing Maskirovska to deceive the intelligence community.[2] The report found only minor differences between these divisions and the '1910' ones, so the report's concept appeared sound.

Technical Intelligence Reports

Technical intelligence reports (TIRs) were detailed analyses of new or modified equipment seen in the GDR. They used all available photographic sources, but predominantly that from AMLMs ground and air tours. Considerable analytical effort was expended in gathering technical intelligence and BCZ light aircraft flights had a unique value because they captured overhead views that were not usually visible to ground tours.[3] They often managed to get close to equipment in barracks when it was opened up for inspection, routine maintenance or modification, with open hatches that often revealed the inner workings. Image 49 reveals the breech details of a 2S5 Giantsint-S 152mm self-propelled howitzer from which analysts produced details of its construction and operation. Image 50 shows the detailed layout of the engine compartment of a Mi-8 Hip helicopter. Analysis of electronic equipment, such as the 'Flat Face B' radar illustrated in image 51, was greatly assisted by the strong shadows on the image, which clearly show the shape of the radar sails. Operations research and procurement staffs used technical intelligence reports to help design future Western weapons systems required to engage and defeat the Warsaw Pact's latest equipment.

Reservists' Reports

The Reservists of 21 Int Coy (V) and 7010 Flt RAFVR produced a series of reports from the late 1970s to meet requests from intelligence staffs in Germany. These reports were not time-sensitive because of the limited time available to the reservists. 21 Int Coy (V) produced detailed studies of static Soviet Petroleum Oil and Lubricants (POL) sites which assessed their capacity and established if they were part of a POL logistics chain of depots along likely land forces' axes of advance into NATO territory. Tactical pipeline storage in these facilities was an important indicator, because it could either provide dispersed refuelling facilities for passing units, or join depots together to establish a forward refuelling chain.

The collapse of the Berlin Wall in 1989 rendered those reports obsolete, so the team were redirected to a series of tasks that HQ BAOR did not have the resources to address. They were an eclectic mix, including: confirming the scrapping of obsolete BA-64 armoured cars issued to factory militias/Kampfgruppen; providing evidence of the removal of sensitive material to Russia from the MfS ('Stasi') Headquarters in Berlin-Karlshorst; assessing the production flow of MBTs through the major workshop at Kirchmöser near Brandenburg; and undertaking a technical assessment of an ionospheric sounding antenna system. The last two reports were attributed to 21 Int Coy (V) and distributed throughout the international intelligence community, much to the amazement of the Volunteers' commanding officer.

In the 1980s, 7010 Flight RAFVR had started a series of studies of minor airfields and Soviet airfield support vehicles to see whether there were sufficient to sustain operations and carry out operational turn rounds of the various aircraft types in use and repair any damage to them. Again the fall of The Wall caught up with these studies that consequently were never published. The TA and RAFVR PIs made a very significant contribution to intelligence-community's Cold War operations in Germany and beyond and was ahead of their time.

Significant Reports and Sightings

Throughout the operations' lives they were at the forefront of many first sightings and incidents, some of which were of historical significance. A selection are briefly described below to demonstrate the breadth of intelligence gained.

Indicators and Warning

In 1956 concentrations of vehicles were seen massing in barracks throughout the GDR. They subsequently deployed to Hungary to quell the uprising. The vacant barracks were then watched to await the return of units from Hungary to ascertain if the same type of unit returned to the same barracks.

East–West relations took a further turn for the worse in 1961 as the second Berlin crisis escalated. Western politicians were understandably nervous and made strenuous efforts to avoid provoking the Soviets. One consequence of this increased tension was a total embargo on British photographic flights in the Corridors and BCZ. The almost overnight building of the infamous Berlin Wall on 16 August 1961 seriously curtailed the output from some intelligence sources and some ceased altogether. This tense atmosphere, coupled with limited hard intelligence, was fertile ground for rumour and speculation: unsubstantiated reports stated that the NVA was in East Berlin, contrary to the terms of the Four Power agreement. Soviet forces from mainland Russia were said to be massing to the east of Berlin. The lack of intelligence meant that the BRIXMIS Chipmunk assumed even greater importance in confirming or refuting these rumours. On the morning of 16 August the Chipmunk made a visual reconnaissance sortie with the crew allegedly still in their pyjamas! They reported the presence of East German Army troops in East Berlin. JIC (Germany) lobbied JIC London and the PM personally approved a single-figure number of Chipmunk photographic flights that had to be executed in a strictly defined time.[4] The photography from the flights showed that the rumours were totally unfounded. There were no Soviet troops massing to the east of Berlin and NVA troops had withdrawn from the city, so the alert state was downgraded. The flights demonstrated that negative intelligence is as vital a component as positive intelligence in the generation of an accurate intelligence picture.

In the spring of 1968 Alexander Dubček's Czechoslovak government contemplated leaving the Warsaw Pact and Soviet sphere of influence. In mid summer, a Corridor flight covered the Dallgow-Döberitz, complex housing 19 MRD. In the barracks the division's vehicles were formed into unit columns, including their logistic vehicles. The presence of these vehicles was significant because they were usually parked in the unit's POL and ammunition storage areas and never joined their parent unit, even for exercises. This was because they were fully loaded with their war stocks. The high level of activity in the complex delayed the production of the First Phase signal. When the PI responsible for the Dallgow-Döberitz input was pressed about the delay, his somewhat testy response was: 'I've just finished counting 300 tanks in

263 [the location number] and I haven't even started on the artillery and APCs.' This caused a fluttering in the dovecotes because of the uncertainty it generated. Was this part of a plan to intervene in Czechoslovakia, or a precursor to invading the West? On 20 August the Soviets invaded Czechoslovakia. As in the previous Hungarian crisis, the PIs monitored the barracks for evidence of units returning and to ensure that the same types of unit returned to their previous locations. In fact, some of the deployed units did not return to the GDR but were replaced by similar units on a 'like-for-like' basis.

History repeated itself in December 1980 and January 1981 at the height of the Polish Solidarity crisis. Speculation was rife that the Soviets planned to intervene to suppress the crisis as they had in Czechoslovakia in 1968. An RAF Corridor mission over the Dallgow-Döberitz complex, now housing 35 MRD, showed that the logistic vehicles had again moved from their normal storage areas to join their parent units. The spectre of Czechoslovakia raised itself and the PI responsible, Peter Jefferies, reported this to his section commander, a WRAC captain who was later promoted to brigadier. They then spent several hours in a series of 'full and frank' exchanges justifying the call to their own immediate superiors and the HQ BAOR Intelligence Staff. In the event the Soviets did not invade Poland but the move of the logistic vehicles indicated that it was a serious option. Based on the call, SACEUR raised the NATO alert state as a precaution.

Another indicator of likely Soviet military intentions in Poland came in April 1981 when an MMFL flight, with Major Roland Pietrini as the observer, photographed vehicles at Schönwalde marked with a prominent 'K' on their roofs (see image 56). Historically, during the interventions in Hungary in 1956 and Czechoslovakia in 1968, the Soviets forces had painted similar identification markings on their vehicles so that they could be clearly distinguished from above to reduce the possibilities of fratricide.

Capability Changes

The Cold War period saw many enhancements to GSFG's and the NVA's capabilities to conduct combat operations.

SA-2 Guideline SAM Deployed into the Forward Area

The deployment of the SA-2 Guideline SAM system into the forward area increased GSFG's capability and posed a credible threat to traffic in some of the Corridors and BCZ airspace. It also ratcheted up the pressure on Berlin, because its appearance had serious political and military implications. The effort expended untangling the facts from the fiction of the SA-2 story used multi-source intelligence to paint the full picture, with Corridor and BCZ photography playing a major part in this effort.

A suspected military construction started in 1957 at Glau, south-west of Berlin, on the edge of the BCZ. It was seen on a Corridor mission and consisted of six emplacements circling a single large central one (image 53 shows a similar site in Cuba). Even at this early stage of construction it was camouflaged and high security was evident.

The Allied interpretation units' initial thoughts were that it was probably a new type of heavy anti-aircraft gun site, and its configuration and the arrival of heavily sheeted equipment in the six outer emplacements tended to confirm this. As construction carried on through 1957 and 1958 doubts began to emerge. The outer emplacements were of a 'drive-through' design, not normally associated with AAA systems, and 'electronic-type' vehicles appeared in the central emplacement area. A BRIXMIS ground tour photographed sheeted equipment on a train that was identical to that seen at Glau. This convinced the APIU (BAOR) PIs that they were not anti-aircraft guns. They took a bold step and reassessed their original findings and now identified Glau as a probable SAM site. The HQ BAOR Intelligence Staff supported this assessment and the importance of the site, which was the first SAM deployment outside Russia, was now fully appreciated. Some intelligence agencies expressed doubts about the reassessment but the appearance of SA-2 Guideline missiles on their transporters settled the matter. This unique opportunity to gather intelligence on a state-of-the-art Soviet SAM system, the missiles' details, the target acquisition and fire control radars, the firing unit's TO & E and the system's support equipment was too good to be missed and was firmly grasped. A major collection effort was set in train, involving AMLM ground tours, Corridor and BCZ photographic flights, the ELINT collectors and technical intelligence staffs pooling their information to produce an all-source assessment.

The site's position on the very edge of the BCZ, the difficult access for AMLM ground tours and the overall sensitivity of the collection effort meant that the best way of photographing it, and the associated equipment, was the BRIXMIS Chipmunk. It could provide detailed, close-up images of the site and equipment from which technical drawings and the system's modus operandi could be compiled. On Wednesday 16 July 1959 the Chipmunk, crewed by Wing Commander Hans Neubroch as pilot and Squadron Leader Harry Nunwick, a specialist electronics officer, as observer, took off from Gatow. They set course for the site, adopting the normal flight profile until very close, when, to preserve an element of surprise, Hans took the aircraft down to 300ft and used the trees to conceal their approach. He then circled over the target twice so that Harry could take photographs. They then returned to Gatow at a normal altitude. The flight was an outstanding success. The following day, Hans and Group Captain J. Boardman, the Deputy Chief BRIXMIS, showed the photographs to the C-in-C RAF Germany, who congratulated Hans on a successful sortie. He arranged for the photographs to be flown to the US intelligence organisation in Frankfurt. By Wednesday 21 July they were on President Eisenhower's desk.[5]

Repeated photographic coverage of the site enabled the determination of an SA-2 battery's TO & E and provided the first and very important initial reports on the missiles, transporters and launchers (image 54) as well as the first technical reports on the Spoon Rest target acquisition and Fan Song fire control radar (image 55). JARIC (UK) provided plans of cable runs and detailed scale drawings of all the system-associated equipment. BRIXMIS provided a steady stream of ground and air photography that showed more detail and new aspects of the equipment.

The final analysis was a combination of the PI's eye and the electronic eavesdropper's ears that enabled the full determination of the radar's appearance, configuration, operational frequencies, range and operation. This combined effort embraced the whole gamut of intelligence reporting by the Germany-based PI units: indicators and warning when site construction started; establishing its function when the first equipment appeared; determining the TO & E of the firing unit; and producing technical and equipment reports. The SA-2 Guideline was credited with downing Powers' U-2 in 1960 and the system, albeit in highly modified form, remains in service today. Over the years the sites were progressively hardened.

Situating the Appreciation

In the 1970s the BMP-1 AIFV progressively replaced the 1950s-era PT-76 light amphibious tanks in divisional reconnaissance battalions. At Bernau the new BMP-1s occupied the vehicle storage bays that had previously housed the PT-76s. These were now parked on the hardstandings outside, with their turret and other hatches open to the elements, clearly awaiting disposal instructions. One US organisation proposed that the reconnaissance battalion organisation should now be amended to include a new BMP-1 company in addition to the existing PT-76 equipped company. There was much discussion between the British and US PIs and the Americans finally accepted that the British view was correct, but only after the US Congress had approved the M3 Bradley armoured reconnaissance vehicle procurement programme.

Maskirovska Strikes

In 1976–77 indicators pointed to the imminent issue of T-72 MBTs into GSFG, with the hot candidate for the first recipient being 6 GMRD of 20 GA at Bernau, on the eastern side of the BCZ. It was then equipped with T-55s. A sighting of all the units' T-55s with exercise markings – a white cross that ran from front to rear and side to side – painted on them caused no concerns. The unit was obviously going out on exercise. Barracks activity then went quiet for far longer than normal, which raised curiosity. Surprise, surprise, three weeks later a BRIXMIS Chipmunk sortie photographed the first 'T-72' in the vacant barracks. In fact it was actually a T-64 but at that time its existence was unknown. Over the next few weeks, 'T-72' numbers increased, confirming the unit's re-equipment. The question now was, 'Where had the T-55s gone?'

About 150km south-west of Bernau, at Bad Langensalza, under the Southern Corridor, there was a heavy tank regiment equipped with obsolescent T-10 and T-10M heavy tanks. Four weeks after the T-55s had left Bernau, a large number of exercise-marked tanks appeared at Bad Langensalza. Some of the experienced PIs reported exercise-marked T-10s but this bubble was burst by a newly qualified PI who identified them as T-55s. Two valuable lessons learned: first, a neat demonstration of Soviet preparedness to practise Maskirovska in peacetime; and second, experienced PIs falling for the old trick of seeing what they expected to see, and not what was actually there.

Command and Control

In the 1970s and 1980s the intelligence community expended a lot of effort trying to determine Soviet command and control at all levels, including the vehicles used, the equipment operated and the relationships between them all. Identifying armoured command vehicles was relatively easy, but identifying other vehicles with a command function relied on them being seen with their armoured brethren. Help in cracking this conundrum came from an unexpected source – the Soviets themselves!

In the early 1980s the Soviets adopted a three-tone camouflage paint scheme, similar to the one used by the US forces at the time, that was reported to be IR suppressant unlike the usual overall dark green scheme. The new paints were either in short supply, or slow in coming down the supply chain. Someone at HQ GSFG decided that the first vehicles and equipment to receive the new paint scheme would be those at a high risk of interdiction in wartime. So the Command, Control, Communications, Computer and Information (C4I) and Reconnaissance, Intelligence, Surveillance and Target Acquisition (RISTA) associated vehicles and equipment got a smart new paint job and the PIs got confirmation, and in some cases a surprise, of the Soviet C4I and RISTA assets at divisional and higher command levels. Regiments were slower to adopt the new scheme but the same principle applied throughout.

Whilst serendipity played its part in the command and control study, the PIs put in a lot of conventional interpretation work needed to determine inter-vehicle relationships. One BRIXMIS Chipmunk sortie photographed a divisional headquarters in the field. The photographs clearly showed every cable run on the ground and using this the analysts ascertained the field layout of a divisional headquarters and the various vehicle associations.

It Pays to Look at Everything

In the mid to late 1980s US imagery was examined selectively based in intelligence requirements (IRs) although some of the more experienced PIs continued to look at all frames for anything unusual. Des Pemberton takes up the tale:

> I was going through a US sortie that was returning to West Germany through the South Corridor. I had nearly got to the end when Eisenach training area (a relatively minor one) appeared in quite small scale imagery. I scanned the imagery for any activity and found 10 BMP-1 AIFVs on a range. The BMP-1 normally carried an AT-3 Sagger anti-tank guided missile (ATGM) mounted over the main armament. To fire the Saqger both it and the main armament had to be pointed at the target. These BMP-1 guns were all pointing in different directions and on each turret there was what appeared to be a tube pointing down range at the target area so it looked as though they were fitted with a new ATGM system.

Subsequent analysis found that the ATGM was the AT-5 Spandrel and this was the first US/UK sighting of the system. A review of imagery embarassingly revealed that the modified BMP-1s had been in the DDR for some time!

Technical Intelligence – 'We wouldn't do it like that'

'We wouldn't do it like that' comes under the heading of famous last words of intelligence officers. A new vehicle was seen on vertical photography whose length/width ratio pointed to it being tracked. The lack of visible weaponry, unusual ancillary attachments, location, and association with a Soviet engineer bridging unit suggested a role connected with river crossing. Later photography showed the machine with a raised snorkel and engaged in a river crossing, confirming the initial assessment. In due course, thanks to BRIXMIS ground and air pictures of the 'beast', the PIs made a detailed assessment of the equipment and its capabilities. The most interesting aspect of the story was the refusal of London's technical scientific intelligence community to accept that the Soviets could produce such a piece of equipment – despite irrefutable evidence. Their reason was 'we have looked at such a concept ourselves and discarded it as un-feasible'. Famous last words – indeed.

The Hunting of the Snark – the SA-9 Gaskin

Every two years, or so, the Letzlinger Heide hosted equipment displays. The late 1972 display featured divisional-level equipment, one of which was a BRDM-2 armoured car with an 'H'-shaped frame on top of it. Shortly before this a BRIXMIS ground tour photographed a peculiar antenna over a barracks fence in Perleberg, which housed elements of a motor rifle regiment (MRR). Some poor-quality US Corridor photography of Köthen airfield, taken earlier in the year, showed a possible BRDM-2 with a peculiar structure on its roof. JARIC (UK) assessed this as some type of meteorological apparatus.

In Germany, the PIs believed that the Perleberg 'antenna', the Letzlinger BRDM-2 and the Köthen vehicle were probably the same equipment. Two PIs, who were keen scale modellers, built models of the Perleberg 'antenna' using matchsticks and cardboard. They agreed that the structures at Perleberg and Letzlinger were identical. Using anglepoise lamps as a light source, the models eventually cast an identical shadow to the equipment at Köthen, demonstrating that the three vehicles were the same – ipso facto, our case rested. They concluded that the system was a new low-level SAM system and this was the first time it had been seen. None of the other Western intelligence agencies had any previous knowledge of it either, so it had quietly slipped into service, undetected by satellite coverage. The system was given the NATO designation of SA-9 Gaskin (see image 57).

A Tale of Two Freds

The late 1970s saw GSFG undergoing a major re-equipment programme, especially of artillery systems. A degree of 'new equipment fatigue' set in and the appearance of a

BMP-1 with a small radar antenna on the rear of the turret (later to be identified as the PRP-3 artillery observation post) prompted the inevitable question – 'What do we call it?' The jaded response was 'Fred' and so it became known as Fred. A few days later an MT-LB with a larger radar antenna at the rear of the turret (later identified as SNAR-10 gun locating radar) was seen and the two vehicles became known in the British PI community as Small Fred and Big Fred (see image 58) respectively. The NATO nomenclature committee disapproved of this departure from normal practice and attempted to bring order by allocating the names Small Wedge and Big Wedge. Their efforts were in vain as US IPIRs instead of using the new official nomenclature continued to report them as Small Fred and Big Fred. The committee gave up the uneven fight and officially sanctioned Big Fred and Small Fred, and Freds they remain to this day.

T-64 Main Battle Tank (MBT)

When the T-64 MBTs arrived in GSFG they sparked off a whole raft of intelligence requirements. Soviet paranoia about the compromise of its technical features led to them issuing strict instructions on preventing photography of it. This included placing tarpaulins over it when undertaking maintenance in the open (e.g. gun barrel or power pack changes). On the whole these measures were successful and any photography normally showed the vehicle closed up. But they were sometimes caught napping, as illustrated in image 60. One priority question was determining the main armament's calibre. Despite many photographs taken by AMLM ground tours and light aircraft sorties, the answer eluded the intelligence community until a light aircraft sortie photographed a T-64 being re-ammunitioned. Alongside the tank were the open ammunition boxes. The photographs revealed markings stating that the contents were 125mm – question answered.

The Zerbst Phantom

A Soviet fighter regiment equipped with MiG-21 Fishbed aircraft was based at Zerbst airfield in the Southern Corridor. An RAF Corridor mission in the early 1970s imaged an F-4 Phantom parked outside one of the hangars. The aircraft had a slightly different nose profile to a normal F-4 and carried no national markings. Much speculation followed as to how and why it had got there. The assessment was that it was a former USAF aircraft that had been shot down in Vietnam and that the Soviets had made it sufficiently airworthy to take round to brief their own fighter pilots on its strengths and weaknesses. After about a fortnight it departed Germany, never to be seen again. Some sources think that the 'Zerbst Phantom' was a mock-up cobbled together by modifying an existing Soviet airframe. The idea has largely been discounted as there was other intelligence indicating that it was the genuine article.

Secure Communications Upgrades

A buried communications array some 5 miles outside the BCZ was photographed by a Chipmunk during its construction in the mid 1970s. The array was thought to use a secure sub-surface propagated Very Low Frequency (VLF) wave system and it belonged to HQ GSFG at Zossen-Wünsdorf for use by senior commanders to communicate with Moscow.

Sometimes we got it wrong

We all make mistakes and the PI community was no exception. Two of the more memorable 'wild goose chases' are recounted below.

BTR-60PB or BRDM-2

The NVA's Beelitz storage depot had over 150 BRDM-2 armoured cars in open storage. One day an Allied agency reported them as BTR-60PB. In their defence the two vehicles are of similar appearance and easy to mis-identify on poor imagery, especially if there were no other vehicles to compare them with. It took ages to convince the agency of their mistake and after one particularly bruising session, one British PI cynically said: 'It requires the simultaneous publication of an act of war, an Act of the British Parliament, an Act of the US Congress and an amendment to a Royal Artillery Drill Book before they will be convinced that a mistake has been made.'

The Saga of the Krampnitz Drill Square

Krampnitz at the southern end of the Dallgow-Döberitz training area housed elements of a TD until the 1980s when an MRD moved in. One of the great mysteries that had exercised minds for at least three decades was: what was held under the Krampnitz parade square? The square was on the same level as the rest of the barracks, but underneath was a large semi-underground storage area with vehicle size entrances capable of giving access to it. Vapour was often seen coming out of the entrances, which generated many theories as to what was there. The first idea was that it held a reserve tank regiment, which caused alarms because it could mean that all GSFG divisions had such a regiment, thus increasing GSFG's overall tank holdings by about 2,000 tanks! The appearance of chemical defence-associated vehicles caused the next alarm – was it now a divisional chemical weapon store, despite there being no other indications of such storage? After much examination of photography from the Corridor and AMLMs, the answer came one sunny morning when washing lines of uniforms were seen being hung out to dry. The under square accommodation housed nothing more offensive than the divisional laundry, which used similar vehicles to the Divisional Chemical Defence Battalion, such as autoclave trucks and a hot and cold washing system, to delouse and decontaminate uniforms before issuing them to new users.

Inter-Allied Co-operation

At the heart of photographic exploitation was the co-operation between the Western Allies. British and French co-operation was mainly confined to the exchange of BCZ flight and ground tour photography and reports under the Tri-Mission agreement.

The British and US intelligence relationships went far deeper and stemmed from the close collaboration forged during the Second World War at the Government Code and Cypher School (GCCS), Bletchley Park and ACIU at Medmenham. During the Cold War this co-operation extended from senior management down to units and even individual PIs. There was regular joint liaison and many joint projects to maximise the use of resources.

From the outset the British and the Americans exchanged photography from the mapping update programme of the early post-war years. This soon extended to exchanging Corridor missions photography and there was a regular courier run from Rheindahlen to the 497 RTS/RTG to facilitate this. From the late 1960s there were regular exchanges of individual PIs with their opposite numbers. The British sent Army and RAF personnel on short-term attachments to 497 RTS/RTG at Wiesbaden and ODCSI at Heidelberg and the USA sent Army, Air Force and in one case a US Marine, to work with 6 Int Coy and PID. These attachments were in addition to those connected with joint projects.

PI Workshops

In the early 1970s Major Lionel Lacey-Johnson, whose previous tour had been as an exchange officer in the USA became OC 6 Int Coy. He believed that regular meetings between the PI units to discuss matters of mutual interest informally would be beneficial to both communities. He initiated quarterly PI workshops that were hosted by the British at Rheindahlen and the Americans at Heidelberg or Wiesbaden in rotation. The workshops achieved much, including avoiding duplication of PI effort and joint programmes where one country would take lead role. Sharing was the name of the game. One definite mutual interest was served on the food front. The Americans would buy various barbecue items from the PX for the British in exchange for Weetabix breakfast cereal that was not available in the American PX facilities. On balance the British probably got the better deal.

Joint Programmes

Until 1962 APIU (BAOR) made amendments to 1: 25,000 maps of the Corridor areas and the immediate environs. Hand-drawn amendments included new construction, alterations to existing facilities and new infrastructure. These amended sheets were regularly sent to 497 RTS/RTG, which incorporated them onto existing map sheets. These were then issued under a very limited distribution to relevant intelligence organisations. The programme was discontinued as satellite imagery became available to the cartographers, although 6 Int Coy continued to maintain the 1: 25000 maps for their own purposes.

When 6 Int Coy reporting emphasis changed from predominantly I&W to unit analysis they started to generate area prints that divided barracks into unit areas. At this stage the USA still used area graphics depicting the whole barracks area. They rapidly saw that the British method would improve their IPIRs' quality and provide deeper analysis of intelligence. The USA proposed a joint programme producing area prints to an agreed standard and a common system of defining areas and sub-areas. This meant that both British and US PI and intelligence units reported in a common way, reducing possibilities for errors. Agreeing common area prints slowed production down slightly but this was more than offset by the efficiencies gained.

The Box-Body Guide

This joint project, led by the US Army's ODCSI at Heidelberg, involved analysing box-bodied vehicles (van trucks in the USA) to enable collectors to associate a particular box with a unit or function. The containers were encoded with a five-digit number that denoted the roof shape, the number of windows on the vehicle's offside and their positions, the number of hatches on the offside and various other characteristics. The last two digits denoted the individual number of a box-body in a series. The vehicle chassis was not included in the encoding because boxes could be moved from one chassis to another.

The offside (left-hand side) was used to define the box-body numbers because it was the view most often seen by the AMLM ground tours who supplied the bulk of the photography used in the analysis. Other views – right-hand side, front, rear and overhead – came from the AMLM ground tours, the BCZ light aircraft flights and occasionally from the Corridor missions if the photographic quality was good enough.

The encoding system is best explained by the following examples: GAZ-66 BB41101 was a GAZ-66-mounted flat- or near-flat-roofed body with one window and one side access panel in the body and was No. 01 in the 411 series of box-bodies. ZIL-131 BB23103 was a ZIL-131-mounted deep-chamfered-roof body with three windows and one side access panel that was No. 03 in the 231 series of box-bodies. The photographic information was collated with other source information (defector reports, association with deployments and units) to determine each box-body's individual function. This was especially important when defining the C4I associated vehicles at unit and formation level. The number of individual box-bodies ran into several thousand that were all faithfully recorded and disseminated in a series of HQ USAREUR books.

SPN-30 Paint Box Radar-Jamming System

Identifying the function and components of the SPN-30 Paint Box radar jamming system (see image 61) was the result of joint British and US analysis over a thirteen-year period. The system consisted of three box-bodied vehicles mounted on URAL-375 or URAL-4320 6 × 6 truck chassis. One vehicle contained the systems generators and was easily recognised by the two large roof-mounted exhausts. The other two vehicles contained the antennae, jamming and other communications equipment. The system first appeared in 1978 in the area associated with the air defence jamming battalion of the Front ECM regiment at Schönwalde. Over the next nine months British and US PIs held regular meetings with the UK MoD in London and HQ USAREUR at Heidelberg to examine their findings. After much debate, discussion, measurement, and analysis of the various cones, antennae, support systems and its deployment, the consensus was that the system was an air defence jammer targeted against the 'E', 'F' and 'G' band terrain-following radars used by RAF Tornados and USAF F-111 fighter-bombers. It was also believed to have the capability to jam the E-3 AWACs system used by the USA, UK and NATO. The final report on the system by 6 Int Coy was accepted by Technical Intelligence (Air) at the UK MoD in its entirety. Further analysis revealed the presence of eight Paint Box systems in the air defence jamming battalion, with each system consisting of a jammer vehicle, an operations vehicle and a generator vehicle. The systems deployed in pairs which gave GSFG four complete mobile systems.

The East Germans also acquired the system and later one of the PIs who had been involved in the 6 Int Coy and BRIXMIS analytical efforts was given the opportunity to examine a former East German Paint Box system. He said that: 'It was gratifying to see that all the time and hard work spent by 6 Int Coy, BRIXMIS and the Americans analysing the system was confirmed, so our time was not wasted.'

Conclusion

The large numbers of installations, unit changes, equipment modernisation programmes and near-constant exercise programmes kept the personnel and aircraft involved in watching them under constant pressure. This was made all the more difficult by the lack of Soviet transparency and a smattering of deception. But diligent work, close co-operation and common sense managed to produce a wealth of carefully organised intelligence reporting on the people and equipment that would face the NATO Allies if the Cold War in Germany went 'hot'. It also begs the question of what the Soviets knew of the West's air reconnaissance activities that collected this intelligence.

Notes

1 The '1910' reports were named after the two Soviet divisions they examined: 19 MRD and 10 GTD.
2 Maskirovska – Russian term denoting concealment and deception efforts designed to mislead the enemy.
3 Bates (2001), p. 19.
4 The National Archive: PRO PREM 11/3698 – minute from Chairman JIC (Sir Norman Brook) to PM, 30 May 1961, and PM's approval of flights, 1 June 1961.
5 H. Neubroch (2001), 'RAF Element BRIXMIS: Further recollections of Operational Experiences 1957–59', *RAF Historical Society Journal*, No. 23, pp. 106–15.

9

WHAT DID THE OPPOSITION KNOW?

While the Kremlin is basically flexible in its reaction to political realities, it is by no means unamenable to considerations of prestige. Like almost any other government, it can be placed by tactless and threatening gestures in a position where it cannot afford to yield.

The Sources of Soviet Conduct (George Kennan, 1947)

The primary question concerning Western Corridor and BCZ flights has always been: just what did the Soviets and East Germans know about them? The simple answer is probably quite a lot. Significant, and growing, anecdotal evidence shows that Soviet military personnel were well aware of the reconnaissance flights. More difficult to determine are the questions following on from that fact, including: what level of detail did they know? Why did they tolerate them? Why did they not protest and harass them more?

Contact with Russian and German embassies in London has yielded little. There was no response from the Russians, although the Germans believe that many of the detailed East German files were probably exported to Russia in the interregnum between the fall of The Wall in 1989 and German reunification in October 1990. Supporting this contention is Peter Jefferies' recollection of seeing photography of the MfS ('Stasi') HQ in Berlin-Karlshorst in early 1990 with military cargo trucks backed up to every available entrance and being loaded with material from the offices.

The limited available official information, together with the accounts of some participants, presents a picture that shows the Soviets and East Germans had a very clear idea of the true purpose of Allied reconnaissance flights and that the knowledge of them was widely disseminated through the military at least. What is more difficult to ascertain are the reasons why the Soviets seemed to tolerate these flights and even appeared to display equipment and operations knowing full well that they would be seen. To start with, there were plenty of simple, overt ways that could have given the Soviets knowledge of Corridor and BCZ reconnaissance flights.

Human Sources – German Employees

The Allied forces in Germany and Berlin employed several thousand German citizens in their installations and offices. Many had relatives, often elderly, in the GDR, which made them susceptible to coercion and possible recruitment as agents. Although most were in relatively low-level positions, such as mess staff and cleaners, there were others who worked in positions such as pay and administration clerks. These employees should not have had any access to operational details but would have been able to observe and report activities, especially unusual ones, unguarded conversations and the personal foibles of military personnel, which could have been used as a potential recruitment tool.

After German reunification in 1990, one of the RAF Gatow Officers' Mess barmen was exposed as having been an East German agent for some time. As a barman he was in a position to overhear conversations, some of which were inevitably 'shop', and to 'talent spot' for potential recruits, either voluntary or pressed. Besides the personnel directly employed by the military, there were also those employed by the various welfare and support organisations such as the British NAAFI, the French Économat and US BX and PX, who could overhear gossip and conversations that would all add grist to the intelligence mill.

Ample opportunities existed to gather low-level intelligence from apparently innocuous sources. For example, in the early days the RAF Gatow Station Flight authorisation book was probably in open view in the hangar office so it could have been overseen by anyone in that office. The phrase 'Berlin Ring – Photo' was entered in the 'Purpose of Flight' column. Doubtless other similar opportunities would have existed.

Military Media

Another open and fruitful low-level intelligence source was the military media with their plethora of official service newspapers such as *Sixth Sense* and *The Stars and Stripes*, together with the many station and garrison magazines that named units and personalities and recorded events. The military radio and TV stations like the American Forces Network (AFN) and the British Forces Network (BFN), later the British Forces Broadcasting Service (BFBS), provided details of units, locations, people and service life in Germany. The extent and value of information gathered by low-level agents and overt sources is now very difficult to determine more than twenty-five years after they stopped. Suffice it to say, they made the work of Soviet and GDR intelligence officers a lot easier than that of their Western counterparts.

Operating Units

Unlike the Red Army, one of the first things an Allied unit erected on arriving at a new location was a sign that proclaimed its presence. Whilst the French were quite open that their unit was connected with electronics, the British and Americans tried to conceal their air reconnaissance activities within apparently innocuous units. The British 'hid' their aircraft in the legitimate Communications Squadron that operated light transport flights within Germany and to Britain. The USA put its aircraft in support squadrons that overtly operated courier flights and carried passengers and cargo to provide a veneer of respectability, as well as operating the reconnaissance flights. A cursory examination of the subordination of the 7405 SS/7405 OS, and the other support squadrons' roles, would have soon made the hidden agenda apparent.

ATC Clearances, Call Signs and Flight Patterns

At a daily routine level, an initial indicator of a possible spyflight in the Corridors would have been the filing of the flight plan with the BASC. The departure bases of RAF Bückeberg or RAF Wildenrath for the British, Lahr or Metz-Frascaty for the French and Wiesbaden or Rhein-Main for the USA were all known by the Soviets to house reconnaissance associated units. However, these airfields also hosted legitimate transport units, so knowing the originating airfield was not conclusive evidence of nefarious activity.

Aircraft call signs depended on the flight's operator and could have been an indicator of a non-standard flight. Until at least 1977, the RAF Communications Squadron used the Transport Command's five-letter identification letter system that began with 'M'. By the early 1980s, 60 Squadron had adopted the RAF transport aircraft call sign 'Ascot' followed by a four-figure flight identification number – Pembrokes used the 'Ascot 8XXX' series. This identified the flight, not the aircraft operating it, so the call sign could not be permanently associated with an individual aircraft.

The French allocated 'civil' registrations as ATC call signs to their military aircraft and each individual aircraft had a unique 'F-XXXX' registration that it carried throughout its service life. Connecting 'F-XXXX' to an individual aircraft was a simple matter.

Until around the mid 1970s, US transport aircraft used call signs that started with the operator (e.g. MAC) followed by a contraction of the aircraft's tail number. Associating the tail number with an individual aircraft was a simple matter. When the C-130s joined the 7405 OS in 1975 they changed to tactical call signs. Training missions often used 'Herky' (as used by many standard transport C-130s), followed by two numbers and 'Ask' followed by two numbers on operational flights.

The Soviets' awareness of call sign associations with particular aircraft and their role becomes clear in an account from US airman David Brogg. Between 1964 and 1975, C-97G 53–0106 operated Project Creek Flea and used its tail number as part of its ATC call sign. To extend and retract the many antennae on the aircraft involved micro-switches that sometimes malfunctioned, especially in winter. From inside the aircraft, it was impossible to tell how much of the antennae might still be extended. In such situations:

> The procedure was to declare an emergency and exit via the Centre Corridor, the shortest one … One December day in 1966, the ice would not let the antennae stow securely for three days in a row. After declaring the third emergency on the same aircraft, on the same week, the Soviet controller in the BASC turned to his US

counterpart and asked: 'What is the matter with your spy plane this week? This is the third time he has not landed here.'[1]

All flightplans recorded the actual numbers of personnel on board the aircraft, for use in case of an accident, rather than trying to disguise the real numbers onboard. This may have helped give away a flight's true purpose to the Soviets.

Once in the Corridors a reconnaissance flight's meandering course and varying altitudes would have been obvious to the BARTCC radar controllers. They were used to the normal Corridor flights that strictly adhered to a course close to the Corridor's centreline and maintained their assigned altitude. The reconnaissance crews explained their deviations as 'equipment failure' or 'crew training', but these must have been glaringly obvious to the Soviet representatives in the BASC. Once in the BCZ the US flights generally flew around it for up to thirty minutes before landing at Tempelhof, unlike normal flights that went directly to their destination airfield.

East German Border Guards watching the RAF's comings and goings at Gatow would have seen how the Pembrokes parked with their passenger door facing the hangar so that the number of personnel onboard could not be observed and verified. At Tempelhof, the 'fence watchers', some of whom were probably East German or Russian agents, would see up to fifteen men disembark from the C-130 and later see the same number of personnel embark again for the return trip – very different from a standard C-130 cargo flight.[2]

The Aircraft

Associating an individual aircraft's identification number with its call signs and known roles provided a reasonable indication of why it was in the Corridors. Efforts were made to conceal sensor hatches and antennae; they were not always successful because they had to be opened to allow the systems to operate. In the Corridors and BCZ where the aircraft flew below 10,000ft, such openings would often be clearly visible from the ground to the naked eye or to watchers using binoculars, or similar optical viewers.

Pembroke pilot Brian King told us that once, when on leave in Berlin with his family, 'I heard a familiar engine tone and looked up to see this Pembroke flying an unmistakable photographic pattern over the city'. RAF PI Andrew Scott recalled seeing a Pembroke flying over Rheindahlen taking photographs of the Headquarters buildings. 'As it came over you could see the hatch open underneath and a camera shutter moving, so I don't think it ever fooled the Russians!' Peter Jefferies also remembers this, or a similar, flight in around 1976 or 1977.

Harassment in the Corridors

From the outset the Russians harassed flights in the Corridors, but this was inconsistent and not directed solely at ICFs. The level of harassment depended on the international political temperature at the time. In the late 1940s/early 1950s there was often harassment of flights and incidences of Russian fighters opening fire on Allied military and civilian aircraft using the Corridors. This was especially true in the lead-up to the Berlin Blockade and Airlift. The fighters sometimes flew very close to aircraft, causing crashes and fatalities, such as the BEA Viking and Yak-3 collision over Dallgow-Döberitz in April 1948.[3]

There were certainly many near misses, but these were generally attributed to accidental miscalculation, or excessive zeal, rather than deliberately planned and officially sanctioned action, although the possibility that there was a mix of both cannot be totally discounted.[4] There were also instances when Soviet fighters practised interception techniques on aircraft in the Corridors. In times of heightened international or local tension, there were likely to be more 'interceptions' and close fly-bys to demonstrate to the West the Corridors' vulnerability. This was especially true in 1961 and 1962 when the second Berlin crisis approached its climax. Incidents that involved large numbers of MiG fighters operating within the Corridors and intercepting aircraft were discussed by the British Cabinet in February 1962.[5] Overall, Corridor incidents may well have been under-reported to avoid drawing unwanted attention to reconnaissance flights.

In 1962 the US complained to the Soviets on a number of occasions about the interception of its Corridor flights, although few resulted in formal diplomatic protests. On 23 July, two MiGs closed to within a hundred feet of a Carol Ann CT-29 (49–1910) some 10 to 15 miles north of Tempelhof. Later on the same day, a US Overseas Airways DC-7 was shadowed for some seven to eight minutes about 70 to 80 miles west of Berlin in the Southern Corridor. The 'interception' took place at around 4,000ft and at one point a MiG was only 20yd from the DC-7 and flying 'in a manner which endangered the DC-7's safety'. The US protest added that this was the fourth serious incident in seven days.[6]

Frank Doucette, flying aboard the Hot Pepper C-54, recounted that:

> Flying in the South Corridor, we got caught with the camera door open, working. The MiG pilot looked and waved. We waved back and took his picture. When we got to Berlin we contacted 'Homeplate' and they said for us to go to Châteauroux Air Base, France. When we got there, we were directed into a large hangar with engines running. We shut down and there was sitting another C-54 with the same tail number. Imagine that!

The crew returned to Wiesbaden in the re-marked aircraft and for the next week continued to 'trail their coat' along the Corridors. 'Captain Stan Sturgill, First-Lieutenant Ron Hummel and I flew the Corridors at maximum altitude and at its edge. We had parachutes, steel pots, and blood chits, but the Soviets didn't take the bait as they could see the distinctive large belly radome was absent.'

One of the most serious harassment incidents was the interception of a Pembroke. On 17 January 1972 XL954 was intercepted by three MiG-17's which thundered by in line astern. Rob Fallon, one of the navigators, described how their Pembroke, flying close to the edge of the Southern Corridor, suddenly started bouncing around:

Immediately the radio became very frantic and we went onto a discrete frequency. The pilot lowered the undercarriage and flaps and brought XL954 down close to its stall speed and moved us back onto the corridor centreline. Meanwhile we were bouncing around in the back, rewinding the film to re-expose it, expecting that we might have to force land. Our cover story suddenly looked very thin. I had been reading the *Gulag Archipelago* at the time and had visions that, even if very lucky, we might end up in Siberia for a very long time!

The MiG-17s couldn't compete with such slow speed, so carried on circling in order to stay with us. Soon another aircraft, this time a MiG-21, came up. It flew on a reciprocal heading beneath us and close enough to see the pilot looking up and waving. We could easily see the missiles loaded under the wings; he was probably at around 2,000ft. Radar was talking to us continually and monitored its approach.

After the event the RAF received an apology for the incident from the Russians through the BASC. The excuse given was that a trainee radar operator monitoring the Corridors had mis-plotted an aircraft, showing it had an apparent ground speed of 600 knots. Checking the inbound flight plans to Berlin, the only thing around was a twin-engined RAF aircraft and he made the assumption that it was one of our new RAF Phantoms commencing an attack run on Berlin to start World War Three! They were told that we were not shot down, or forced to land, because the first CAP MiG to buzz us told his control that the aircraft was not a Phantom and perhaps they should check again.[7]

One significant piece of intelligence came out of this incident. The intercepting pilots could be heard talking in Russian. This confirmed Soviet involvement in CAPs because until then the intelligence suggested that only East Germans operated the alert and CAP aircraft.

A number of possible reasons explain the near misses experienced by Allied reconnaissance aircraft in the Corridors, such as high cockpit workloads causing distraction, failing to understand ATC instructions, and some because individual pilots wanted to 'show off' or be 'mischievous'. Despite the harassment, not a single Allied aircraft operating in the Corridors or BCZ on reconnaissance operations was brought down, although the Soviets had shown on many occasions that they were quite prepared to bring down overflights and peripheral missions and to harass civilian and military flights en route to Berlin. There are instances of Allied aircraft leaving the relative safety of the Corridors but these were rare and largely undocumented. When they happened noisy Soviet protests usually followed, but not always. On 6 May 1975 an RAF Pembroke strayed from the Centre Corridor, penetrating into GDR airspace by 3½ miles. It eventually regained the Corridor after flying some 15 miles further before flying on to RAF Wildenrath. The British BASC element reported: 'no contact was possible on any frequency' with the aircraft until after it re-entered the Corridor. The Soviet controller in the BASC was not told of the incursion and no protest was filed.[8]

Official records cast no light on the reasons for this 'diversion' so any explanation is speculative. Deliberately leaving the Corridor, even just by a few miles, was very risky. Such action would have to be approved at a very high level and justified by an intelligence priority of the highest order. Close-in 'looks' happened very rarely. They were never 'officially' authorised and there would be no official instructions. At the crew brief it could be suggested that, if conditions allowed, they might fly to the very edge of the Corridor to photograph a target of great importance but the final decision rested with the crew. In the event of a Soviet protest, the crew might receive an 'interview without coffee and biscuits from their CO', which was then instantly forgotten. The simple explanation is that there was probably a navigational error and the pilot eased the aircraft back into the Corridor rather than make an abrupt turn, in the hope that no one would notice it.

However, in this instance, the following day another Pembroke, most likely a passenger aircraft flying from RAF Gütersloh to Gatow along the Centre Corridor, adjacent to where the previous day's Pembroke had left the Corridor, was subjected to a frightening airmiss:

> the twin jet came from the South [and] passed in front of Pembroke by approx. 50yd. Then made a left turn onto a Southerly heading and disappeared from the Pembroke pilot's view.

Unable to identify it definitively, the pilot described it as a 'twin jet, swept wing with red star on fuselage'.[9]

No other details of this incident are available, but the airmiss could indicate that the previous day's excursion had indeed been noticed by the Soviets and was a sign of their displeasure.

As serious as reconnaissance flights were, a number of incidents, with a humorous side, illustrate that the Soviets had a very clear picture of what the Allies were doing. Phil Chaney described that during his tour: 'one week before Christmas at an airfield on the Centre Corridor trampled out in the thick snow, just in front of the tower, in English and in time for the routine Pembroke's overflight was "Happy Christmas".'[10]

Others have recounted similar messages. Indeed, snow seems to have been a popular medium for Soviet communication with overflying aircraft. As well as simple greetings there were also forthright expressions of the desire that the recipients 'go away' – or words to that effect. Phil Chaney describes another contact with the Russians around 1980 during a darts match against members of the BASC in the Gatow Officers' Mess. 'While I was playing against the Russian Colonel, he turned to me and asked, very slowly, if I was visiting on "The Pembroke" – then winked!'

Major General Peter Williams, who did two tours with BRIXMIS, was convinced that even the East German population knew precisely what the Chipmunks did. He recalls:

> On one occasion a forester stopped us on tour as we were trying to creep up on a Soviet radar deployment in a forest north of Potsdam and, taking no notice of our protestations of incomprehension, announced: 'Sorry, but you're too late! The

Russians were here for four days with about a dozen trucks, but they went home to Schönwalde late this morning. But don't worry, your little plane came over and buzzed them earlier!'[11]

Similarly, on 26 March 1981 there was a BASC Senior Controllers meeting. At the time there were a number of ongoing disputes between the western allies and the Soviets over a number of issues. These included a very close 'airmiss' between a Soviet helicopter and a Panam airlines B-727, a bullet that had struck an RAF C-130 landing at RAF Gatow and the Soviets unhappy with the conduct of western light aircraft flights within the BCZ, but especially the British and their Chipmunk in parts of the zone. At the time the Soviet Chief Controller, Colonel Evstigneyev was seen as rather a testy and excitable man and during the meeting he protested a number of times about alleged low flying transgressions in the Karlshorst and Werneuchen airfield areas of the Chipmunk and said: 'Earlier this week the British Chipmunk was near Karlshorst taking pictures. The pilot took some of me walking between buildings. May I have copies please.'[12] Roy Marsden has also asserted that the Soviets knew exactly what the RAF Chipmunks were up to. He has said that in meetings with Soviet SERB officers they 'often made oblique references to those who participated, about the Chipmunk aircraft and where it had been seen over installations both inside and allegedly outside the BCZ'. He believes that the Soviets largely turned a blind eye to many of the West's intelligence-gathering activities in and over Berlin and the GDR. He thinks many senior Soviet officers, up until the late 1970s, had served in the Great Patriotic War (the Second World War) and did not want to repeat that experience. They perhaps thought the way to deter a Western pre-emptive attack was to let them see just how strong Warsaw Pact forces were and that this would dissuade 'any reckless Western politicians' from risking conflict for a 'quick victory'.[13]

Why not Stronger Countermeasures?

If well aware of Allied reconnaissance flights, why did the Soviet forces not undertake stronger countermeasures? There are a wide range of possible explanations for this.

Some British participants expressed the view that the lack of strong action against Western aircraft was a quid pro quo from the Soviets for the occasional wanderings of allegedly camera-equipped Aeroflot and Interflug flights that deviated from their assigned flight track to overfly military installations in Federal Germany. They would not respond to ATC instructions until they had returned to their assigned route.[14] For example, on 29 October 1976, Aeroflot Flight SU297 from Moscow to Madrid, via Luxembourg, made a substantial deviation from its assigned track and flight level to overfly the USAF's Bitburg Air Base. At the time the TAB-V aircraft shelters there were being modified to accept F-15 aircraft and it was strongly believed that SU297 had deliberately deviated to conduct aerial reconnaissance of the base.[15]

Similarly Peter Jefferies recalls the time that a Mi-26 Halo heavy-lift helicopter was en route to France for its first appearance at the Paris Airshow in 1981. It transited the Corridors, as it was entitled to do, exiting into West German airspace, then deviated from its approved flight plan to overfly the USAF bases at Bitburg and Hahn. During the deviation it failed to respond to any ATC transmissions. On arrival in Paris the rear clamshell doors opened to reveal a camera on an oblique mount in the rear fuselage.

The Risks of Deliberate Shoot Downs

To deliberately bring down a Corridor reconnaissance flight without prima facie evidence of its activity would have been a very high-risk strategy for the Soviets. It would certainly have resulted in an international incident and immediately increased local tension, with the possibility of Western retaliation.

Proving aerial espionage in international airways such as the Corridors would have needed the airframe and reconnaissance equipment to survive sufficiently intact to be put on public display, like Powers' U-2. It would have been entirely unpredictable whether such a result could have been achieved from a forced landing, or shoot down. Even if the Soviets could publicly demonstrate 'aerial espionage', it would probably have bothered few politicians and diplomats on either side. Intelligence gathering was practised by both parties, so apart from some faux diplomatic indignation and posturing followed by tit-for-tat responses, inevitably temporarily damaging local relationships, it would have made little difference overall. The main outcome would have been a Soviet propaganda victory and there might have been a short-term suspension of reconnaissance flights, but they would have resumed after a decent interval. Western retaliation might have included harassing of Aeroflot and Interflug flights over West Germany or barring them from Western airports. The possibilities were endless but would have depended on Western political will. The only real value in shooting down an aircraft would have been to apply political and military pressure on the city and there were easier, and more predictable, ways to do that around Berlin.

Capturing a reconnaissance aircraft intact, with the crew alive and being able to put them on public display, would have been a very different matter. There were often attempts to lure aircraft out of the Corridors by 'spoofing' – giving false instructions or signals by Soviet and GDR forces. This came in many forms, such as suggesting that an aircraft was off-course and needed to correct its heading.[16] If a genuine in-flight emergency was ever declared, a 'helpful voice' would come on to the frequency offering landing options at a Soviet or GDR airfield along the route.[17] In 1981, Peter Jefferies was a passenger on a training flight which started to receive suspicious instructions that would have directed them into Werneuchen airfield. The day was '8/8ths blue and gin clear' so it was a fruitless exercise by the Soviets, but nevertheless they tried.

Equipment Displays – Showing Us Too

Periodically the Soviets put on equipment displays to show senior officers their latest 'kit'. They would show examples of each equipment item to be found in a formation, or present a themed display of equipment associated with a particular function, such as the Army-level air defence equipment display shown in image 66. These displays were often mounted under a Corridor and there was considerable speculation that besides their stated purpose they were also intended to be a 'show and tell' for the West's benefit.

The foregoing is compelling enough evidence that the Soviets and East Germans were fully aware of the reconnaissance flights. What they may not have been aware of was the quantity and high quality of the photography produced and the intelligence extracted from it.

As well as putting equipment on display that would be very visible to reconnaissance flights, there is some evidence to the contrary, that the Soviets sometimes tried to conceal the presence of specific equipment items until they were ready to reveal them. In early 1977, the SA-8 Gecko SAM system was the 'hot' intelligence 'flavour of the month'. Was it in East Germany or not? Peter Jefferies remembers being on a training flight in Pembroke XL953, which was not 'in fit' on 15 March 1977. The flight landed at RAF Gatow in the late morning and after lunch they took off to 'do' the BCZ. As the aircraft approached Dallgow-Döberitz, three SA-8 Gecko TELAR were seen moving at high speed across the former airfield towards the hangars. Was this just a normal return to barracks? Or had the garrison been warned of the 'spy-plane' and was it quickly attempting to conceal the SA-8's presence?[18]

Why did the Soviets and East Germans not locate their forces in areas out of Corridor and BCZ camera range? Most GSFG and NVA forces were housed in former Reichswehr barracks that had been taken over at the end of the war, although the NVA possessed some new-build barracks. The cost of building all new facilities out of camera range would have been prohibitive. Locating forces out of camera range would also have created a huge gap in the centre of the GDR devoid of military forces, which would need to be repopulated with forces prior to any hostilities. Moving forces to fill such a gap would have been an important indicator in its own right that would have been hard to ignore. In any case constructing bases in almost any part of the GDR would still have left them vulnerable to some level of AMLM observation and aerial reconnaissance.

Allied Secrecy

If the Soviets knew so much, why were the Allies so secretive about their reconnaissance flights? A cursory glance suggests that much of the secrecy practised by Allied military and governmental bodies was directed at concealing this knowledge from elements of their own, and other, military services and governments, although proving this would be extremely difficult. Openness would certainly have confirmed for the Soviets what they had long suspected. Reconnaissance operations were restricted to the three Allies. The British, French and US products were only shared directly between them and not widely with other NATO Allies. The West German government was never formally informed about the British flights until after they ceased in 1990. The Germans would almost certainly have insisted on the USA and UK sharing their information and material with them in return for allowing the flights' continuation. Given the extent of the FRG government's penetration by hostile intelligence services, the Soviets would soon have become totally aware of the operations and probably their products. Keeping the flights' existence from them, and other less secure NATO nations, was considered necessary to reduce the risk of the operation's compromise.

The use of transport and training aircraft meant that the intelligence-gathering operations were not overtly flaunted in the Soviets' face, especially as they were integrated into the normal supply and VIP flights to and from the city. The sensors carried were very discreetly mounted and the numerous tell-tale external blisters and aerials associated with dedicated reconnaissance aircraft disguised as far as possible. Whilst the real role was kept largely hidden from the casual observer and was not an open affront to Soviet sensitivities, there was no immediate need for any 'face-saving' retaliation. This was a repetition of the situation created by early overflights of the USSR. Aware of the realities, as long as Corridor and BCZ flights were not too obvious, or provocative, the Soviet government was not forced into a political position where it was forced to act against them.

Conclusions

Politicians generally appeared to have recognised the military need for overflights to acquire intelligence. British politicians, senior MoD and FO/FCO officials saw political benefits of co-operation with the USA. Sharing British-collected imagery was a way of maintaining good relations with the US intelligence community and contributing something tangible to the US–UK intelligence 'special relationship', which was inevitably dominated by the Americans. But British politicians and officials were considerably more nervous about Soviet awareness of the programmes than the French and Americans. The British wanted the Corridor flights kept on a short leash, with a high degree of political control and 'low visibility'. Their US counterparts treated Berlin operations in a more relaxed manner, important, but essentially 'routine' in nature. Both countries quickly developed procedures to balance the potential gains against the political and military risks involved until operations ended in 1990. The combination of AMLM activities and overflights of the GDR resulted in considerable information sharing between the three Western Allies and provided their intelligence agencies with rich pickings over the duration of the Cold War.

Britain, France and the USA devoted significant resources to the collection and exploitation of airborne intelligence in the Corridors and BCZ and from peripheral flights. The operations grew in both extent and sophistication and were vital for several reasons. Until the mid 1960s they provided the only regular, relatively low-risk, surveillance of the most forward-based Soviet and East German forces. The priority was to try to gauge the level of direct threat to West Germany and Berlin, especially during the turbulent period of the second Berlin crisis between 1958 and 1962 and when The Wall was erected. Later, the priority changed to assembling more processed intelligence on the huge number of troops and their equipment stationed in the GDR and around Berlin that were widely observable from the Corridors and BCZ. This vast array of equipment was often the latest and best that the Soviet forces possessed. Corridor and BCZ flights produced a prodigious quantity of high-quality imagery and were in a strong position to record the evolution and development of Soviet and GDR force structures over the forty-five years of the Cold War.

The operations were conducted in great secrecy, despite the circumstantial and anecdotal information that the Soviets and East Germans were well aware of them. These flying activities went largely unhindered by Soviet and GDR forces. Indeed the Soviets became complicit in the whole process by being prepared to keep their knowledge of the Western flights largely to themselves. The Allies conducted the flights covertly, keeping them largely secret from their own armed forces, let alone the wider public. This allowed the Soviets to 'turn a Nelsonian eye' to them, largely impotent as they were to prevent them, without provoking a serious crisis with the West. Had the Soviets been determined to hide their activities and equipment from the West, they could have done so more effectively. By not constantly trying to hide

The Wall comes down in 1990.

all their operations and equipment, sometimes doing the complete opposite by putting them openly on display, the Soviets helped foster an element of stability, even at very tense times across a vulnerable divided city at the heart of the Cold War.

Notes

1 David Brog to Stephen Barranco communication, 26 February 2008.
2 van Waarde (2010), p. 9.
3 Aldrich (2011), pp. 111–12, 126–31.
4 Interviews with David Clark and Brian King.
5 The National Archive: CAB/128/36, CC 14 (62), 15 February 1962, p. 3.
6 The National Archive: FO371/163670. Telegram No. 645, Berlin to FO, 23 July 1962, and Telegram No. 648, Berlin to FO, 24 July 1962.
7 Interview with Paul Fallon.
8 The National Archive: PRO DEFE 71/8, Doc's 2A to 2C, 6 May 1975.
9 The National Archive: PRO DEFE 71/8 '*BASC Form 11*', Doc. 3.
10 Wright (2011), p. 27.
11 Williams (2006), p. 23.
12 The National Archive: FCO 33/5043, BASC/1/1/AIR, 27 March 1981. Although his protest was rapidly dismissed, if it was was in any way accurate, it again illustrates the Soviets were well aware of the Allies activities.
13 Marsden (1998), p. 192.
14 Aircrew interviews.
15 http://aad.archives.gov/aad/createpdf?rid=312848&dt=2082&dl=.
16 Aircrew interviews.
17 Aircrew interviews.
18 Peter Jefferies' Flying Logbook entries for 1977.

Appendix

Targets Covered by the Corridor and BCZ Flights

Location	Corridor	Nationality	Target type
Allstedt	South	Soviet	Airfield and SA-3 Site
Alt Rüdersdorf	BCZ	Soviet	Barracks
Bad Frankenhausen	South	East German	Barracks
Bad Langensalza	South	Soviet	Barracks
Bad Salzungen	South	East German	Barracks
Basdorf	BCZ	East German	Barracks
Beelitz	South	Soviet/East German	Barracks/hospital
Behnsdorf	Centre	Soviet	Radar Site
Berlin-Karlshorst	BCZ	Soviet/East German	Barracks and headquarters
Bernau	BCZ	Soviet	Barracks
Bernberg	South	Soviet	Barracks
Biesenthal	BCZ	Soviet	Logistic
Bittkau	Centre	Soviet/East German	Training area
Börgitz	Centre	Soviet	Barracks
Born	Centre	Soviet/East German	Barracks
Brand	BCZ	Soviet	Airfield
Brandenburg	Centre	Soviet/East German	Barracks

Location	Corridor	Nationality	Target type
Brandenburg-Briest	Centre	East German	Airfield
Brück	South	Soviet/East German	Logistics installation and training area
Burg bei Magdeburg	Centre	Soviet	Barracks and logistics
Cochstedt	South	Soviet	Barracks
Colbitz	Centre	Soviet	Barracks
Dallgow–Döberitz	BCZ	Soviet	Barracks
Damgarten (Putnitz)	North Coast	Soviet	Airfield
Dessau	South	East German	Barracks
Eisenach	South	Soviet/ East German	Barracks
Eisenach-Haina	South	Soviet/East German	Airfield and training area
Finow (Eberswalde)	BCZ	Soviet	Airfield
Finsterwalde	BCZ	Soviet	Airfield
Gardelegen	Centre	Soviet	Barracks
Genthin	Centre	East German	Logistic
Glau	BCZ	Soviet	Barracks and SAM site
Gotha	South	Soviet/East German	Barracks
Gross Behnitz	North	East German	Barracks
Gross Dölln (Templin)	BCZ	Soviet	Airfield
Gross Glienicke	BCZ	East German	Barracks
Hagenow	North	Soviet/East German	Barracks
Havelberg	North	East German	Barracks
Hillersleben	Centre	Soviet	Barracks
Jävenitz	Centre	Soviet/East German	Training area
Jüterbog	BCZ	Soviet	Airfield, barracks and training area
Jüterbog (Altes Lager)	BCZ	Soviet	Airfield

Location	Corridor	Nationality	Target type
Kehnert	Centre	Soviet/East German	River-crossing area
Kirchmöser	Centre	Soviet	Logistics and radar site
Kochstedt	South	Soviet	Airfield
Königs Wusterhausen	BCZ	Soviet	Workshop
Köthen	South	Soviet	Airfield
Krampnitz	BCZ	Soviet	Barracks
Kummersdorf	BCZ	Soviet	Barracks
Ladeburg-Lanke	BCZ	East German	Logistic
Lehnin	South	East German	Barracks
Letzlinger Heide	Centre	Soviet/East German	Training area
Ludwigslust	North	Soviet/East German	Barracks
Lübtheen	North	East German	Training area
Mahlwinkel	Centre	Soviet	Airfield and barracks
Mittenwalde	BCZ	East German	Logistic
Mühlhausen	South	Soviet/East German	Barracks
Neuruppin	North	Soviet	Airfield
Nordhausen	South	Soviet	Barracks
Oranienburg	BCZ	Soviet/East German	Airfield and barracks
Parchim	North	Soviet	Airfield and barracks
Peenemünde	North Coast		Airfield
Perleberg	North	Soviet	Barracks
Planken	Centre	Soviet/East German	Barracks
Potsdam	BCZ	Soviet	Barracks
Rangsdorf	BCZ	Soviet	Barracks and logistics
Rathenow	Centre	Soviet	Barracks
Rechlin-Lärz (Mirow)	North Coast	Soviet	Airfield
Ribnitz-Damgarteh (Pütnitz)	North Coast	Soviet	Airfield

Location	Corridor	Nationality	Target type
Ringfurth	Centre	Soviet/East German	River crossing area
Rosslau	South	Soviet	Barracks and training area
Schlotheim	South	Soviet	Barracks and airfield
Schönfelde	BCZ	East German	Airfield
Schönwalde	BCZ	Soviet	Barracks
Sondershausen	South		Barracks
Sperenberg	BCZ	Soviet	Airfield
Stahnsdorf	BCZ	Soviet	Barracks
Stendal	Centre	Soviet	Airfield and barracks
Storkow	BCZ	Soviet	Logistic
Strausberg	BCZ	East German	Barracks and airfield
Tangermünde	Centre	Soviet/East German	River crossing area
Templin	North	Soviet	Airfield
Töpchin	BCZ	Soviet	Logistics
Werder	BCZ	Soviet	Logistics
Werneuchen	BCZ	Soviet	Airfield and SAM site
Wittstock	North	Soviet	Airfield
Zerbst	South	Soviet	Airfield
Zossen-Wünsdorf	BCZ	Soviet	Headquarters

Glossary

2ème Bureau	Intelligence Branch (France)
10 GTD	10 Guards Tank Division
10 RG	10th Reconnaissance Group
10 PCS	10th Photo Charting Squadron
16 TAA	16 Tactical Air Army, previously 24 TAA
20 GA	20 Guards Army
19 MRD	19 Motor Rifle Division
21 AGPIU	21st Army Group Photographic Interpretation Unit
21 Int Coy (V)	21 Intelligence Company (Volunteers)
24 TAA	24 Tactical Air Army, later 16TAA
2ATAF	Second Allied Tactical Air Force – NATO formation
2TAF	Second Tactical Air Force – RAF command
3 Int & Sy Coy	3 Intelligence and Security Company
3 SA	3 Shock Army
35 MRD	35 Motor Rifle Division
4 MFPS	4 Mobile Field Photographic Section
4 MFPU	4 Mobile Field Photographic Unit
4025 SRS	4025th Strategic Reconnaissance Squadron
45 RS	45th Reconnaissance Squadron
6 Inf Regt	6th Infantry Regiment
7 Avn Flt AAC	7 Aviation Flight Army Air Corps
6911 RS (M)	6911th Radio Squadron (Mobile)
6916 RS (M)	6916th Radio Squadron (Mobile)
7 Flt AAC	7 Flight Army Air Corps
7 SOS	7th Special Operations Squadron
7010 Flt RAFVR	7010 Flight Royal Air Force Volunteer Reserve
7167 TS	7167th Transport Squadron

7405 SS	7405th Support Squadron
7406 SS	7406th Support Squadron
7407 SS	7407th Support Squadron
7499 SS	7499th Support Squadron
7499 SG	7499th Support Group
7575 OG	7575th Operations Group
7580 OS	7580th Operations Squadron
A-26/B-26 Invader	US twin-engine light bomber used on Corridor photographic missions
AAA	Anti-Aircraft Artillery
AB	Air Base
ACC	Allied Control Commission
ACIU	Allied Central Interpretation Unit
ADF	Automatic Direction Finder(ing)
ADIZ	Air Defence Identification Zone
AdlA	Armée de l'Air – French Air Force
AFB	Air Force Base
AFN	Armed Forces Network
ALAT	Aviation Légère de l'Armée de Terre (France)
AMARC	Aircraft Maintenance and Regeneration Center
AMLM	Allied Military Liaison Mission(s)
Andover	British twin-engine transport aircraft designed by Hawker Siddley
Anson	British twin-engine light transport aircraft manufactured by Avro
AO	Aerial Observer
AOB	Air Order of Battle
AOP	Air Observation Post
APC	Armoured Personnel Carrier
APIS	Army Photographic Interpretation Section
APIU (BAOR)	Army Photographic Interpretation Unit (British Army of the Rhine)
APU	Auxiliary Power Unit
APR	Air Photographic Reading
ASF	Aircraft Servicing Flight
ASTAC	Analyseur Superhétérodyne TACtique
ATC	Air Traffic Control
ATCC	Air Traffic Control Centre
AVM	Air Vice-Marshal
B-17G	Flying Fortress US Bomber aircraft used on Corridor and BCZ flights 1947–53
BAOR	British Army of the Rhine
BARTCC	Berlin Air Route Traffic Control Centre

BASC	Berlin Air Safety Centre
BCZ	Berlin Control Zone
BE	Bombing (later Basic) Encyclopaedia of targets
BFBS	British Forces Broadcasting Service (formerly BFN)
BFLB	Berlin for Lunch Bunch. Title bestowed on 7405 SS crews
BFN	British Forces Network (later BFBS)
BGÉ	Bureau de Guerre Électronique
BIB	Berlin Infantry Brigade (UK)
Big Bertha	US camera system, *see* Pie Face
Big Item	Nickname for the KA-82 H-Pan camera in the C-130E-II
BMG	British Military Government in Germany and Berlin
BN	Briefing Note
Bordertown	Peripheral reconnaissance missions flown by 4025 SRS
Boston Camera	Original version of the Pie Face (K-42) camera
BOZ	British Occupation Zone of Germany
BRD	Bundesrepublik Deutschland; also Federal German Republic and West Germany
BRIXMIS	British Commander-in-Chief's Military Liaison Mission to the Commander-in-Chief Group of Soviet Forces in Germany
BSF	Base Security Forces
BX	Base Exchange, *see also* PX
C-47 Skytrain	Military version of the Douglas DC-3 airliner
C-118 Liftmaster	Military version of the civilian DC-6 airliner
C-130E-II Hercules	US Transport aircraft modified for photographic and SIGINT duties
C4I	Command, Control, Communications, Computers and Intelligence
CAP	Combat Air Patrol
Carol Ann	US project name for photographic flights in Corridors and BCZ
CATac	Commandant Aérien Tactique
CC FFA	Commandant Chef du Forces Français en Allemange
CEAM	Centre d'Experiénces Aériennes Militaires
CERT	Centre d'Exploitation du Reseignement Tactique
CFS	Central Flying School
Chucker	US description of the outline of the Corridors and BCZ because it resembled a baseball field
Chukka	Alternative term for BCZ
CIA	Central Intelligence Agency (US)
C-in-C	Commander-in-Chief
C-in-C 2TAF	Commander-in-Chief Second Tactical Air Force
C-in-C BAFO	Commander-in-Chief British Air Force of Occupation

C-in-C BAOR	Commander-in-Chief British Army of the Rhine
C-in-C RAFG	Commander-in-Chief Royal Air Force Germany
CINCSAC	Commander-in-Chief Strategic Air Command (US)
CINCUSAFE	Commander-in-Chief United States Air Force in Europe
Cindy Fay	US project name for conversion of C-97 aircraft to photographic role
COMEL	Communications Électroniques
COMINT	Intelligence derived from the intercept of communications
Comms	Communications
CONUS	Continental United States
Corridor Airspace	20 statute miles wide with height limitations from 2,500 to 10,000ft connecting Berlin to Hamburg, Hannover and Frankfurt-am-Main
COTAM	Commandement du Transport Aérien Militaire (Military Air Transport Command)
CPSU	Communist Party of the Soviet Union
Creek Field	US project name for Corridor photographic flights by C-97 and CT- 29 aircraft
Creek Flush	US project name for Corridor photographic flights by C-97 and CT-29 aircraft
Creek Misty	US project name for Corridor photographic flights by C-130 aircraft
Creek Rail	US project name for Corridor ELINT flights by C-47 aircraft
CWO	Chief Warrant Officer (US Army)
Daisy Mae	US camera system fitted to C-97G aircraft (see Pie Face)
DDR	Deutsches Demokratik Republik, *see* GDR
DETALAT BERLIN	French Army Light Aviation Detachment based at Berlin-Tegel
DHC-1 Chipmunk	Two-seat training aircraft manufactured by De Havilland (Canada)
DIS	Defence Intelligence Staff
DISC	Defence Intelligence and Security Centre
DM	Deutschemark – West Germany currency
DV	Double Vision Joint 6 Int Coy and PID IT system introduced in the 1980s
EC-97	Designation erroneously applied to C-97 in SIGINT role
ECM	Electronic Counter Measures
Économat	French equivalent of the British NAAFI
ECCM	Electronic Counter-Counter Measures
EÉ 54	Escadre Électronique 54 (Electronic Squadron 54 – EE 54)
EÉT 54	Escadre Électronique Tactique 54 (54 Tactical Electronic Wing)
EGAF	East German Air Force

EGN	East German Navy
ELA	Escadrille de Liaison Aérienne (Air Liaison Squadron)
ELINT	Intelligence derived from the intercept of electronic equipment emissions (e.g. radar)
Elisa	French ELINT intercept system
EOB	Electronic Order of Battle
ERA	Explosive Reactive Armour
ESC	Electronic Security Command
ETA	Estimated Time of Arrival
ETD	Estimated Time of Departure
EU	European Union
EWO	Electronic Warfare Officer
F.49	UK air camera usually used for survey work
F.52	UK air camera fitted with either 14in or 20in lens (vertical-split pair) and either 36in or 48in lens (oblique) for Corridor flights
F.95	UK tactical air camera fitted with lenses up to 12in and operated in either hand-held or fixed mounting
F.96	UK air camera fitted with 12in lens (vertical) and 48in (oblique) for Corridor flights
F.126	UK air camera fitted with 12in (vertical) lens and reworked 48in (oblique) lens for Corridor flights
F-6K	Photographic reconnaissance variant of P-51 Mustang
FAA	Federal Aviation Administration
Fabian	UK code name for RAF Corridor photographic flights *c.* 1962
Farnborough, UK	Code name for BRIXMIS Chipmunk flights
FATac	Force Aérienne Tactique
FCO	Foreign and Commonwealth Office
FFR Bn	Free Flight Rocket Battalion
Flintstone	US project name for conversion of C-97 aircraft to photographic role
FLIR	Forward Looking Infrared
FMLM	*See* MMFL
FO	Foreign Office
FOZ	French Occupied Zone of Germany
FRG	Federal Republic of Germany – West Germany
FROG	Free Rocket over Ground – unguided rocket system
FROGMIS	Affectionate nickname for the MMFL (qv)
GA	Guards Army
GDR	German Democratic Republic. Alternative for DDR or East Germany
GÉ 30.450	Groupement Électronique 30.450 (Electronic Group 30.450)
GÉT 30.341	Groupement Électronique Tactique (Tactical Electronic Group 30.341)

GHL	Groupe d'Hélicoptères Légères
GKM	Grenzkommando Mitte – East German Border Guard Centre Command
GMRD	Guards Motor Rifle Division
GOC Berlin	General Officer Commanding British Troops Berlin
GSFG	Group of Soviet Forces in Germany
GSOFG	Group of Soviet Occupation Forces in Germany
GTD	Guards Tank Division
H-Pan	Horizontal (or High) Panoramic camera
Hallmark	Code name for RAF Corridor photographic flights
HÉT	Hélicoptère Électronique Technique
HF	High Frequency
HQ 21 AG	Headquarters 21st Army Group
HQ BAOR	Headquarters British Army of the Rhine
Huebener–Malinin	Agreement between C-in-C USAREUR and C-in-C GSFG governing relations between GSFG and HQ USAREUR
I&W	Indicators and Warning
IA	Image Analyst
ICBM	Inter-Continental Ballistic Missile
ICF	Intelligence Collection Flight
IFR	Instrument Flight Rules
IGB	Inner German Border
IMINT	Intelligence derived from multi-spectral imagery
IPIR	Initial Photographic Interpretation Report
IR	Infrared
IRIS	Intégration du Renseignement et des Informations SIGINT
IRLS	Infrared Linescan
IT	Information Technology
JAC	Joint Analysis Centre
JAPIC (G)	Joint Air Photographic Interpretation Centre (Germany)
JARIB	Joint Air Reconnaissance Intelligence Board
JARIC (UK)	Joint Air Reconnaissance Intelligence Centre (United Kingdom) (later JARIC)
JCS	Joint Chiefs of Staff
JIC	Joint Intelligence Committee based in London
JIC(G)	Joint Intelligence Committee (Germany)
JNCO	Junior Non-Commissioned Officer
JRC	Joint Reconnaissance Center
JSPI	Joint School of Photographic Interpretation
K-17	US camera system producing 9in × 9in images
K-18	US camera system producing 9in × 9in images
K-22	US camera system producing 9in × 9in images
K-30	US camera system producing 9in × 18in images

K-38	US camera system producing 9in × 18in images
K-42	US camera system producing 36in × 18in images, *see* Pie Face
KA-81A	US panoramic camera system producing images on 5in-wide film
KA-82	US panoramic camera system producing images on 5in-wide film
KA-95	US panoramic camera system producing images on 5in-wide film
KA-116	US-origin sideways-looking panoramic camera fitted with 72in lens
Ladbrook	UK code name for RAF Corridor photographic flights circa 1965–66
Live Oak	NATO contingency planning staff in Paris to prepare military responses to possible Soviet restrictions to Allied access to Berlin
MAC	Military Airlift Command
MANPADS	Man–Portable Air Defence System
MASDC	Military Aircraft Storage and Disposal Centre (later AMARC)
Maskirovska	Russian military term for all forms of deception and concealment
MBRL	Multi-Barrel Rocket Launcher
MBT	Main Battle Tank
MD	Military District
MEDEVAC	Medical Evacuation
Medius	Code name for BRIXMIS Chipmunk flights 1967–71
MF	Medium Frequency
MFPS	Mobile Field Photographic Section
MFPU	Mobile Field Photographic Unit
MfS	Ministerium für Staats Sicherheit
MI5	*See* Security Service
MI6	*See* SIS
The 'Mission'	Slang name for BRIXMIS
MMFL	Le Mission Militaire Français de Liaison. French equivalent of BRIXMIS, affectionately known as FROGMIS
MND	Ministry of National Defence
MoD UK	Ministry of Defence United Kingdom
MRR	Motor Rifle Regiment
MT-LB	Soviet tracked armoured personnel carrier
NAAFI	Navy, Army and Air Force Institutes
NATO	North Atlantic Treaty Organisation
NCO	Non-commissioned officer
NIIRS	National Image Interpretability Rating Scales
NORTHAG	Northern Army Group – NATO ground force command

NRO	National Reconnaissance Office
NSA	National Security Agency
NSC	National Security Council
NVA	Nationale Volks Armee – East German Army
Nylon	UK code name for BRIXMIS Chipmunk flights
Oberon	UK code name for BRIXMIS Chipmunk flights circa 1990
ODCSI	Office of Deputy Chief of Staff for Intelligence
Olive Harvest	US project name for U-2 flights over the Levant
ORB	Operations Record Book
ORBAT	Order of Battle
OSIRIS	Organisation Système d'Intégration du Renseignement et des Informations SIGINT
P-51 Mustang	US fighter aircraft used in photographic role
PAP	Plotter Air Photography
PARPRO	Peacetime Airborne Reconnaissance Programmes
PDI	Photographic Data Index
Pembroke	British twin-engine light transport aircraft manufactured by Percival
Philaria	UK code name for BRIXMIS Chipmunk BCZ photographic flights 1966–67
PHOTINT	Intelligence derived from optical photographic material
PI	Photographic Interpreter or Photographic Interpretation
PID	Photographic Interpretation Detachment. Became Photographic Intelligence Department
Pie Face	Project name for K-42 camera, *see also* Big Bertha and Daisy Mae
Plainsman	UK code name for RAF Corridor photographic flights
PM	Prime Minister
POL	Petroleum Oil and Lubricants
PPMS	Precision Parameter Measurements System
PR	Photographic Reconnaissance
PR	Public Relations
PRA	Permanently Restricted Area
PSMS	Phase Stability Measurement System
PX	Post Exchange – US equivalent of the British NAAFI, *see also* BX
QFI	Qualified Flying Instructor
R and D (R&D)	Research and Development
RADINT	Radiation Intelligence
RAF	Royal Air Force
RAFG	Royal Air Force Germany
RAFG PRU	Royal Air Force Germany Photographic Reproduction Unit
RAFVR	Royal Air Force Volunteer Reserve

Raindrop	Project name for corridor photographic flights in circa 1965
Raven	US nickname for electronic warfare officers
RB-26 Invader	US twin-engine light bomber converted to the photographic role
RB-36D	Reconnaissance version of the Convair B-36 Peacemaker aircraft
RC-97	Designation erroneously applied to C-97 aircraft in photographic role
RC-135	Electronic reconnaissance version of the C-135 Stratotanker aircraft
RECCEXREP	Reconnaissance Exploitation Report
Red Owl	US project name for photographic operations in the Corridors and BCZ 1950–58
Reichswehr	Collective name for the German armed forces during Nazi era 1933–45
Remote	UK code name for Pembroke photographic operations in the Corridors and BCZ 1967–71
RISTA	Reconnaissance Intelligence Strike and Target Acquisition
Rivet Flare	US project name for conversion of C-97 aircraft to photographic role
Rivet Giant	US project name for conversion of C-97 aircraft to photographic role
Robertson–Malinin	Agreement between C-in-C BAOR and C-in-C GSFG governing relations between GSFG and BAOR, including BRIXMIS
RPF	Radio Proving Flight
RWR	Radar Warning Receiver
SA-330 Puma (HÉT)	SA-330 Puma Hélicoptère Électronique Technique (HÉT)
SAC	Strategic Air Command
SAM	Surface-to-Air Missile
Sarigue	Système Aéroporté de Recueil des Informations de Guerre Électronique
Schooner	UK code name for BRIXMIS Chipmunk flights circa 1970s
SCIF	Special Compartmented Imagery Facility
Security Service	UK agency responsible for the security of the UK mainland, *see also* MI5
SED	Sozialistische Einheits Deutschland – German Unity Party
Senior Reach	US project name for KA-116 SRIS camera system
SENSINT	Sensitive intelligence programme
SEO	Special Equipment Officer
SERB	Soviet External Relations Branch. Responsible for liaison between the AMLMs and HQ GSFG at Zossen-Wünsdorf
Sergeant III	Thermal Imaging System proposed for fitting to Andover

Six Ps	Prior Preparation and Planning Prevents Poor Performance
SIGINT	Overall term covering intercept of electronic emissions that covers COMINT (qv) and ELINT (qv)
SIS	Secret Intelligence Service, *see also* MI6
SMLM	Soviet Military Liaison Mission(s) in West Germany
SNCO	Senior non-commissioned officer
SOXMIS	Soviet Commander-in-Chief's Military Liaison Mission to the Commander-in-Chief BAOR. Russian equivalent of BRIXMIS
SOZ	Soviet Occupied Zone of Germany
SPIR	Special Photographic Interpretation Report
SRIS	Senior Reach Imaging System, *see* KA-116
SRS	Strategic Reconnaissance Squadron
SRW	Strategic Reconnaissance Wing
SSI	School of Service Intelligence based at Ashford in Kent
Stasi	*See* MfS
STOL	Short Take Off and Landing
Sqn	Squadron
T-29A/CT-29A	Military version of CV240 civil airliner
TA	Territorial Army
TAS	Tactical Airlift Squadron
TAW	Tactical Airlift Wing
TEL	Transporter-Erector-Launcher
TELAR	Transporter-Erector-Launcher and Radar
Texas Postcard	Unofficial name for the 36in × 18in images produced by the K-42 Pie Face camera
The Wall	Concrete wall constructed in August 1961 dividing East from West Berlin
The Wire	Border between West Berlin and the GDR
TO & E	Table of Organisation and Equipment
Tokay	UK code name for RAF Corridor photographic flights 1959–64
TR	Tank Regiment
TRS	Tactical Reconnaissance Squadron
TTW	Transition to War
UAS	University Air Squadron
UHF	Ultra High Frequency
UN	United Nations
US	United States
USA	United States of America
USAAF	United States Army Air Force
USAF	United States Air Force
USAFE	United States Air Force in Europe

USAFSS	United States Air Force Security Service
USAREUR	United States Army in Europe
USCINCEUR	United States Commander-in-Chief Europe
USCOB	United Sates Command Berlin
USMLM	United States Military Liaison Mission
USN	United States Navy
USSR	Union of Soviet Socialist Republics
VCAS	Vice Chief of the Air Staff
Venton	Code name for RAF Corridor photographic flights 1987–90
VFR	Visual Flight Rules
VG	Vugraph: transparent positive image that could be projected for briefings
VHF	Very High Frequency
VLF	Very Low Frequency
WAC	World Area Chart
Wg	Wing
WGF	Western Group of Forces
Witch Doctor	Project name for USAF covert airborne photographic programme
WO	War Office, British Ministry responsible for the Army until the formation of the Ministry of Defence
WO	Warrant Officer: highest non-commissioned rank in the British forces
WOZ	Western Occupied Zones

ABOUT THE AUTHORS

Kevin Wright, PhD

Attending university as a mature student, Kevin Wright was awarded his PhD by the University of Essex in 1998 on the role of expert communities in arms control policy formulation. He went on to teach with the Government Department at Essex for over fifteen years, lecturing in international security studies and international relations. He is now a freelance aviation writer and photographer, living in Ireland with his wife Sue and son Stefan.

His current research interests are Cold War intelligence gathering, the development of an EU military identity, peace-keeping doctrine, arms control and Confidence and Security Building Measures in Europe. Recent published works include items on military policy and history for defence and web-based journals covering British Cold War intelligence gathering in Germany, the Treaty on Open Skies, Japanese Air Defence, JASDF fighter history, Polish airlift assets, US civilian airlift capabilities and the Vienna Documents.

Peter Jefferies

Peter Jefferies enlisted into the Intelligence Corps in 1962 after a short period in the Royal Artillery (Territorial Army). He served in Germany, Malta and Cyprus in intelligence, counter intelligence and security duties before qualifying as a Photographic Interpreter in 1969. Until he left the Regular Army in 1983 he mainly served in PI units in Germany and Britain and Northern Ireland. During his time as a PI he spent over nine years exploiting the imagery from the Allied photographic reconnaissance operations in the Berlin Air Corridors and BCZ. Peter rejoined the Territorial Army in 1984 and one of his appointments was commanding the section exploiting the Corridor and BCZ imagery during training weekends and annual continuation training camps.

After leaving the Regular Army in 1983 he became a civil servant with the UK MoD and remained with them until he retired in 2007.

Peter lives in Cambridgeshire with his wife Valerie. They have three children and eight grandchildren.

References and Bibliography

R. Aldrich (1998), 'British Intelligence and the Anglo American "Special Relationship" during the Cold War', *Review of International Studies*, Vol. 24, No. 3, pp. 331–51.

R. Aldrich (2001), *The Hidden Hand: Britain, America and Cold War Secret Intelligence* (London: John Murray Books).

R. Aldrich (2011), *GCHQ* (London: Harper Press).

R. Bates (2001), 'BRIXMIS – History and Roles', *RAF Historical Society Journal*, No. 23, pp. 10–19.

M.R. Beschloss (1986), *Mayday: Eisenhower, Khrushchev and the U-2 Affair* (London: Faber & Faber).

W.J. Boyne (2012), *The Berlin for Lunch Bunch*. Available at: http://www.airforcemag.com/MagazineArchive/Pages/2012/July%202012/0712berlin.aspx.

D.A. Brugioni (2010), *Eyes in the Sky: Eisenhower, the CIA and Cold War Aerial Espionage* (Annapolis, MD: Naval Institute Press).

W.E. Burrows (2001), *By Any Means Necessary: America's Secret Air War* (London: Arrow Books).

R. Cargill Hall and C.D. Laurie (2003), *Early Cold War Overflights 1950–1956: Symposium Proceedings*, Vol. 1: *Memoirs* (Washington DC: Office of the Historian, National Reconnaissance Office).

R. Cargill Hall and C.D. Laurie (2003), *Early Cold War Overflights 1950–1956: Symposium Proceedings*, Vol. 2: *Appendixes* (Washington DC: Office of the Historian, National Reconnaissance Office).

D. Cockburn, 'Chipmunk Pilot 1985–1990: A Personal Boring Story' (unpublished memoir).

Comité Historique de l'Association Guerrelec (2009), *Les Avions de Renseignement Électronique* (Panazol: Lavauzelle Graphic).

J. Crampton (1997), 'RB-45 Operations', Air Intelligence Symposium, RAF Historical Society, Bracknell Paper No. 7, pp. 124–32.

L. Davies, 'BRIXMIS Member April 1975 to August 1978: My Re-acquaintance with the Chipmunk' (unpublished memoir).

T. Geraghty (1997), *BRIXMIS: The Untold Exploits of Britain's Most Daring Cold War Spy Mission* (London: Harper Collins).

S. Gibson (2012), *Live and Let Spy: BRIXMIS – the Last Cold War Mission* (Stroud: The History Press).

D. Gordon (2006), *Tactical Reconnaissance in the Cold War* (Barnsley: Pen & Sword Books).

W. Grimes (2014), *The History of Big Safari* (Bloomington, IN: Archway Publishing).

P. Kuhrt (1968), 'Looking Down on Berlin's Wall', *Stars and Stripes*, 11 August 1968.

P. Lashmar (1996), *Spy Flights of the Cold War* (Stroud: Sutton Publishing).

P. Magnificat (2008), *Propousk! Missions derrière le rideau de fer (1947–1989)* (Panazol: Lavauzelle Graphic).

R. Marsden (1998), 'Operation "Schooner/Nylon": RAF Flying in the Berlin Control Zone', *Intelligence and National Security*, Vol. 1, No. 4, pp. 178–93.

R.G. Miller (1998), *To Save a City: The Berlin Airlift 1948–49* (Washington DC: Bolling AFB). Available at: http://www.afhso.af.mil/shared/media/document/AFD-101001–053.pdf.

G. Mindling and R. Bolton (2011), *US Air Force Tactical Missiles 1949–1969* (Morrisville, NC: Lulu.com publishing).

H. Neubroch (2001), 'RAF Element BRIXMIS: Further Recollections of Operational Experiences 1957–59', *RAF Historical Society Journal*, No. 23, pp. 106–15.

A. Paringaux (1996), *Le Règne du Mirage IV* (Paris: La Mâitrise du Ciel).

G.W. Pedlow and D.E. Welzenbach (1992), *The Central Intelligence Agency and Overhead Reconnaissance, 1954–1974* (Washington DC: History Staff, CIA). Available at: http://www2.gwu.edu/~nsarchiv/NSAEBB/NSAEBB434/ Appendix D.

R. Pietrini (2008), *Vostock, missions de renseignement au coeur de la Guerre froide* (Les Echelles: Mission Speciale Productions).

C. Pocock and C. Fu (2010), *The Black Bats: CIA Spy Flights over China from Taiwan 1951–1969* (Atglen, PA: Schiffer Publishing).

J. Richelson (1987), *American Espionage and the Soviet Target* (New York: William Morrow Inc.).

P. Rodgers (2001), 'Photographic Reconnaissance Operations', *RAF Historical Society Journal*, No. 23, pp. 69–77.

R. Saar, 'Sqn Ldr Ops 1970–1973 BRIXMIS Memories' (unpublished memoir).

J. Smith (1998), *The Cold War* (London: Blackwell) (2nd edn).

L. Tart (2013), *Freedom through Vigilance: History of US Air Forces Security Service (USAFSS)*, Vol. 2 (West Conshocken, PA: Infinity Publishing).

L. Tart and R. Keefe (2001), *The Price of Vigilance* (New York: Ballantine).

W. Taylor (2003), *Royal Air Force Germany since 1945* (Hinckley: Midland Publishing).

A. and J. Tusa (1988), *The Berlin Blockade: Berlin in 1948* (London: Hodder & Stoughton).

J. van Waarde (2010), *Target Iron Curtain*. Available at: http://www.16va.be/ TargetIronCurtain-JanvanWaarde2010.pdf.

P. Williams (2006), *Brixmis in the 1980s: The Cold War's 'Great Game' – Memories of Liaising with the Soviet Army in East Germany*. Parallel History Project on Cooperative Security (PHP). Available at: http://www.php.isn.ethz.ch/collections/colltopic.cfm?lng=en&id=27 752&nav1=1&nav2=3&nav3=5.

K. Wright (2009), 'Opening the Skies: The Fascinating World of Open Skies Overflights', *Aircraft Illustrated*, Vol. 42, No. 5, pp. 60–4.

K. Wright (2009), 'War of Intelligence', *Aircraft*, Vol. 42, No. 11, pp. 64–70.

K. Wright (2011), 'The Photo Pembrokes', *Aircraft*, Vol. 44, No. 3, pp. 22–8.

K. Wright (2014), 'Cold War Reconnaissance Flights along the Berlin Corridors and in the Berlin Control Zone 1960–90: Risk, Coordination and Sharing', *Intelligence and National Security*, DOI: 10.1080/02684527.2014.890467.

K. Wright and P. Jefferies (2015), 'Berlin Air Corridors US Peace Missions', *Aviation News*, February 2015, pp. 50–6.

H. Wynn (1997), *RAF Nuclear Deterrent Forces* (London: HMSO).

Index